ADDITIONAL PRAISE FOR
THE CARING COMPANY

"As someone who's worked hands on with staff empowerment for their full dedication to customers and seen its correlation to superior profitability, I found this book to be both timely and essential. The authors' insights are sharp, the research is thorough, and the writing is compelling."

—Anders Bouvin, former Handelsbanken CEO

"*The Caring Company* is making the case for fundamentally re-channeling business. If we want our companies to be future-proof, we cannot be satisfied with making only slight changes to the way they operate (the "How"). In fact, we must reshape their "What," i.e., their core activities. As Isaac and Laurent clearly illustrate in their book, this profound shift can only occur through authentic and caring face-to-face relationships."

—Isabelle Kocher, former Engie CEO; Chairman and founder of Blunomy

"You know that Isaac and Laurent are right. This is a Socratic volume that plays the melody of the Saint-Exupéry in us. The point of the book is to make us admit that our internal mechanisms of self-correction need a French Revolution."

—Esa Saarinen, Philosopher

"Organizations built on trust, care, and high purpose are not a utopian dream—they exist today and are thriving. At Viisi, we believe these values form the essential foundation of sustainable success. *The Caring Company* offers a compelling blueprint for leaders who are ready to embrace this path."

—Tom van der Lubbe, founder and CEO of VIISI

"I recognize in *The Caring Company* the same spirit that guided me in building Buurtzorg: the belief that organizations succeed when they truly care for people. This book is a vital reminder that caring is the future of business."

—Jos de Blok, founder of Buurtzorg

"With the dawn of the AI era upon us, people must focus on what only human beings can bring to any enterprise. At the heart of what only people can do, that AI will never be able to do, is actually feel care for another person, and feel cared for by another person. The essence of any enterprise is the quality of relationships that make up its members, customers, suppliers, the local community, and shareholders. Leaders and corporate cultures that genuinely care will attract and retain the best talent and build the trust from which the strongest brands are made."

—**Jeff Westphal**, former CEO and Chairman of Vertex;
founder of MeaningSphere.com

"At Decathlon, and through our investments, I witnessed firsthand how a company thrives when it embodies trust and the intrinsic motivation of people—whether they are customers, associates, or shareholders. Isaac and Laurent have captured this spirit and demonstrate how caring organizations not only outperform, but also—like a successful family business—leave an empowering legacy for future leaders to reimagine the vision. This book offers a compelling roadmap for any leader seeking to build a truly caring company."

—**Matthieu Leclercq**, former President of Decathlon;
founder of ForTalents

"*The Caring Company* is not yet another management handbook, but an invitation to profoundly transform the way we conceive of business. By placing care and relationships at the heart of practices, Isaac Getz and Laurent Marbacher demonstrate that lasting prosperity arises from trust and from serving stakeholders. This book outlines a new path for capitalism: more human, more responsible, and more effective."

—**Arnaud Naudan**, Chairman, BDO France

"This is an important book for those seeking to understand how to create more human and adaptive organizations in a viable way. Highly readable and highly recommendable!"

—**Bjarte Bogsnes**, Chairman, Beyond Budgeting Roundtable

"Want to future-proof your organization by attracting and keeping the next generation of talent? Start caring. This book shows you how."

—**Joost Minnaar,** co-founder of Corporate Rebels

The Caring Company

The Caring Company

HOW TO SHIFT BUSINESS AND THE ECONOMY FOR GOOD

ISAAC GETZ *and* LAURENT MARBACHER

WILEY

Published by John Wiley & Sons, Inc., Hoboken, New Jersey.
Published simultaneously in Canada.

For general information on our other products and services or for technical support, please contact our Customer Care Department within the United States at (800) 762-2974, outside the United States at (317) 572-3993 or fax (317) 572-4002.

Wiley also publishes its books in a variety of electronic formats. Some content that appears in print may not be available in electronic formats. For more information about Wiley products, visit our web site at www.wiley.com.

Library of Congress Cataloging-in-Publication Data Applied for:

Hardback ISBN: 9781394315437
ePDF ISBN: 9781394315475
ePub ISBN: 9781394315468

Cover design by Wiley
Cover Image: © miobuono/stock.adobe.com
Printed and bound by CPI Group (UK) Ltd, Croydon, CR0 4YY

C9781394315437_261025

To Isaac's parents, Simon and Cilia, and to Laurent's parents, Jean-Paul and Monique, to whom we owe our lives and much of what we have endeavored to achieve through them.

CONTENTS

CONTENTS

PART II
THE CARING COMPANY WAY   97

INTRODUCTION

I t is 7 a.m. when Wladek's truck enters the huge parking lot of LSDH, a European leader in packed milk and juices. After 10 hours of night driving to this Loire Valley warehouse, he is tired, hoping to load his shipment quickly and leave.

At most warehouses around the world, what Wladek would do next is entirely predictable: Wait for your turn, adapt to the supply chain constraints, and hope to be able to maintain your human dignity – not an abstraction in this case. For truckers, that means to take a shower, eat a snack, and, possibly, to rest. Usually, they are deprived of these opportunities, but not at LSDH.

After signing in, Wladek can settle down in a lodge on the property called the Trucker's House. There he can wash himself, have food, watch TV in a lounge, and even take a nap in one of the bedrooms – all at no cost.

This facility is certainly nice, but is investing in such creature comforts for your drivers economically rational? LSDH is a 2,250-strong business with more than $1 billion in annual revenue. If caring for hundreds of anonymous truckers for free had proven profitable, it would have been copied by all of LSDH's competitors. At first glance, it seems more like a folly than sound business.

But LSDH's case, along with the many others you will discover in this book, is significant, and it speaks to the heart of the predicament currently facing our economic system. Once, the free-market economy was widely praised. Today, it is under scrutiny, even attack. And one of the most frequent angles of attack concerns the treatment of workers under capitalism.

Modern capitalism, to be sure, has worked economic wonders. From 1820 to 2001, per capita income increased 20-fold in the free-market West, while it rose only sixfold in the rest of the world.[1] Historically, the free-markets in Europe, by allowing masses to engage in direct trade relationships, have been a major catalyst for the emancipation of the lower classes from the dominance of nobility and clergy, as well as for wives from their husbands' economic control.[2] More recently, through initiatives like microcredit, this economic system has proven to be a powerful tool in the fight against extreme poverty. At the same time, critics are right that this unparalleled growth of prosperity and many social conquests have come at a significant cost and has not benefited everyone equally, either within a given country or across the globe. From the deplorable working conditions of the Industrial Revolution to the plundering of resources from countries in the Global South and to the present environmental damages, corporations are accused. They are viewed as making profits thanks to the collective efforts of communities while shifting social and environmental costs onto society at large.

Today, younger generations are the most disillusioned with business-as-usual. According to a Deloitte survey, 87% of millennials believe that "the success of a business should be measured in terms of more than just its financial performance."[3] And according to the most recent Deloitte study, younger generations go beyond simple beliefs, with many translating them into professional decisions: "44% of Gen Zs and 45% of millennials have left a role they felt lacked purpose, and around 40% of both groups have declined an assignment, project, or even a potential employer based on their personal ethics or beliefs."[4] With millennials and Gen Z making up between 65% and 80% of the workforce in 2025, their expectations cannot be ignored by business.

No matter your age, you may also believe that something must be done to address the contradiction between the interests of the corporations and those of society at large. You may even question whether it is possible to reform capitalism as we know it. However, you don't want to throw the baby out with the bathwater. You don't want to abandon the free-market economy or the idea that business can be part of the solution – not only a source of problems.

Companies have long been trying to be part of the solution to social problems. For centuries, this took the form of corporate philanthropy, mostly conducted outside their core business processes, and in the last decades, through Corporate Social Responsibility (CSR), marginally integrated within them. Recently, in response to criticism about the social and environmental ineffectiveness of philanthropy and CSR, companies have started to balance their focus on profit with two additional priorities: people and planet. By the early twenty-first century, thousands of companies were seeking external validation for their efforts, earning the status of "B-Corps," or incorporating these three priorities into their corporate charters to become "Benefit Corporations." However, the balancing efforts haven't stopped there.

In December 2022, a Wall Street Journal Intelligence Survey found that 59% of 350 CEO respondents confirmed that their organizations had a well-established purpose – typically involving social and environmental goals.[5] The survey concluded that companies had learned that "they must collaborate for the greater good."

Yet, a cynic might dismiss these "wider social impact" initiatives as merely the latest effort by unrepentant capitalists to maintain the status quo – and there is evidence to support this view. A Deloitte 2023 Gen Z and Millennial Survey reveals that only 26% of Gen Z and 30% of millennials are content with the social impact of their company.[6] Despite the recent surge of attention paid to corporate purpose, with thousands of business leaders trying to balance social and environmental values and profits, the jury is still out.

Regarding LSDH, you might wonder whether the Trucker's House is something more than a well-orchestrated PR campaign for the sake of the CSR report. For sure, LSDH would not be the first company accused of social- or green-washing. So, let's look at another story from LSDH.

At the beginning of 2016, Nicolas Chabanne, a French social entrepreneur promoting sustainable consumption, comes to the Loire Valley to meet LSDH's CEO, Emmanuel Vasseneix. Chabanne has the idea of creating a milk product that will simultaneously offer a fair return to farmers, nutritional value for consumers, and environmental sustainability. Moreover, it will be consumers themselves who will devise this product and decide how much they are willing to pay for it. Concretely, for a 1-quart carton of milk, they will be invited to a website where they can indicate their preferences along the following dimensions: How many hours a day do they want the animals to graze outside? Should the farmer enjoy two weeks of annual vacation? What food quality do they want for the cows? They will be able to directly observe on the website the impact of each choice on the retail price of the milk. To finish, Chabanne explains to Vasseneix that to implement his idea he needs a milk producing and packaging partner and that LSDH is a perfect fit for it. Though Vasseneix finds Chabanne a bit over the top, the project resonates with him, and he accepts the deal.

In July 2016, 6,823 people take part in the web-based simulation, with the characteristics most favored by these consumers becoming the specifications for this new milk product. They also indicate the retail price they are ready to pay for it. Now it's Vasseneix's turn to find the farmers willing to supply such a milk. He happened to be in contact with a cooperative of 81 milk farmers who are on the verge of bankruptcy because the price they are getting for their milk is so low. So Vasseneix offers them almost double the price they are receiving, provided they respect the conditions laid out for what will become the Consumer's Milk brand. This turns out even better than they imagined. The first year, Consumer's Milk sells 5.8 million gallons, instead of the 2.6 million gallons projected. As of today, the brand has sold more than 114 million gallons – the biggest commercial success in the French food industry in the past 30 years.

But that came later. In 2016, when LSDH's Vasseneix agreed to lead this project, he had neither a business plan nor certainty of profits. Moreover, Chabanne's visit was the last-ditch effort – all of France's biggest industrial diary producers had already rejected his idea. Is this another LSDH folly?

In fact, we have seen other LSDH follies, and many more in dozens of other companies we have studied and will describe in this book. And though we have not uncovered a clear-cut "method in their madness," we have discovered a deep reason why they engage in seemingly unprofitable activities that their competitors avoid.

The reason is simple: They care. And not in the abstract, remote sense of the word we are all used to, as in "customer care" or "health care." Put differently, they care not for all humankind or for nature in general. Nor is it for global causes like fighting epidemics or promoting the arts. Importantly, they eschew these types of care not because they are indifferent. Rather these companies believe that the most authentic and effective way to care is to care about the people right on their doorsteps, those with whom the company is continuously interacting – its customers, suppliers, and the local community.

Such caring focus has for these companies one logical and one surprising consequence. The logical consequence is that since the company aims to care about those with whom it interacts, it has to make sure that its processes allow and reinforce these caring interactions. This often means radically transforming these processes, since they were devised in the first place not to maximize care but to maximize profit. Specifically, this means transforming them from being designed for transactions based on self-interest and mistrust to being designed for relationships based on serving others' needs and trust.

And now, the surprising result: Once their transformed business processes allow companies to care unconditionally about the members of their business ecosystem, these companies enjoy a continuous and amazing prosperity.

This book does not prescribe a new ideology. Nor does it pretend to get us out from all the shortcomings of modern capitalism. Rather, it tells the story of outstanding, yet often discreet companies – small and large, public and private, in diverse industries and geographies – that are quietly reinventing what it means to operate a business successfully while meeting our world's biggest challenges. Their stories are so counterintuitive to traditional business thinking that you will probably hear your inner voice telling you that they are too good to be true.

We heard the same inner voice. Like many others, we are suffused with the dominant paradigm: That running a business successfully means maximizing its profits. Treating anonymous truck drivers well – and for free – or saving an economically strangled community of milk producers without any solid business plan does not seem to fit this paradigm.

You may suspect that we exaggerate. Maybe your company has a solid CSR program and even a C-suite executive in charge of it. Or you may work in finance and witness Environmental, Social, and Governance (ESG) criteria increasingly impacting the investment decisions or work for a corporation adhering to the World Economic Forum or the Business Roundtable stakeholder capitalism pledges. There's a chance that you may even work for a B-Corp or a Benefit Corporation. Most of these approaches try to balance the shareholder interests with those of employees, clients, suppliers, and the local community. Profit or shareholder value as the sole measure for business success seems almost outdated. Balancing profit with social and environmental considerations seems to be the new zeitgeist.

Yet, despite this recent surge of attention to measures of business success beyond the financial, with thousands of business leaders trying to transform their companies to balance social and environmental value with profits, for all the well-meant words and some actions, the jury is still out. And that's because research shows that these efforts are largely unsuccessful or insufficient.

Yes, businesses may care *somewhat* about society and the environment, but they do not *fully* care about them. As the famous adage goes, these companies are chasing multiple rabbits at the same time, ultimately catching none. Or, despite their balancing declarations, they focus on the rabbit they are most familiar with chasing – profits. The world – whether business leaders, employees, investors, academics, politicians, consultants, or coaches – is still pondering what kind of transformation can allow businesses to truly serve the common good while remaining prosperous.

This challenge of finding an alternative and successful way of running business has gnawed at us for the past decade. In our respective fields, we have been deeply – and for some time – involved in searching and putting into practice a different way of running organizations, one that allows human dignity, potential, and creativity.

Isaac, a leadership scholar at ESCP, the world's oldest and top-ranked business school, co-wrote with Brian M. Carney *Freedom, Inc.* in 2009 (Crown Business), which has since been translated into 15 languages. It has become France's best-selling business book of the past decade, sparking a corporate transformation movement involving hundreds of companies, including multinationals. Drawing on his observations and business learnings, he also advised and inspired senior leaders of corporations, such as Michelin and Decathlon, on building an organizational setting that allows for responsibility and freedom of action.

Laurent, right after graduating from France's top business school, went to Chile and launched the country's first micro-credit bank in the early 1990s with some friends and the support of Nobel Prize winner Muhammad Yunus. Since then, he has devoted himself to supporting and coaching transformation journeys based on the capacity of ordinary people to achieve extraordinary results, if only they are given the freedom to create the future they truly desire. This experience led him to play a role and witness exceptional transformations in dozens of remarkable companies. In addition to constant dialogues with CEOs, he designs and coaches leadership development programs for top executives.

It was their shared passion and belief in the possibility of responsibility- and freedom-based companies that led to their meeting in July 2010. Jean-François Zobrist, a pioneering French transformational CEO, invited both of them to spend a Sunday at his country house. They clicked, and one year later, together with a dozen other pioneering CEOs, Isaac and Laurent launched a movement of companies seeking to build workplaces that allow workers both responsibility and freedom of action. This movement has since spread from France and Belgium to five continents and today involves close to 500 companies and public administrations. Zobrist, who, since 1983, had built the first so-called "liberated company" in Europe, also took a very active part in this movement. He was relentless in spreading this philosophy, both in his speeches to thousands of executives and through his writings. To our immense regret, in March 2025, Zobrist passed away. He had been, for us and for hundreds of thousands, a source of profound inspiration.

As the movement of liberated companies grew, we realized that focusing solely on the internal dynamics of companies – how to provide employees with trust, growth, and autonomy – was only half of the equation. It was clear to us that companies do not operate in isolation, focused only on their internal workings. They are embedded in a free-market system and constantly collaborate with other economic actors. We also realized that the self-interest basis for these interactions had never been fundamentally questioned. We asked if it's possible for companies to base their interactions with their clients, suppliers, and the local community on something different – on unconditional care and trust.

This question led us to embark on a five-year research journey. Much like Darwin, who sailed the *Beagle* to observe the natural world, we set out to observe the business world, studying several dozen companies of various types, sizes, and industries across three continents. These observations, once compiled and reviewed, revealed an answer to our question. We felt like we were discovering a new business species, one that had not yet been described. We call it *The Caring Company*.

The caring company is a company that serves its business ecosystem – clients, suppliers, and the local community – unconditionally and through its core business processes. By doing so, it enjoys unrivalled long-term prosperity.

The caring company is not a model. It's a business philosophy – or should we say a *way of life* – that LSDH and dozens of other companies have articulated, each in its own way transforming its core business processes to focus on unconditional care. As a result, in the past 15 years, LSDH's revenues grew from $205 million to $1.12 billion, and it has been voted the best food-industry business in France. Other companies we studied boast similar outstanding results. But their achievements have implications beyond the discovery of a novel way of running business.

Our combined 50 years of close observation and work with hundreds of businesses convinced us that a core of select companies routinely discover solutions to the major problems facing the economy and society. Family therapists refer to this as *system's competence*, meaning that for any problem a family generates, it has the competence to resolve it – if only the right environment is established for solutions to emerge. Applied to companies, we believe that by identifying, conceptualizing, and effectively conveying such corporate solutions, we can accelerate the transition toward this unusual, yet tried and tested paradigm for running businesses. And by describing the conditions needed for their emergence, we could pave the way for enough companies to adopt these practices so that entire industries, regions, and economies would be revitalized.

All these corporate transformations, some done decades ago with their social – and therefore economic – results still lasting, prove that caring companies' approach is not a flash in a pan, soon replaced by another management fad. It is not based on some new tool or recipe. Rather, it is based on a unique view of a company's purpose – a single-minded pursuit of the social good of the clients, suppliers, and the local community – and on the ensuing transformation of all its business processes from focusing on a self-interested transaction to focusing on an authentic relationship. That's why it's not a methodology but a paradigm – that is, a set of beliefs and values of how to run a business and the practices that flow from that. Yet, besides the caring companies' long-lasting record and the fairly well-known business practices that led to it, their competitors continue to rely on a transactional framework – and to underperform.

The reason for this puzzling state – we found – is that transformation is not easy. That is why *The Caring Company* is not just about describing a paradigm of how to run a business for social good and therefore prosper. The caring company paradigm is distinct from the traditional approaches such as CSR or ESG. Rather than balance the cost of doing "good" against profit goals or shareholder returns, as we see all too often, caring companies *single-mindedly* care about its clients, suppliers, and their host communities – and therefore, prosper. This focus on unreserved care for the company's ecosystem members, rather than on transacting with them, requires a fundamental shift of nearly all elements of the corporate way of functioning, such as managerial framework and processes, traditionally conceived with a profit-first mindset. This fundamental transformation of all the business processes sets this paradigm apart from the balancing approaches and the CSR alike. This is also what makes it so difficult to adopt.

It is a bit like making exercising part of your life. We all know and admire some colleagues or neighbors who are in shape because they exercise consistently. Some of us even resolve to change our behavior – especially once a year, on New Year's Eve. So we purchase an annual subscription to the local gym, go there a few times, then, a bit less, and a bit less, until finally we slip back to our old ways. Aware that even the most proven exercise routine will be ineffective if we don't change our behavior, many among us still can't do it. Those that do succeed because they don't make their physical condition an afterthought or a "nice to have" – they make it a core belief.

Shifting to the caring company paradigm requires a similar dedication to a core belief – the belief that a company can focus on the social and environmental good, and as a consequence, prosper economically. Moreover, such a belief runs against many truths taken to be self-evident. For instance, business schools and strategy firms tell you that you should focus on your core business and that any move outside of it is dangerous. Yet, because LSDH is focused on the social and environmental good first, it did exactly the opposite.

One Friday, in June 2017, Emmanuel Vasseneix, LSDH CEO, learned that a packed salad company 10 miles away from LSDH was about to be sold to a large food corporation. The deal was to be closed next Monday. So on Saturday, Vasseneix reached the company's owners and made a counter-offer. By Sunday, the parties finalized the deal, with LSDH becoming the new owner.

There was absolutely no strategic reason for LSDH's packed milk and juice business to acquire a salad one. The reason was LSDH belief in caring – in this case about the local community. Specifically, Vasseneix feared that relatives or friends of his employees could lose their jobs since acquiring corporations often proceed with cost reductions.

But while neither profit maximization nor strategic thinking guided LSDH's decision, the economic benefits soon appeared. Salad is a light product, while packed milk and juice are heavy ones. Because of the latter's weight, a truck can be loaded only up to two thirds of its volume, which led to Vasseneix's insight. Since the trucks go to the same food retail clients, use the empty space to transport the light salads, thus reducing the salad delivery costs to practically zero and improving the salad business's margins. But this came later. When Vasseneix decided on the salad business acquisition, he did not have a clue about this possibility. His decision was based on his fundamental belief in caring about LSDH's business ecosystem – not on a cost-benefit calculation of the anticipated gains from the purchase.

That is why *The Caring Company* goes beyond a description of the paradigm and provides the principles that allowed the companies we studied to adopt it – and will allow others to do so as well. These companies prove that business can become the solution to the world's major problems, starting at their doorsteps. When enough companies transform themselves using this paradigm, collectively they will have the potential to revitalize entire economies, thereby setting the conditions for another two centuries of prosperity – this time, social, environmental and, consequently, economic. We hope this book will make a significant contribution to this movement.

YOUR JOURNEY THROUGH THIS BOOK

R eady to see where this journey will take you? The following illustration maps the big questions, bold ideas, and surprising insights
that lie ahead—as we move from businesses' past and present
approaches to doing good, to becoming caring companies, and ultimately
to reimagining the future of business—and of the broader economy.

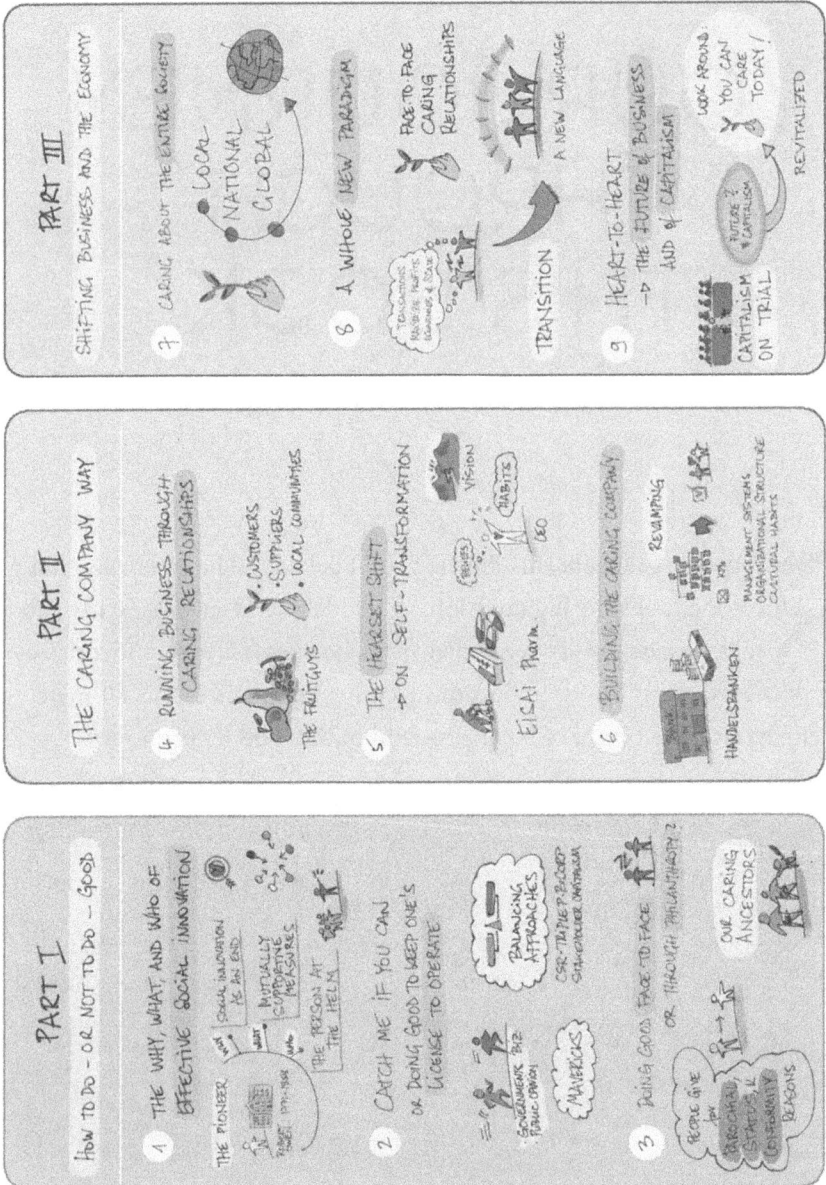

PART I

HOW TO DO – OR NOT TO DO – GOOD

CHAPTER ONE

THE WHY, WHAT, AND WHO OF EFFECTIVE SOCIAL INNOVATION

Utopia is the truth of tomorrow.

– Victor Hugo

As business sage Peter Drucker put it some 40 years ago, the book he'd like to write is: "How to make a million and still go to heaven."[1] This tension between achieving success and doing good in business can be traced at least to the Industrial Revolution. Its division of labor and economies of scale have led to the rise of large, modern enterprises. Simultaneously, they also led to the emergence of a labor class subject to harsh working and living conditions similar to those of today's workers in many countries over the world. All early industrialists faced these deplorable conditions. Some of them turned to philanthropy – usually after selling their business or retiring from it – in order to "give back." Yet, a select few took "the road less traveled" and sought to transform the workers' miserable social situation while they were still at the helm of their company.

These industrialists were pursuing lives aligned with their humanistic or religious principles or were simply guided by their inner moral compass. In other words, they didn't just lament the negative social impacts of business – unbearable living conditions, child labor, the mistreatment of workers, alcoholism, drug use, or crime – they acted to alter them.

In the 1770s and 1780s, Josiah Wedgwood gave us one of the earliest examples of such social innovations in his pottery factory, one of Britain's largest, employing 700 workers. His innovations included shorter working hours, improved safety and hygiene, healthcare, better housing, apprenticeship and training opportunities, and worker participation in manufacturing decisions.

A decade later, in the 1790s, David Dale – founder and owner of New Lanark cotton mill – launched his own series of social innovations. These included high-quality, multi-story tenement buildings to house laborers and their families, reasonable working hours, fair treatment and healthcare for workers, as well as part-time education for children, who worked shorter hours to attend school.

However, it was Robert Owen, Dale's future son-in-law, who pioneered the most audacious social innovations, not only for his time but for many decades to come.[2]

THE PIONEER OF SOCIAL INNOVATION

Between 1815 and 1825, a particular scene regularly unfolded close to the small Scottish village of Lanark, about 25 miles southeast of Glasgow, on the banks of the River Clyde. Industrialists and prominent figures from all over the world – including two Austrian princes and the future Russian tsar – visited the place. The object of their fascination was the cotton mill at New Lanark, an economic and social complex unlike anything seen before.

This industrial site was very different from other early industrial plants. Working hours were limited, and the site included a nursery school – the first of its kind in the world – as well as a primary school, the first free one in the United Kingdom. An educational and cultural center was open to everyone, a store provided workers with quality goods at below-market prices, a health insurance plan and retirement system were established, and finally, children were not allowed to work in the factory before the age of 10.

Many of these measures were so far ahead of their time that it would take more than a century for them to become widespread in Europe and the United States.

From Apprentice Draper to Industrialist

An apprentice draper and later a cloth merchant in Manchester, Robert Owen was 18 when he borrowed the current equivalent of about $20,000 from his older brother to launch a small business with two partners.[3] This venture lasted only a few months, but he soon started another that succeeded, earning him a weekly profit equivalent to $1,177.

Confident in his abilities, at only 20, Owen applied for the role of general manager at one of the largest spinning mills. He quickly set to expand the mill, which soon employed 500 people, thanks to his technological and social innovations. Later on, driven by his belief that a good physical and moral environment was essential for economic success, Owen improved workers' welfare. However, his ambition to possess his own business, where he could fully implement his vision, remained strong.

When, along with eight other partners, Owen purchased the New Lanark Mills from his future father-in-law David Dale in 1799, it was already Britain's largest cotton mill, with 1,300 workers. He began with what we would call today "business process improvements," introducing quality, cost, and inventory controls, as well as time tracking. Owen did not hesitate to fire workers for theft, chronic absenteeism, or alcoholism, earning him the reputation of being "crabbit." His methods proved effective. Between 1799 and 1810, the mill generated the present-day equivalent of more than $10 million in cumulative profit, and its value nearly doubled over this period.

These harsh policies did not mean that Owen had abandoned his aspirations for improving worker welfare at New Lanark. Strict as it might seem today, his management was vastly more humane than was typical at the time, when corporal punishment for workers was legal. Owen, of course, never permitted this at his mill. He also abolished summary dismissals, thus improving job security. Furthermore, many parents who worked together, with neither of them thus available to cook, could get good food from the communal kitchen. Finally, he established contributory disability, health, and retirement plans and opened a home for retired workers.

Interestingly, Owen not only cared about his employees but also about his customers. Knowing in advance about the future rise or fall in yarn prices, he advised customers to rush their orders in the first case and to delay them in the second. In both cases, the customer got better prices. We return to this customer-caring theme later in the book.

However, Owen encountered challenges in implementing more radical social innovations in his mill.

Getting Radical

When he sought to reduce the long working hours from 13 to 10 hours per day – the world's shortest workday at the time – he first faced strong opposition from the workers themselves.[4] His ultimate vision was of "eight hours of labor, eight hours of recreation, and eight hours of rest," but accustomed to exploitative owners, workers feared that Owen was simply looking for an excuse to pay them less. This fear persisted even after Owen kept their salaries the same for the shortened work hours. To win them over, Owen appealed to what today would be called the "influencers," to whom he patiently explained his intentions, in the hope that they would accept them and convince their colleagues. He understood that he couldn't force transformation on the resisting workers and proceeded slowly.

Unexpectedly, in 1807, the United States helped him. Due to America's embargo against British trade, all of Britain's textile manufacturers put their workers on furlough – except Owen, who continued to pay all salaries for four months until business resumed. This convinced many workers to trust him.

Another constituency that resisted many of his social innovations were his eight business partners. They were what we call today "value extractors," and they believed that Owen's social innovations did nothing but eat up their dividends. In 1809, they asked him either to change course or to buy the co-owners out. Owen chose the latter, finding eight new investors. But they proved to be even more impatient with Owen's "philanthropy" – as they called it – at the expense of their earnings.

Owen had to wait seven years before he could implement his educational projects. David Dale had already built a school for apprentices, primarily poor children, to learn reading, writing, arithmetic, sewing, and religion. However, Owen's vision was different: he wanted to ban all children under the age of 10 from the factory and ensure they attended school. He also envisioned a new facility, the "Institute for the Formation of Character," aimed at providing educational and cultural activities for local adults. In 1813, despite his partners' opposition, Owen finally succeeded in opening both nursery and primary schools. But his partners could not imagine that improving the well-being of workers and their families – a goal in itself – could also lead to better company performance. Like the former co-owners, they too instructed Owen to end his social innovations. He resigned, and the mill was put up for sale. But Owen outwitted his erstwhile partners. He went to London and found new investors – including several Quakers and the philosopher Jeremy Bentham, founder of utilitarianism – who were supportive of Owen's social innovations and also agreed to cap their dividends at 5% of profits.

On 10 January 1814, when Owen returned as director and new co-owner, the workers' families greeted him with the village orchestra, flags, and cheers of joy.

Going National and Beyond

Imagine yourself in Owen's situation. You've succeeded in realizing your beliefs about taking care of workers, their families, and your local community on a large scale. The social reality of your factory draws the admiration of tens of thousands. Your employees are not only better treated, but they have also become more productive, just as you believed. As a result, your company is doing extremely well. Your "activist" stockholders left; you now have co-owners who fully share your beliefs. Wouldn't you like your fellow industrialists to adopt similar practices, effective both socially and economically? That's what Owen did, but the results were disappointing.

Besides inviting his peers, Britain's influential personalities and opinion leaders, to New Lanark, Owen published *A New View of Society* outlining his ideas.[5] They were praised by many of Britain's elite, including Prince Edward, Lord Lansdowne, the poet Samuel Taylor Coleridge, and Jeremy Bentham, all of whom viewed him as a visionary. Owen also appealed to his fellow industrialists, asking them why, if they invested time and capital to maintain the effectiveness of their "lifeless machines," they didn't want to invest a fraction of this time and capital in "living machines" even more advantageously. The owner of the most profitable mill in Britain, he thus publicly showed them that not only do they mistreat their workers, but they are underperforming. They didn't like it. The prevailing view was that improving workers' welfare didn't directly contribute to a company's profitability and was therefore a waste. Most considered him overly idealistic, some even calling him a political lunatic.

But sure of his approach, Owen pushed ahead. He investigated the working conditions in British factories and presented his findings to the House of Commons, pointing to the severe exploitation of workers, particularly children, who often worked up to 14 hours a day in appalling conditions. In 1819, the parliament adopted the *Factory Act* prohibiting work for children under 9 and limiting the workday for those aged 9–16 to a maximum of 12 hours per day. It applied only to the textile industry; British *laisser faire* politicians didn't want to go further. Consequently, none of Owen's other social innovations were widely enacted. Even the textile industry largely ignored the 1819 act, as it had no clear enforcement mechanism and relied on mill owners' compliance, which was minimal.

You might expect that after such disappointing results Owen would give up. Yes and no. He gave up on his peers, but he had a grander plan: to reform the entire society. Robert Owen saw that rapid industrialization led not only to economic growth, but also to economic crises, poverty, and unemployment. He was concerned with their impact on workers.

His solution was the self-sufficient, cooperative communities he called the "villages of cooperation." In 1817, he submitted to the British government his "Report to the Committee of the Association for the Relief of the Manufacturing Poor" outlining his project. But it would not be the British authorities, but the American ones, including seven sitting and former presidents of the United States, who welcomed his ideas. In 1825, Owen purchased a town in Indiana, which he named New Harmony, and there he established his first village of cooperation. It attracted many idealists, but few skilled laborers. The diversity of their beliefs led to many ideological debates, but little agreement on how to run the village's economic activities. Productivity was low, the community struggled financially, and the turnover among residents was high. After two years, Owen's New Harmony project failed. Altogether, he had invested the current equivalent of $20 million – 80% of his fortune – in this endeavor.

Mixed Record Rich in Lessons

Owen's record was mixed. But it's rich in lessons. His social innovations in New Lanark were highly effective both in social and, subsequently, economic terms. The flow of visitors to admire them never stopped. And as one more sign of their success, Marx made them the object of his harsh critique, as they placed in doubt his cherished belief that workers would never be reconciled with a capitalist enterprise. Still today, New Lanark, a UNESCO World Heritage Site showcasing all of Owen's social advances, attracts countless visitors. But even though his innovations in the mill were highly effective, Owen's later attempts to persuade other British industrialists to follow his example or his later projects to transform entire communities failed.

Of course, Owen's case is just one example, but we believe that its depth and diversity can point to what works and what doesn't in carrying out social innovations. In particular, we can draw from it some preliminary lessons about the key success factors for effective social innovations. By effective, we mean social innovations that significantly improve the welfare of employees, their families, and the host community, ultimately resulting in improved economic performance for the business.

Based on Owen's experiences, we propose three factors for social innovations to achieve this kind of effectiveness. We call them the WHY, WHAT, and WHO of social innovation.

- **Why:** These innovations should be *ends in themselves*, not simply the means to increase profits – though profits should follow.
- **What:** They must consist of a bundle of *mutually supportive measures*, systematically transforming both the way the business operates and the social conditions of employees, their families, and the local community.
- **Who:** These transformations should be *led by businesspersons at the helm* of their companies and with the cooperation of employees.

In the following three sections, we examine each one of these factors and muster scientific evidence in support of them.

One more point. Because social challenges have historically been at the heart of the transformational efforts of business leaders, in this chapter we focus mostly on them. However, in the rest of our book, we show how the same factors are key to effective environmental innovations.

THE WHY OF SOCIAL INNOVATION

Start with Why is the title of Simon Sinek's renowned 2009 book on business leadership.[6] The same year, Isaac's book *Freedom, Inc.* with Brian Carney opened with a section on "HOW Companies and WHY Companies."[7]

When looking at the effectiveness of social innovations, we examine the WHY factor by asking why a leader has attempted a given innovation: Is the innovation an end in itself, or merely a means to greater economic performance? In other words, putting in place social innovations and expecting that economic performance will follow is a bet. Such a bet runs against the typical way companies operate. Typically, they fix economic targets, such as 14% EBITDA margins, and then design a business model – with its business processes and metrics – which is supposed to generate such an economic result. It's mechanical and linear. Of course, most business leaders know that the assumptions put into a business model rarely come true. They make assumptions about demand, interest rates, inflation, or oil prices that almost never prove accurate, to say nothing of unexpected economic, health, or geo-political crises that frequently make these business models obsolete by the end of the year, if not before. And the world is getting more – not less – unpredictable. Yet, businesses continue betting on such assumptions, although they may "rebrand" it as strategic forecasting or scenario planning.[8]

Instead of pursuing the economic WHY through betting on assumptions about the future, we propose a different type of bet: pursuing the social and environmental WHY and believing that economic performance will follow. Such a bet may seem idealistic. Yet the following economic theory may render it more realistic.

It is called the *Theory of Obliquity*, and it has been developed by London School of Economics professor John Kay.[9] He defines obliquity as the indirect way of achieving one's goals. Literally, obliquity signifies a relationship between two lines that are neither perpendicular nor parallel. In other words, this relationship exists, but it's not apparent to the naked eye.

For example, when researchers study people who describe themselves as happy – that is, experiencing simultaneous feelings of well-being and vitality – almost none report having directly pursued happiness through their actions. Athletes say they train to improve their time or technique, artists paint to achieve a new effect in color or rhythm, architects design to create a new solution for dwelling or working, and entrepreneurs undertake ventures to pursue a personal dream and to invent a new way of satisfying customers. It's when they succeed in achieving what they were aiming for that they describe themselves as happy, happiness being an oblique benefit of these intrinsically motivated actions.

You may agree that athletes are not aiming at happiness, but they do aim at winning, don't they? Well, John Wooden, ESPN's Coach of the twentieth century, who won 10 college basketball championships with UCLA, disagrees. He aimed not at winning but at success, which he defined as "peace of mind, which is a direct result of self-satisfaction in knowing you made the *effort* to become the best that you are capable of becoming."[10] In other words, each player's – and Wooden's – WHY is the effort of realizing one's potential. All else, he adds, "fame and fortune, power and prestige, trophies and titles, as well as outscoring an opponent, are merely by-products of *effort*."[11]

Entrepreneurs are not an exception to obliquity theory. Researchers Xu and Rueff, one from Princeton and the other from Stanford, have investigated why entrepreneurs start their businesses.[12] The commonly accepted answer is to make a profit, an answer that they decided to test. They randomly called 65,000 people, identifying 830 among them as nascent entrepreneurs. Next, they administered a test to pinpoint the factors that motivated these individuals to start their businesses. Surprisingly, the two main factors they found were not financial in nature: autonomy – being their own boss and self-directing their life; and identity fulfillment – living their dream and establishing an enduring personal legacy by offering a product or service useful to society.

That said, entrepreneurs do not eschew profits, but they are very careful not to maximize them. They seek enough profit to sustain the business that provides them with autonomy and self-fulfillment. Put differently, they are aware that aiming for *too much profit* endangers their business and hence, their chances for autonomy and self-fulfillment. We will explore this sweet vitality spot between efficiency and resilience in Chapter 8.

You may still believe that despite this, if an entrepreneur seeks investors, she must present a business model that will directly demonstrate how the company plans to achieve economic performance. Listening to a renowned entrepreneurship thinker and venture capitalist like Guy Kawasaki might alter your belief, however. Reflecting on the business models presented to investors, Kawasaki notes that "like the Holy Grail, the business plan remains largely unattainable and mythological; [it] is of limited usefulness for a startup because entrepreneurs base so much of their plans on assumptions, 'visions,' and unknowns."[13] It is by acting and engaging that entrepreneurs begin to better understand the complex environment in which they operate. Simply put, they try to explore it rather than to model it. Instead, most approaches to entrepreneurship are oblique, such as "learning by doing," "tinkering," "design thinking," "prototyping," "low-cost experimentation," or "lean start-up" – all creative processes.[14] In other words, business models and projected revenues are important, but as financial communication tools, not as the entrepreneur's WHY.

Some renowned entrepreneurs think similarly. Thus, Steve Jobs was disturbed to hear young Silicon Valley entrepreneurs talking about "exit strategy" – a quick, highly profitable sale of a start-up to a larger company: "It's a small ambition, instead of trying to build companies that last for decades, if not a century or more."[15] Several years later he added: "Being the richest man in the cemetery doesn't matter to me. Going to bed at night saying we've done something wonderful ... that's what matters to me."[16] And Michel Leclerc, the founder of Decathlon, a world-leading sports-equipment retail chain said: "You should never seek money; you should seek how to contribute to people's well-being."[17] These entrepreneurs became extremely prosperous without actively pursuing wealth through their professional activities. Instead, they pursued their freedom and self-fulfillment through the creation of useful and novel solutions for customers, which – obliquely – generated immense fortunes.

Finally, there is one ubiquitous business activity – sales – which practices obliquity every day. As any good sales person will tell you, good client relationship lead to good sales. Therefore, she will concentrate on the first and expect the second to follow. The caveat is that, although most businesses adhere to this idea, they still view caring for clients as means to sales rather than a purpose itself. We will return to this point.

To sum up, the WHY factor of seeing social innovation as the end in itself and betting that the economic results will follow is not only backed by economic science but by the research and practice of entrepreneurship.

Later in the book, we show how caring companies organize their activities in pursuit of their social and environmental WHY – and as a result prosper. To achieve that, they have all thought through the WHAT of social innovation.

THE WHAT OF SOCIAL INNOVATION

On numerous occasions, we have observed something very human in business leaders. Once they are filled with the social or environmental WHY and once it provides meaning to their professional lives, they want to fulfill it fast – they crave action. It's a very human impulse, yet it is one that often renders social innovation ineffective. The reason is that haste most often leads to a one-off measure, perhaps a couple of them – instead of a thought-through and carefully elaborated set of measures. Take alpinism as a metaphor.

If you dream of climbing a high mountain peak, you wouldn't assume that simply buying the best alpine gear is enough to reach the summit. Such a "silver bullet" approach is destined to fail, and if these failures accumulate, a general skepticism will likely set in, doubting that the mountain is climbable at all. Fortunately, in the real world, experienced alpinists advise aspiring climbers that top physical condition, rigorous high-altitude training, a qualified team, and several other conditions are necessary – though not sufficient – for reaching a high mountain summit. In other words, while your dream to climb may impress friends and family, disregarding the necessary and comprehensive set of measures and expecting success is not only naive but potentially life-threatening.

There is no "silver bullet" – no single measure that will bring success.

Like the alpine WHY – which can't be accomplished without an appropriate WHAT bundle of mutually supportive measures – the social and environmental WHY can't be accomplished without an appropriate WHAT bundle. This bundle idea is backed by science.

The evidence comes from studies on innovative work practices, also called high performance work practices, such as extensive recruiting and careful selection, flexible job definitions and problem-solving teams, gain-sharing-type compensation plans, employment security, and extensive labor-management communication.[18] They are called "high performance" because their implementation is supposed to impact employee well-being, measured by lower absenteeism or higher engagement, and subsequently, result in higher economic performance. Researchers have looked at the factors that generate high performance. Reviewing dozens of studies, they found that high performance results only when these work practices are implemented as a mutually reinforcing coherent bundle; they concluded that "changes in *individual* work practices have no effect on performance."[19]

Companies still often overlook these decades-old findings on the effectiveness of the innovative work practices. Many wrongly believe that adopting individual practice, be it a four-day work week, offering remote work, providing flexible hours, or gain-sharing compensation plan, will meaningfully impact employees' welfare, and consequently, the company's performance. Netflix and Gravity Payments are two such examples.

Netflix's Unlimited Vacation Policy

In 2003, Netflix CEO Reed Hastings introduced an unlimited vacation policy, giving employees the freedom to take as many vacation days as they deemed necessary. Hastings provided several motives for this measure.[20] First, what mattered for him "is what you achieve, not how many hours you clock," and since the company didn't control how many hours employees work, it seemed to him incoherent to control how many vacation days they took. Next, he thought it would be good for creativity, noting that employees returning from vacation often have many great ideas. Finally, he recognized that the policy also appealed to the younger generations.

Hastings recounts that it took years until this policy worked with the majority of employees. Indeed, without any regulation, employees would look at their superiors and colleagues' behavior. Those surrounded by workaholics would not dare to take many days off. On the other hand, there were cases of irresponsible behavior, such as an accounting team member who took two weeks off at the beginning of January's busy period and made the department miss its reporting deadline. Over time, Hastings encouraged leaders to be good examples, and teams started to coordinate taking vacations in advance so that important deadlines would not be compromised.

We can see that the launch of this social innovation ignored both key factors to make them effective. In terms of WHY, it was not introduced as an end in itself – the well-being of employees – but as a means to spur employee creativity and loyalty, valued by the company. But most importantly, this social innovation ignored the WHAT factor. Netflix did not bundle it with other mutually supportive social measures, such as exemplary leadership by superiors and respect-based relations between colleagues.

To Hastings' credit, he became aware of the need for a comprehensive bundle of measures to be put in place and gradually implemented them. Several years later, together with Netflix chief talent officer, Patty McCord, he created – and in 2009, rendered public – the *Culture Deck*. The deck consists of more than one hundred slides that detail the company's values, such as freedom and responsibility, and how they are articulated through various organizational practices.[21] Unlimited vacation policy is there, but so are numerous other people-centered practices forming a mutually supportive bundle, which form the core of Netflix' culture. To this day, it remains widely influential in Silicon Valley.

Dan Price's $70,000 Salaries

In 2015, American screens and social media exploded with news of a new star CEO very few people had heard of – Dan Price. Price founded a Seattle-based credit card processing company, Gravity Payments. Paradoxically, he was hailed not because he was earning a $1 million salary, but because he cut it by 90%. Moreover, he used these funds to raise every one of his 13 employees' salaries to $70,000.

Price credited his idea to a study coauthored by Nobel Prize winner Daniel Kahneman, which argued that: "Emotional well-being [doesn't] progress beyond an annual income of ~$75,000. Low income exacerbates the emotional pain associated with such misfortunes as divorce, ill health, and being alone … High income buys life satisfaction but not happiness."[22]

Price put the bar at $70,000 for every employee. According to some, in the following years, they were able to buy a house or start a family. Price also cited the company's attractiveness to new hires and said that employee turnover fell by half. Finally, the company's revenue tripled and the number of employees quickly grew. All in all, the increase in salaries looked like a "silver bullet" social innovation.

Yet, by 2022, the effectiveness of this social innovation came into question. In terms of corporate performance, concerns arose regarding product innovation and sources of growth. As a former director of engineering noted, Gravity's attempts to develop new products fell short, making it difficult to compete with larger rivals. Furthermore, regarding the company's revenue growth, some employees attributed it not to the inherent quality of its products and services but to Price's fame: "Gravity did not sell credit card processing. We sold Dan Price."[23]

Moreover, according to our definition of social innovation's effectiveness, it must, first and foremost, significantly improve the welfare of employees, their families, and the local community. Indeed, Price frequently appealed to "invest in people," and his salaries' increase was supposed to contribute to employee welfare. However, several dozen former employees reported that working at Gravity took a mental or emotional toll on them, including crying at work, panic attacks, and stress-induced health issues. When a dozen employees brought their concerns to HR, they were intimidated rather than supported.

In addition, many of the interviewed people spoke of Price's behavioral issues, such as being prone to outlandish requests, grand entrances, outbursts, and contacting employees at all hours. Moreover, there were also ethical concerns about Price's decisions and behavior. When the marketing team raised them openly, 12 of its 14 members were pushed out of the company. To cap it all, there were several allegations of Price's sexual misconduct, following which he resigned as CEO in 2022. Currently, Price is charged in one of the cases, while the other cases are pending.

There may be debate over whether the failure of the salary increase measure stemmed from it being a one-off initiative, the toxic culture within Gravity, or both. However, had it been implemented alongside – or preferably after – other social measures, particularly reforming the CEO's behavior and transforming managerial practices that mistreated employees, it might have had a chance to succeed.

The Netflix and Gravity Payments cases would be of little value if they were unique. They are not. For decades and up to today, we have heard about one-off innovations such as casual Friday, four-day work weeks, flexible work hours, remote work, or even gain sharing and shared-ownership schemes. Often, each of them is painted by corporate management or by the human resources department as a "silver bullet" that radically improves employee welfare. In reality, after the initial buzz, employees soon discover that the purpose of the innovation is not their welfare but achieving corporate goals such as retaining and attracting talent, limiting salary increases, making a PR point, or signaling "social virtue." In other words, they realize that aside from this isolated innovation, it's "business as usual" in their company. Day after day, they observe that all other workplace aspects that hamper employee welfare remain in place, which provokes in them a feeling of double-bind and malaise. Most importantly, employees always suspect that the one-off measure, however enjoyable, is a PR stunt. They can be convinced that their company walks the social talk only if it rolls out a bundle of coherent social measures.

But even if business leaders have an ambitious WHY and have elaborated a comprehensive bundle of social measures as their WHAT, they can still miss the WHO factor and doom their social innovation.

THE WHO OF SOCIAL INNOVATION

The last factor for effective social innovation requires that it be carried out by the business leader at the helm of the company. Among the three factors, it is perhaps the most controversial one. Indeed, as you will see in Chapters 2 and 3, all the existing corporate approaches to social and environmental challenges – philanthropy, corporate social responsibility, triple bottom line, B Corps, benefit corporations, stakeholder capitalism, or ESG (environmental, social, governance) – are most often conducted by dedicated managers and executives, and not the leaders who head these companies.

Moreover, even if leaders at the helm of the company wish to be involved, there is a deep reason why most often they are not able to do it: "important and urgent tasks." Through the lens of Eisenhower's classical matrix for organizing priorities, we have seldom seen leaders able to really allocate time for "important but nonurgent tasks." The result is that they don't invest enough in the future and are condemned to the continuous flow of urgent issues.

John Wooden, whom we've already mentioned, would teach every new basketball player how to tie his shoelaces. Wooden would explain that not taking this time would haunt the player during training, not only requiring him to pause and retie his shoelaces, but worse, it may cause blisters, thus leading to missed training and perhaps games. Furthermore, tying shoelaces is just the step zero of training, which for Wooden was the key to everything he did. It's through practice that his WHY of realizing the human potential of his players would be accomplished. There is a common saying in sports: "You play the way you train." For Wooden, the coach's most important job is to conduct the best possible training sessions for his players: "Once a game began, I felt my job as coach [is] complete and I could go into the stands and watch without having to give constant instructions … micromanaging."[24]

Social innovation is like training sessions. Some business leaders understand the importance of elaborating and conducting such innovations by themselves. Yet for most, running their most visible and rewarding tasks – managing the games – is too demanding to dedicate sufficient time for social innovation – training sessions. Thus, they delegate the latter to the "assistant coach." As a consequence, their corporate "club" rarely wins. Unlike them, many pioneers of effective social innovations have been fully involved in implementing them. Let's visit the Hall of Fame of such pioneers.

HISTORY'S WHO'S WHO OF SOCIAL INNOVATION

In the United States, at the start of the twentieth century, James Cash Penney, founder of a department store chain originally named Golden Rule, implemented social innovations. These innovations supported customers (never profiting at their expense), employees (job security, vacations, sick leave, life insurance, continuous training, profit-sharing), and the host communities (requiring each store to contribute to the city in which it operated).

In Europe, pioneers implemented social innovations as early as the nineteenth-century. This was the case in France with the Schneider family in Le Creusot, as well as with Alsace and Northern France entrepreneurs who provided housing, open schools, and established local social security and retirement funds.

In the 1920s and 1930s in the United Kingdom, Michael Marks and his successors at the Marks & Spencer chain introduced social innovations that benefit customers (offering quality goods at low prices for the working class), suppliers (long-term, loyal relationships), and employees (advanced working conditions for the time, including canteens, medical services, a retirement system, etc.). In Czechoslovakia in the 1930s, Tomáš Baťa pioneered a series of social innovations at Europe's largest shoe manufacturer, including a company town with housing, healthcare, and educational facilities for employees and their families, along with a profit-sharing scheme and participative decision-making in daily activities.

History has more business owners, beginning with Wedgwood, Dale, and Owen, who have adopted similar social innovations. Remarkably, all of the historical social innovations we have described have resulted in better economic results. James O'Toole, after reviewing more than two dozen such cases across two centuries, concluded that social innovations "proved compatible with profitability at all the companies, starting with the New Lanark Mills on down to Ben & Jerry's."[25]

All these cases of social innovation had the right WHY and used a comprehensive WHAT bundle. Most importantly, their WHO, the person who led the implementation of this WHAT bundle, was at the helm of the company. In this book we describe and analyze other contemporary cases of effective social and environmental innovations in which leaders respected the WHY, WHAT, and WHO factors. But first we need to describe the existing approaches to social and environmental challenges, approaches that the leaders in our book have mostly eschewed, though they dominate the current debate on the topic.

CHAPTER TWO

"CATCH ME IF YOU CAN" OR DOING GOOD TO KEEP ONE'S LICENSE TO OPERATE

It is impossible to chase two rabbits at the same time.

– Popular wisdom

Having explored the principles that make social innovation effective – and seen how maverick leaders like Owen thrived by embracing them – we now turn to the prevailing approaches to doing good that most companies have adopted in recent decades. Unlike the rare few who acted out of genuine conviction, most businesses have attempted to do good while remaining within the safe confines of profit-seeking. This chapter examines these strategies and poses a critical question: Have they fundamentally reshaped corporate behavior, or merely served as tools to adapt to an evolving public opinion and maintain a satisfactory reputation?

To start, let us challenge you to guess the author of this critique of capitalism:

> Giant, monetized, shareholder corporations ... have become a superb instrument for the capitalization of gain and socialization of cost.
>
> When a corporation rips from the Earth irreplaceable energy or resources, no matter how much it pays for them; when it uses any resources more rapidly than they can be replaced, or at less than full replacement cost, it has socialized the cost (spread it to society as a whole; the people at large) and capitalized the resultant gain.
>
> When a corporation "downsizes" workers, abandons a community, or pays less than a living wage; when it creates and dumps waste in the process of manufacturing or marketing a product, or at the end of its useful life; when it receives a subsidy, guarantee, or relief from taxation by government, it has socialized a cost and capitalized the gain ...
>
> The possibilities for socializing cost and capitalizing gain are endless, as those who hold power or wealth within monetized corporations have discovered to their endless benefit. [And t]his effect of this vast corporate socialization of cost and capitalization of gain is no longer limited to the current generation ...[1]

Then, the author delivers his verdict:

> If the purpose of each corporation is not primarily the health and well-being of the Earth and all life thereon, if its principles are not based on equitable distribution of power and wealth, if it avoids responsibility for the sustenance of family, community, and place, if it has no belief system, or one devoid of ethical and moral content, it is difficult to see why it should have the sanction and protection of society through the arm of government.[2]

You may think the author is a Marxist economist, an anti-capitalist politician, or a leader of a militant anti-system movement. He isn't. In fact, he spent all his professional life at the heart of our global financial system. His name is Dee Hock, the founder and the first chairman of VISA International, the world's largest credit card company.

Indeed, Hock wrote these lines in 2005, but the challenges to corporations' right to operate are not recent. For more than 50 years already, governments – pressed by the public – have been trying to regulate corporations, forcing them more and more to comply.[3] We call it the "Catch me if you can" game.

THE "CATCH ME IF YOU CAN" GAME

There are four main players in this game: the general public, government and authorities, thought leaders, and corporations. There are, in addition, some maverick players, business leaders who operate outside the main field of play and test different rules for the game.

At first glance, the interaction among these players seems linear: the general public elects politicians into government, the government regulates the corporations, thinkers propose new approaches on how to take into account these regulations, and the corporations follow the new rules. Yet a deeper look reveals that corporations routinely influence governments and the general public, while thought leaders often influence corporations and governments (see Figure 2.1). To further complicate matters, additional players, such as the media and non-governmental organizations (NGOs), influence the four main players. But to make the description simpler, we leave them out for now.

Figure 2.1   Players of the "catch me if you can" game.

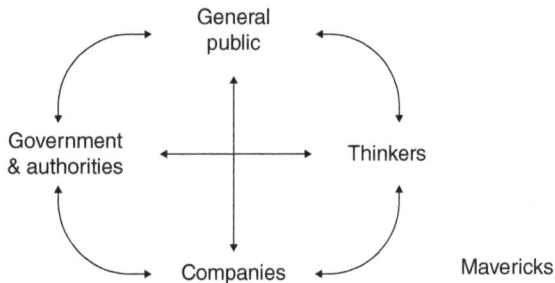

The Public Gets Uneasy

Do you remember the day your youngest child asked you: "Mommy, why are all these birds dying trapped in oil?" Or the day you first investigated the conditions in which your favorite pair of sneakers had been produced? Have you ever thought about the fact that you, as a taxpayer, might have, even indirectly, been asked to pay for the cost – financial and social – imposed by the greed of a few people, such as after the subprime mortgage crisis between 2007 and 2010?

In democracies at least, everything starts with public opinion. Over the decades, industrial accidents, ethical scandals, and global crises have gradually eroded the trust between the general public and corporations. This brief overview explains why.

Industrial Accidents

The most palpable negative effect of business is a sudden destruction of nature or a catastrophe affecting numerous victims. Table 2.1 lists major industrial accidents since 1980 and their consequences.

You may think that the root causes of these catastrophes were human error. Yes, that often played a role. But if you look closely at most of these events, you will find in the background a cost-minimizing corporate approach to safety or simply an arrogant management deaf to signals from the frontline.

Table 2.1   Major Industrial Accidents Since 1980

Year	Name	Country	Type	Effects
1984	Bhopal	India	Gas Explosion	3,787 deaths, over 558,000 injured
1984	San Juanico	Mexico	Fires and Explosions	500–600 deaths, 50–60,000 with severe burns
1986	Chernobyl	Ukraine	Nuclear Disaster	3,940 deaths from radiation-induced cancer and leukemia
1988	Piper Alpha	North Sea	Oil Platform Explosion	167 deaths
1989	Exxon Valdez	USA (Alaska)	Oil Spill	100–250,000 seabirds killed
2001	AZF Total	France	Plant Explosion	31 deaths, 2,500 injured
2005	Texas City	USA	Refinery Explosion	15 deaths, 170 injured
2010	Deepwater Horizon	Gulf of Mexico	Oil Spill	11 deaths, largest marine oil spill (4.9 million barrels of oil released)
2013	Rana Plaza	Bangladesh	Building Collapse	More than 1,100 deaths
2022	Fukushima Daiichi	Japan	Nuclear Disaster	164,000 displaced people

Source: Caiazza, et al., 2023/John Wiley & Sons.[4]

Without excusing anyone, you might point out that while these were very unfortunate events, not all accidents can be avoided. Any industrial activity involves risk, and a small percentage of accidents is the price to pay collectively for the benefits that corporations bring to us – just as we accept car accidents as the price of the benefits that come with automotive transportation. But this line of argument doesn't work as well with corporate ethical scandals – another element that degrades general public trust in corporations.

Ethical Scandals

Thinking about ethical scandals, what immediately pops into our minds are the massive frauds associated with Enron, Madoff, or more recently Sam Bankman-Fried. You may still believe that these cases are so exceptional that they don't prove anything about typical business ethics. The following cases of entire industries entering in fraudulent activities may, however, alter your belief. In 2012, an important international interest-rate benchmark, the London Interbank Offer Rate, or LIBOR, was found to have been manipulated by the following institutions: Barclays, Citigroup, Deutsche Bank, HSBC, JP Morgan Chase, Royal Bank of Scotland, Société Générale, UBS Group. If this list does not point to a whole industry engulfed in fraud, what does?

But there is more. The list of ethical scandals that you find in Table 2.2 can further alter your belief that this is just about "black sheep." The truth is that the accumulation of cases has tarnished – in people's eyes and for a long time – the image of prestigious industries and global brands.

This extensive list, spanning various industries and geographical regions, provides compelling evidence that large corporations frequently breach the ethical standards they have publicly pledged to uphold.

Global Crises

"An empty and misleading work … best summarized … as a rediscovery of the oldest maxim of computer science: Garbage In, Garbage Out." This is how an April 1972, *New York Times* article harshly criticized the Club of Rome report *Limits to Growth,* based on an MIT study that for the first time modeled the obstacles to endless economic expansion.[5] Only 18 months after the *NYT* article, the warning of the possible depletion of resources became real – with the unexpected first global oil crisis in 1973.

Table 2.2   Scandals Involving Global Companies by Type (2000–2020)

Corruption, Fraud, and Bribery		
ABB	2004	Pension scandal
Adecco	2004	Accounting scandal
Alcatel-Lucent	2010	Bribery payments
Alibaba	2010	Methodical fraud against Alibaba dealers
BAE Systems	2004	Corruption
BAE Systems	2009	Corruption and bribery payments
BASF	2010	Corruption
Credit Suisse Group	2012	Tax scandal
Daimler	2010	Bribery payments
Deutsche Bank	2012	CO_2 emission certificate scandal
Facebook-Cambridge Analytica	2018	Improperly obtained and used data
Glaxosmithkline	2013	Bribery of physicians
Glaxosmithkline	2012	Illegal distribution practices for drugs
Hyundai Motor	2006	Corruption
IBM	2011	Bribery payments China and South Korea
Infineon Technologies	2005	Bribery payments
MAN	2009	Bribery
Olympus	2011	Accounting fraud
Pfizer	2004	Illegal marketing practices
Siemens	2007	Bribery
Telia Company	2013	Bribery payments, corruption, money laundering
Volkswagen	2005	Bribery payments
Wells Fargo & C°	2012	Property loan fraud

(Continued)

Table 2.2 (Continued)

Dangerous Products		
Baxter Intl.	2008	Fatalities caused by tainted heparin in 11 countries
Mattel	2007	Toy recall due to toxic lead color
Merck & Company	2004	Vioxx recall and increased heart attack risk
Nestlé	2008	Tainted milk powder in China
Pfizer	2007	Unauthorized drug testing on children in Nigeria
Roche Holding	2009	Tamiflu
Servier	2010	Mediator scandal
Toyota Motors	2009	Recall scandal in US
Working Conditions and Child Labor		
Apple	2010	Suicide wave and bad working conditions
Apple	2012	Bad working, safety, health conditions
Apple	2013	Bad working, safety, health conditions, child labor
Coca Cola	2004	Child labor on sugar plantations
Deutsche Telekom	2008	Spying on own executives
Foxconn Technology	2012	Bad working, safety, health conditions
GAP	2007	Child labor in India
Microsoft	2010	Reproach of child labor at supplier KYE
Monsanto	2007	Child labor
Philip Morris Intl.	2010	Child labor on tobacco plantation
Samsung Electronics	2012	Child labor
Tesco	2010	Child labor at suppliers
Walmart Stores	2009	Bad labor conditions and child labor
Walmart Stores	2013	Child labor in textile factory in Bangladesh
Walt Disney	2010	Child labor at suppliers

Source: Sebastian Utz (2019)/Springer Nature.[6]

In fact, since 1972, the scientific community has been warning us relentlessly about the perils to human life on Earth. Due to the wide dissemination of the Intergovernmental Panel on Climate Change (IPCC) reports, global warming due to greenhouse gas emission is the most publicized of these perils. However, it is only one of the systemic limits that are on the verge of being crossed – biosphere integrity and novel entities being the main risks (see Figure 2.2). The responsibility of businesses in this planetary crisis cannot be avoided: partly as the cause of some of these problems, but more importantly as a major partner in finding solutions.

Figure 2.2   Current status of control variables of nine planetary boundaries.
Source: American Association for the Advancement of Science/CC BY-NC 4.0.[7]

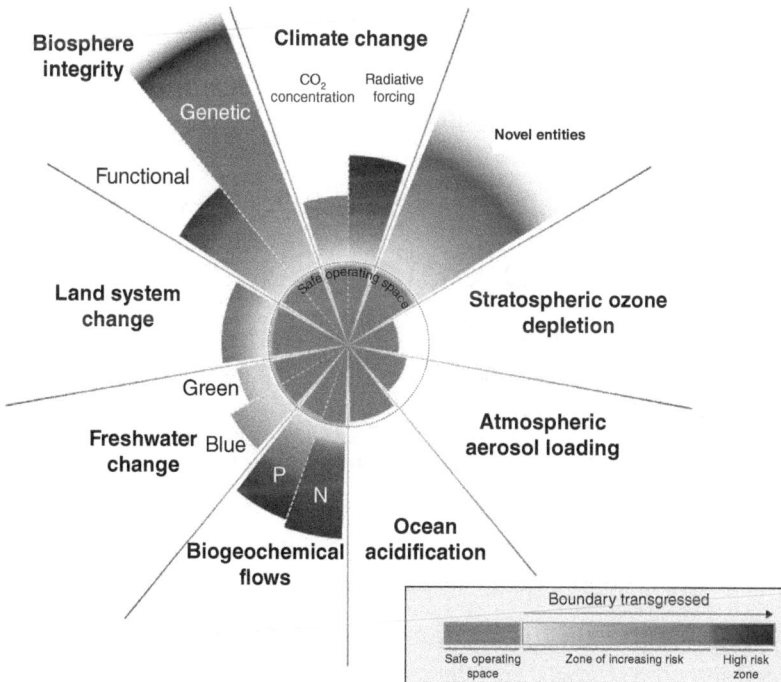

Moreover, environmental crises share the spotlight with many social crises, such as unprecedented inequality, the economic weight of criminal organizations, urban violence, and forced migration. And we all know that many conflicts around the world have an economic root – such as fights for control of raw materials and sources of energy or water.

Taken together, these accidents, scandals, and global disorders have proven to the public that corporations' contributions to the environment and to society are insufficient, and even negative. No wonder then that large companies are among the least trusted institutions by the American public, and the situation is not much different in other developed countries.[8] Not surprising either that the public pressure on governments to constraint businesses grows continuously. Enter the second player of the "catch me if you can" game – public authorities.

Governments and Authorities Trying to Catch Businesses

"Get out! Get out! Killers!" This is how an enraged crowd greeted Spain's Prime Minister Pedro Sanchez, King Felipe VI, and Queen Letizia in the town of Paiporta in early November 2024. A few days before, torrential rains killed more than 150 people in the region of Valencia, with the national and regional governments both appearing overwhelmed by the event.[9]

In democracies, public authorities are supposed to care for the safety of the people who elect them. They must show that they are responding to public concerns. Whether local, national, or international, it leads them to define political goals, translate these goals into law, and finally, create administrative bodies to enforce them.

A detailed description of the actions undertaken by different governments or by the United Nations would definitely be too boring. We don't want you to fall asleep before we move to next chapter. A quick look at Table 2.3 will suffice. It shows you the main milestones set in the past 50 years by public authorities to control or limit the power of businesses.

Table 2.3   Initiatives Taken by Governments, Public Authorities, or the International Community to Address Social and Environmental Challenges

Year	Country or geography	Action	Type
1970	USA	Creation of Environmental Protection Agency	Admin body
1971	USA	Creation of Occupational Safety and Health Administration	Admin body
1972	USA	Creation of US Consumer Product Safety Commission	Admin body
1987	International	Montreal Protocol	Political goal
1987	UN	Brundtland Commission	Political goal
1988	International	Creation of IPCC	Research body
1990	European Union	Creation of European Environment Agency	Admin body
1992	UN	UN declaration on Environment and Development (Rio)	Political goal
1997	International	Kyoto Protocol	Political goal
2000	UN	Global compact (10 principles for businesses)	Political goal
2010	UN	17 Development Objectives	Political goal
2014	EU	Directive to disclose nonfinancial and diversity information (large companies)	Law
2015	International	Paris Agreement	Political goal

(Continued)

Table 2.3 (Continued)

Year	Country or geography	Action	Type
2020	China	Carbon-neutrality for 2060	Political goal
2021	EU	European Climate Law	Law
2022	USA	Inflation Reduction Act (−40% on carbon emission for 2030)	Political goal
2024	EU	Corporate Sustainability Due Diligence Directive (CSDDD) -> effective in 2027	Law

Source: Adapted from Latapí Agudelo, et al., 2019.[10]

You can conclude from this quick review that governments and public authorities have mostly defined political goals and created administrative bodies for public action. That doesn't "catch" many businesses. Only recently have they started enforcing relevant legislation, which catch some businesses unprepared and put more pressure on many others to comply or be condemned by courts. Thus, the 2021 European Climate Law allows citizens to sue governments or companies for insufficient efforts to comply with its rules. And it is already happening. A coalition of four NGOs has sued the French government for climate inaction and won. Similarly, in 2021, a Dutch court ruled against Royal Dutch Shell, ordering the company to reduce its global emissions by 45% by 2030.[11]

We will see in the future how companies respond to all this – perhaps, they will initiate "soft laws" to prevent more "hard laws" from being imposed upon them. But before that, let's see how thought leaders – particularly those influencing the corporate world – have dealt with this growing public consciousness and with the declarations and actions of public authorities.

Thinkers Enter the Field

In the 1950s, some thinkers had already started to reflect on the social responsibilities of the business leaders.[12] But it is really only in the 1960s that the theme of "social responsibility" became popular in the US public debate. This is the decade that birthed Rachel Carson's *Silent Spring*, which exposed the wide-ranging ecological effects of Monsanto's DDT pesticide, helping give rise to the modern environmentalist movement. Three years later, Ralph Nader published his seminal attack on General Motors, *Unsafe at Any Speed*, which argued that America's large carmakers knowingly sold unsafe cars, abandoning their corporate social responsibility in the single-minded pursuit of profit. Nader's work would help spawn an entire industry, so to speak, of consumer activism that railed against the social irresponsibility of large corporations.

Milton Friedman's Critique and Its Unexpected Consequences

This advocacy and the public's and authorities' mounting pressure on businesses to assume social responsibility didn't escape the attention of one very sharp and influential thinker – Milton Friedman. A decade earlier, with an eye on the Cold War, his book *Capitalism and Freedom* made a vibrant case for a free-market economy.[13] In particular, Friedman argued that free markets promote individual choice, personal responsibility, and innovation, while any government intervention in the economy leads to waste and diminished personal freedom. Faithful to his views, in 1970, Friedman published his now-famous article in the *New York Times Magazine*: "The Social Responsibility of Business Is to Increase Its Profits."[14]

What Did Friedman Really Say?

Friedman's landmark article focused on the salaried business executives' decisions to use corporate resources for social or environmental goals instead of for profit maximization. Friedman criticized such a decision on three grounds:

First, by diverting corporate resources, the executives bias the free markets, leading to reduced dividends to the stockholders, higher prices for customers, or reduced wages to employees. Neither the stockholders, the customers, or the employees, he argues, has given the executives these powers of "imposing taxes and enacting expenditures" on them.

Second, Friedman noted that these latter powers are those of the elected government, which are limited through the democratic executive, legislative, and judicial powers. Unlike the elected government, executives who spend a corporation's resources on social causes take these powers for themselves in a uniquely undemocratic fashion, acting as a self-appointed authoritarian according to their personal desires.

Friedman's third and final charge was that these executives have no competence in choosing the best way to allocate corporate money to help social causes. Most social and environmental causes, he noted, be it bad education, insufficient affordable housing, or pollution, are very complex phenomena, and amateur decisions will rather worsen them than help.

Despite his harsh critique, Friedman was not totally dismissive of corporate social action. There was one reason he viewed as justifying them: He accepted corporations contributing to social and environmental causes as a tax-deductible way for them to generate goodwill from the public and the government. For example, corporations contributing to the local community may attract desirable employees or reduce their wage bill. Such contributions make good business sense and were justified for Friedman in terms of shareholders' interest.

Friedman's opponents usually quote his conclusion about the only social responsibility of business being "profit maximization within the rules of the free-markets, law, and ethical custom." But Friedman inadvertently did something else his critics rarely notice: He signaled a way for businesses to buy the public's goodwill, all the while sacrificing little and changing only minimally the way they operate.

> It's not "how to do good, while doing well," but "how to signal doing good, while continuing as usual."

Paradoxically, Friedman wanted businesses to reject the argument for social responsibility, but he contributed to the massive adherence of business to *signaling* social responsibility while doing as little as possible. And thus, companies started to increasingly use the escape route Friedman pointed to and continue doing so up to this day. Their earliest, and still influential, escape route in the "catch me if you can" game is called corporate social responsibility (CSR).

The CSR Escape

Since 2019, IKEA has supported more than 3,500 refugees and asylum seekers looking for employment opportunities. In 2023, Starbucks installed 50 fast chargers on the route between Denver and Seattle. In 2024, Glossier donated $300,000 and free mentoring for Black-Owned Beauty Business entrepreneurs. What is the link between the three companies leading these initiatives? Business magazine *Fast Company* named them among "the most innovative corporate social responsibility companies in 2024."[15]

First defined in 1979 by the American scholar Archie B. Carroll, the concept of CSR gained momentum in the 1980s mainly through what

Carroll identified as the fourth level of CSR: What is desired by society. That is, firms seek to meet philanthropic expectations – basically, to be good corporate citizens.

In this decade, companies engaged in an array of activities under the umbrella of CSR, from sponsoring art in the West to subsidizing schools or water supply in poor countries. Most of these activities had no direct link with the core business of the firm. In many cases, just as Friedman envisioned, these philanthropic activities often reflected the CEO's personal preferences for specific causes.

With time, CSR has expanded into activities to meet environmental and ethical expectations of the public, with the aim of reducing a corporation's negative impacts or to contribute to solving society's most pressing challenges. Thus, for example, food producers act to ensure their developing-country suppliers pay a "living wage" and ensure that they don't use child or slave labor.

A lot of great and useful projects would not happen without these CSR initiatives. However, the Friedmanite critiques of CSR often have a point. Just as Friedman argued, many companies are spending their money on CSR initiatives not because they truly care about their causes but because it varnishes their corporate or brand reputation and hence buys public goodwill.

That said, some companies do seek to maximize their social responsibility all the while doing everything to pursue their economic goals. In other words, these companies believe they can *balance* their social and environmental responsibilities with profit maximization.

The Triple Bottom Line and the First Balancing Escape

SMART, NPS, OKR, TQM, USP, KPI, BSC, SWOT, BPR, MVP, POC – welcome to the world of acronyms. Companies love them and consultants adore them. Facing the first wave of CSR initiatives, managers asked for some unifying framework that they could easily integrate in their strategies and in their reporting. At the end of the 1990s, British consultant John Elkington proposed just such a framework.[16] He also had a knack for the easiest-to-remember acronym to name his approach: 3Ps, standing for Profit, People, Planet – companies seeking to obtain positive results on all three dimensions. Since profit is often referred to as "the bottom line," Elkington designates his 3Ps as the Triple Bottom Line (TBL). When a business operates with a TBL, social and environmental goals take their place alongside the financial results, becoming part of the duty of top executives and the measurement of their performance. Consequently, implementing TBL required a new accounting and reporting system to make sure they do it – Elkington offered to help with that.

In the following years, Elkington led TBL implementations in many companies and expected more to voluntarily adopt it. After some time, their overall number reached several thousand.

The Shared Value Creation Escape

Observing that CSR and TBL were gaining momentum among business leaders, strategy thinkers didn't want to be left behind. In 2005, two American business strategy professors, David Chandler and William Werther, argued that CSR was moving from minimal commitment to a strategic necessity.[17] Half a decade later, Michael Porter, Harvard Business School strategy professor, co-published an article "Strategy and Society: The Link Between Competitiveness and Corporate Social Responsibility." The authors argued that "mere" CSR had too narrow a mindset – looking at social and environmental consequences of business only as externalities to be managed. They advocated for creating "Shared Value," which they defined as the "policies and practices that enhance the competitiveness of a company while simultaneously advancing the social and economic conditions of the communities in which it operates."[18] They added that shared value creation links societal progress to economic success. Companies such as Nestlé, Unilever, and Google adopted this approach.

In comparison to TBL, the Shared Value strategy is less balanced, as it clearly puts profit as its main goal, with social and environmental goals present, yet secondary.

To complete this quick overview of key thinkers, let's go to Davos, Switzerland, and visit its key influencer.

Stakeholder Capitalism and the Davos Escape

In 1971, a little-known German scholar co-authored a book, inspired by the cooperation in his country between companies, worker councils, and the local communities.[19] He described the 1950s German economy as typical of a capitalism conscious of its responsibilities toward other entities that also have a stake in a company's fate and grouped them all together as stakeholders – shareholders/owners, lenders, customers, suppliers, employees, state and society, economy.[20]

To advance his idea of stakeholder capitalism, he created an annual gathering in a small Swiss mountain resort, where business leaders, academics, and politicians started discussing a more responsible capitalism. More than 50 years after his first writings, the scholar – Klaus Schwab – has become one of the world's most influential thought leaders and personalities. And his World Economic Forum in Davos is the most prestigious event of the world for business and political elites.

Today, at least in Northern Europe, there are still many companies that would identify with stakeholder capitalism. Schwab, on his part, continues to evolve his model, particularly taking into account new environmental issues, all the while keeping its fundamentals intact.[21]

How People Understand Stakeholder Capitalism

R. Edward Freeman is an academic who is often called the "father" of stakeholder capitalism.[22] In this excerpt of an interview, he states that there are at least four ways to understand stakeholder capitalism:

The first way to understand this is … virtue signaling. "There's nothing to it, it's just PR."

Second view … "Well, it's virtue signaling but companies mean it. You know it's corporate social responsibility, that's what it is." The

---

problem with that view is that it only thinks about stakeholders on social or societal issues … Stakeholders are the civil society …

There's a third view: It's about top-down elites, getting CEOs and executives and political leaders and governments in a room and have them decide about some new agencies or rules, or that sort of thing. That comes close, I think, to what some have thought about this, like the World Economic Forum and others. There's some usefulness and truth in that.

But my version of this, and this is the fourth version: It's a business model, it's about how you create value for customers, suppliers, employees, communities, and people … and what if lots of companies did that?[23]

CSR, TBL, and stakeholder capitalism are all escape routes that initiated from outside the corporate world and are all based on balancing shareholders' goal of profit maximization with the goals of other stakeholders.[24] We discuss this balancing view later in this chapter – both in terms of its results and in terms of its consistency.

Before that, let's see how the corporate world has organized itself to face the pressures, trends, and theories from the public, from authorities, and from thought leaders we have just described.

How Companies Are Playing the Game

Companies have proved quite resourceful and devised many practical ways to escape in the "catch me if you can" game. Here is a brief review of these ways.

First, we observe organizational reshuffling and different ways of reporting. In its early stages, CSR initiatives are managed by PR departments or by separate foundations. In the past two decades, with pressure from the public and from the governments increasing, CSR has moved to dedicated sustainability vice presidencies, and even to the CEO and the board of directors. The number of chief sustainability officers (CSOs) in listed companies grew from 29 in 2011 to 95 in 2021.[25] With the more strategic role of CSR executives comes additional reporting. In some countries, TBL translates into the legal obligation for large firms to publish an annual social and environmental responsibility report, but many companies now do it on their own. The number of firms publishing such information – voluntarily or under obligation – has grown dramatically, from less than 20 companies in the early 1990s to more than 10,000 in 2019.[26]

The second way to show clean hands is certification. This means that all the activities of the firm are screened for their effects on society and the environment. That approach was pioneered in 2006, by the B-Corp movement aiming to "change our economic system."[27]

How Does B-Corp Certification Work?

B-Corp certification starts with an online self-assessment. A company needs to collect at least 80 out of a possible 200 points in order to be certified. These points are self-assessed on different items, such as governance, environment, workers, community, and the offering of the company, and are validated by B-Lab staff. For example, at the time of its certification in 2018, Danone North America became the largest certified company in the world, with a score of 85. It is showing progress year after year, reaching a total of 103 points in 2024.[28] Today, there are more than 3,000 certified B-Corps in the United States and more than 9,000 worldwide.[29]

The B-Corp approach is compatible with stakeholder capitalism, as certification is based – among other criteria – on a "legal commitment by changing their corporate governance structure to be accountable to all stakeholders, not just shareholder."[30]

The third practical way to escape in the "catch me if you can" game is to change the corporate statutes. In 2010, Maryland became the first state to legalize Benefit Corporation statutes, defined as a for-profit entity whose goals include making a positive impact on society. Although the names B-Corp and Benefit Corporation sound similar and thus are confusing, the main difference between a B-Corp and a Benefit Corporation is that a B-Corp is a certification, while a Benefit Corporation is a legal status.

One characteristic of Benefit Corporation statutes is the delineation of a "corporate purpose." The premise is that CEOs would risk legal action from shareholders in case they fail to prioritize their interests over those of other stakeholders – although the research shows that US courts have consistently upheld directors' discretion to consider broader stakeholder interests alongside shareholder primacy in their decision-making.[31] These legal statutes are now available in 38 states and in Washington, D.C., and similar statutes have been introduced in the United Kingdom as Community Interest Companies, in Italy as Società Benefit, in Canada as Benefit Companies, in Colombia as Beneficio e Interés Colectivo, and in France as Entreprise à Mission. Currently, the high estimation is that 10,000 Benefit Corporations exist in the United States alone.

The final practical way to win in the "catch me if you can" game are nonfinancial metrics. They are called ESG – Environmental, Social, and Governance – a set of criteria for extra-financial reporting. In their desire to mitigate risks linked to social and environmental issues – reputational risks vis-à-vis customers and communities as well as compliance risks vis-à-vis regulation – banks, insurance companies and investment funds are developing new standards for reporting the corporate activity. Though stimulated by governments, ESG reporting aims primarily at shareholders as well as other stakeholders. Thanks to their popularity, an array of ESG reporting standards has emerged: ISO 14001, Global Reporting Initiative

(GRI), Carbon Disclosure Project (CDP), ISO 26000 standards, etc. Seeking their convergence, the World Economic Forum (WEF) recently launched an initiative for "Stakeholder metrics" in cooperation with the Big Four accounting firms. One hundred fifty multinationals are already using it.[32]

The ESG escape route goes in line with the development of impact investment. In the United States alone, capital flow into ESG and sustainable investment funds has increased from $1 trillion in 1998 to $15 trillion in 2020.[33] Globally, according to KPMG, the value of "sustainable assets" is $30 trillion in 2019, having increased 38% between 2017 and 2019.[34] As of 2022, Europe seems to be leading that trend, with European-domiciled responsible-investment funds accounting for 90% of such funds globally.[35]

You may have deduced from this review that the practical escape routes used by the corporate world – organizational reshuffling, certification, legal structure, and financial metrics – reflect the same managerial mindset. It's a mindset in which "doing well while doing good" is something that can be achieved with a specific organizational structure, with processes and key performance indicators (KPIs). Something, in other words, that executives can control – in exactly the same manner that they control other aspects of their businesses. If you conclude that, so far, no mainstream alternative mindset considers the challenges of our times, you are right. As Einstein noted: "We cannot solve our problems with the same thinking we used when we created them."

Meet the Mavericks

Even though, since the 1970s, most companies have not changed profoundly the way they think and operate, some maverick entrepreneurs have done just that. They launched businesses whose core activities were specifically conceived with environmental concerns in mind. The best-known among them are the apparel company Patagonia, which Yvon Chouinard launched in 1973, the Body Shop cosmetics chain, which Anita Roddick opened in

1976, and Ben Cohen and Jerry Greenfield's eponymous ice-cream maker, Ben & Jerry's, founded in 1978.

They were the first mavericks: entrepreneurs who refused to enter the "catch me if you can" field and decided to play a different, truly transformative game. Instead of merely reacting to mounting public and government pressure via various escape tactics, these mavericks, and others who would follow, tried to proactively transform their companies – and with them potentially capitalism itself.

Bottom of the Pyramid Movement

In 2004, Roberto Bocca, a bright young Italian-born corporate executive found himself seated on the floor of a very humble straw house in rural India. When the poor villager welcomed him with a cup of tea, he was deeply moved by the hospitality of the woman. This was not a private trip, however. He was on a mission for his company: the giant energy multinational BP.

Earlier, in 2002, C. K. Prahalad, a Harvard Business School professor, wrote a landmark article: "Serving the world's poor, profitably."[36] He emphasized that not only is there an entirely untapped potential for business among poor people, but enlightened companies can contribute greatly to solving social problems – and consequently make profits. He called this approach the "Bottom of the Pyramid" strategy.

Two years later, John Browne, CEO of BP, decided to launch an initiative in India through a project managed by the young maverick Bocca. Cooperating with Prahalad and some NGOs, Bocca and his team spent more than 100 days in the homes of very poor people learning how BP could help them. This led to an innovative solution to the respiratory diseases caused by traditional ovens in poor people's homes. Specifically, BP conceived an energy system consisting of a $17 portable biomass stove that emitted 70% less carbon dioxide than gas ovens, without any emissions of toxic indoor gas. In April 2006, BP sold its first stove. By December 2008, they had sold 375,000 stoves – all at a profit. The Indian project was then replicated in South Africa, China, and Vietnam.

In the same spirit, in 2006, Franck Riboud, then CEO of Danone, the food industry leader, met Muhammad Yunus, the founder of Bangladesh's micro-credit Grameen Bank. Together they launched a pioneering joint venture, Grameen Danone Food Ltd. Based on the experience of Grameen Bank, serving nearly 10 million people through microfinance, Yunus had theorized about "social business," which he described as a company dedicated to solving a particular social issue and adhering to the principle: "No dividend. No loss." On these principles, the joint venture launched a yogurt called *Shokti Doi* aimed to supplement underfed children with protein, vitamins, iron, calcium, and zinc. The factory producing the yogurt was much smaller than what Danone would have built normally to address a market like Bangladesh. Their distribution of *Shokti Doi* is also peculiar: clients of Grameen Bank, called "Grameen ladies," would come to the plant and then go from village to village to sell it directly to the customers.

Such special side projects by large corporations are nice, but some maverick entrepreneurs think bigger. As CEOs, they have chosen to turn their entire company into a pioneer organization.

Industry-wide Mavericks

John Mackay was one of these entrepreneurs. Together with associates, in 1980, he founded in Austin, Texas, the first Whole Foods supermarket, committed to selling natural and organic products. The company also built a culture based on autonomous teams, which hired their team members and made a host of other decisions. In 2016, the chain boasted more than 450 stores in the United States, Canada, and the United Kingdom and was the market leader in upscale natural and organic food.

Meanwhile, in the early 2010s, while still CEO, Mackay, together with Babson College professor Rajendra Sisodia, codified his Whole Foods experience under the rubric of "conscious capitalism."[37] It was based on four pillars: higher purpose, stakeholder orientation, conscious leadership, and conscious culture. In comparison with classical CSR, conscious capitalism focused on leadership and presented itself as a movement of CEOs and companies determined to "rewrite the narrative of capitalism."[38] The movement also called for compassion – along with freedom and prosperity – to take center stage. In 2024, the movement had more than 30 chapters in large US cities and abroad.

About the same time, there emerged another maverick, Paul Polman, CEO of Unilever from 2009 to 2019. He could have acted as a typical corporate CEO, oriented toward shareholders' interests and public authorities' pressures. But in the first months of his tenure, he stepped outside of this game, and started to play a different one, based on his deep values. Right after his nomination, he spoke about "the difference between being a half person and a full person" and that he hates "to have, the day when [he] passes on, people talk about [him] building market share" and that he would rather "have them talk about [him] making a difference in society."[39]

And Polman walked his talk. He stopped quarterly reports to shareholders in order to focus on a long-term strategy, redefined Unilever's purpose, and sought to align its product line with it. He also announced and monitored ambitious social and environmental goals, such as creating five million jobs on small farms or having 100% of its factories sending no waste to landfills. Remarkably, during Polman's tenure, Unilever's commitment to social and environmental goals did not impair its financial performance: its revenues doubled and returns to shareholders grew 290%. Moreover, the purpose-led "Sustainable Living Brands" grew 69% faster than the rest of Unilever's brands.

The Mavericks' Record

"Maverick" cases have been impressive in their ambition to meet the environmental and social challenges and, hence, have been widely hailed and publicized. But except for Polman, their financial results had been so far less impressive.

For the inside projects, despite their clear social and environmental benefits, BP judged its Indian stoves business as insufficiently profitable relative to shareholders' expectations and sold it. The high-profile Grameen Danone venture never broke even. The original plan to build nine additional plants was never implemented.

Regarding maverick entrepreneurs, Patagonia remains an independent company and iconic brand. However, Ben & Jerry's, after becoming publicly traded, ran into financial difficulties and under pressure from shareholders, sold itself to Unilever in 2000 (before Polman's tenure). It managed to keep its environmental focus, however, and its original founders are still active in the company. The Body Shop was acquired too, and founder Roddick left. First it was sold to L'Oréal, which altered its environmental focus, then to Natura & Co., which reinstated it, and finally – after serious economic difficulties – to a private equity fund. For its part, Whole Foods Market, publicly traded since 1992, was acquired in 2017 by Amazon, following financial difficulties and activist shareholder pressure, with Mackay leaving the company. Currently, it seems to maintain its environmental focus, but its people- and autonomous-teams-focused social practices have been altered.

Regarding Polman's tenure, despite his excellent financial results, his conviction that purpose drives the long-term financial success was doubted by some Unilever investors as detracting from shareholder value. In 2019, the board removed Polman as CEO.

At the end of the day, we can see that, with few exceptions, the mavericks have not survived. Some companies, however, managed to preserve their environmental focus after being acquired, perhaps because that was their brand identity and market value. Despite this record, mavericks have proven that business leaders can adopt a mindset with environmental and social goals being the focus, all the while keeping their company profitable enough. Unfortunately, just as with Robert Owen two centuries earlier, their "enough" has often not been enough for their shareholders with a profit maximization mindset. But, as we show later in this book, this situation can be different.

HAS THE CORPORATE WORLD FINALLY MANAGED TO ESCAPE?

In August 2019, 181 CEOs of leading US corporations within the Business Roundtable made history. They signed a Declaration on the Purpose of a Corporation, which changed this most powerful American business association's 22-year-old orientation toward maximizing shareholder returns:

> While each of our individual companies serves its own corporate purpose, we share a fundamental commitment to all of our stakeholders … We commit to deliver value to all of them, for the future success of our companies, our communities and our country.[40]

Later on, Larry Fink, CEO of BlackRock, the world's largest investment fund, and one of the signatories made a similar move. In his annual 2022 letter to investors, he used the term "stakeholder" 18 times. He wrote:

> In today's globally interconnected world, a company must create value for and be valued by its full range of stakeholders in order to deliver long-term value for its shareholders. It is through effective stakeholder capitalism that capital is efficiently allocated, companies achieve durable profitability, and value is created and sustained over the long-term.[41]

In the same letter, he announced the creation of the Center for Stakeholder Capitalism to:

> … further explore the relationships between companies and their stakeholders and between stakeholder engagement and shareholder value.[42]

It seems that stakeholder capitalism has triumphed over shareholder capitalism. There remains, though, the question of how effective stakeholder capitalism and other balancing approaches have been in meeting social and environmental challenges.

The Effectiveness Record of Stakeholder Capitalism

Have you ever seen a respected and successful writer and practitioner acknowledging that his concept deserves a safety recall – just as cars are recalled when they turn out to be flawed? And if you found yourself in that position, would you dare to do that 25 years after your ideas had been praised and adopted by a vast number of leaders and companies?

That's exactly what John Elkington, the inventor of the already discussed TBL, did in 2018, in a *Harvard Business Review* article titled "25 Years Ago I Coined the Phrase 'Triple Bottom Line.' Here's Why It's Time to Rethink It." Interestingly, the URL of the article reveals an even harsher subtitle – "Here's Why I'm Giving Up on It."[43] In this piece, Elkington reviews TBL's results and concludes that it has failed to deliver on its promise because of corporate executives' mindset:

> Fundamentally, we have a hard-wired cultural problem in business, finance, and markets. Whereas CEOs, CFOs, and other corporate leaders move heaven and earth to ensure that they hit their profit targets, the same is very rarely true of their people and planet targets. Clearly, the Triple Bottom Line has failed to bury the single bottom line paradigm.[44]

In other words, executives haven't walked the TBL talk.

Now, let's talk about ESG.

In November 2021, Yves Le Masne was a proud CEO. The third quarter of activity had been better than expected with +10.8% revenue growth.

Occupancy rates of Orpea, a world leader in long-term care, including nursing homes, assisted living, and more, was excellent. Le Masne describes this performance as a result of the company's operating model, especially strong on quality. Moreover, he said that "a demanding care and services offer meet the expectations of stakeholders."[45] Nonfinancial rating agencies were also praising Orpea, putting the company in the top 10 of the industry. One of them even praised Orpea's high level of transparency.

Two months later, a book called *The Gravediggers* was released in France, shocking readers. Based on more than 250 interviews, it revealed a systematic mistreatment of the elderly at Orpea.[46] In order to maximize profit, health treatments, hygiene services, and even food were rationed, leaving people macerating in their feces during hours or forcing them to skip a meal. All this for $7,400 a month.

A similar thing happened to Volkswagen prior to the famous Dieselgate in 2015, leaving many observers wondering whether good-looking sustainability and ESG reports are sufficient evidence of good corporate citizenship.

In 2022, Stanford and Yale researchers Larcker, Tayan, and Watts tested just that. In their article "Seven Myths of ESG," the authors detailed the limits – and myths – of ESG criteria.[47] One myth particularly relevant to our discussion is that "ESG is value-increasing." Based on a meta-analysis of numerous empirical studies, the authors found no clear evidence that a company's better CSR or ESG orientation leads to better financial returns, either short term or long term. One of the most comprehensive studies that the authors quote concluded that "the financial performance of ESG investing has on average been indistinguishable from conventional investing."[48]

We can add to that a well-known fact: "You can make the figures say whatever you like," as CEO Jean-François Zobrist puts it.[49] This holds true not only for financial reporting but also for ESG and other social metrics.

So much for the ESG results. Let's turn now to the results of that 2019 Business Roundtable Declaration. In 2020 and 2022, Harvard researchers

Bebchuk and Tallarita analyzed whether this declaration's signatory corporations followed up on it with concrete corporate actions.[50] They found that, after two years, none of the 181 signatories had translated their commitment into their legal corporate acts or operating methods. This is despite the fact that shareholders themselves had suggested 43 concrete proposals in some signatory companies to implement their declaration of corporate purpose. None of these proposals had been implemented; they were all either rejected at shareholder general assemblies or never presented to them in the first place by the boards. The authors concluded that these companies signed their declaration not to commit to stakeholders but for public-relations purposes.

Our final remark relates to the momentum that B-Corp or Benefit Corporations have had in recent years.

Both movements have generated a lot of hope and have attracted an extraordinary media attention. Yet currently, there are just over 3,000 certified B-Corps in the United States and more than 9,000 in the world. Given that in the United States alone there are 33 million businesses, B-Corps represent 0.009% of them. That is not much of a change in the way that the corporate world functions.

Regarding the Benefit Corporations, today, there are more than 10,000 of them in the United States – that's 0.03% of American businesses.[51] Slightly better than B-Corps, but also not a sea-change in corporate functioning.

As for the number of business signatories of the UN Global Compact, with some 25,963 companies from more than 160 countries who have signed up – it is just twice the number of Benefit Corporations and thrice the number of B-Corps.

We must conclude that, despite good intentions and a lot of hope, neither B-Corps nor Benefit Corporations nor the UN Global Compact have significantly impacted the corporate world, which has largely ignored them.

Recently, we interviewed a CEO of a medium-sized real estate advisory firm working with local public authorities.

"I was really upset several months ago by losing a $2.5 million offer. I thought it was in the bag, and you won't believe what I discovered," he started.

We wanted to know more, of course.

"I asked to see the client in charge of the offer, with whom we worked really well in the past, and he was really sorry. He explained to me that our offer was at the right price and even of a better quality, but we haven't won because the offer missed one point: our firm's lack of social and environmental commitment."

"So, what are you going to do," we inquired.

"I've done it already. I didn't even ask for any help within the firm. I just went to see the winner's website and immediately discovered there the UN Global Compact logo. Wow!"

"So, what did you do?" we pressed.

"Easy. I typed into ChatGPT: 'What is required for a small company to get the UN Global Compact logo?' I almost fell off my chair when I saw that all I needed to do was to sign a letter by the CEO, to make a commitment to their 10 principles, and to contribute a few hundred dollars.[52] I am the CEO, so I handled all that myself. I still can't believe that I lost a two and a half million dollars deal over it."

This real story reveals why the UN Global Compact is so popular. A letter and an annual contribution, that's all. Besides that, companies have to fill in the digital self-assessment online once a year. This is the easiest and the cheapest escape route that has ever been offered to the corporate world in the "catch me if you can" game – no wonder it's so popular around the world.

At the end of this examination, it seems obvious that the array of approaches that can be categorized as balancing do not have a lot to show for themselves. Companies are either not walking the talk, as with TBL, extra-financial reporting, the Business Roundtable declaration, and mostly with the UN Compact; have no impact, as with ESG; or remain marginal to the corporate world, as with B-Corps and Benefit Corporations. There is a reason why this is so.

THE PROBLEM WITH BALANCING AND WHAT COMPANIES OUGHT TO BE

You may be surprised that, despite all the publicity they get, the balancing or stakeholder capitalism approaches have so little to show by way of results. There is, however, a serious reason for it.

Popular wisdom tells us that it is impossible to chase two rabbits at the same time: you end up with none. This wisdom is supported by linear programming, a mathematical discipline for solving complex problems. It teaches us that you cannot optimize several separate variables at the same time. For example, you can't simultaneously maximize environmental protection and minimize corporate costs. One of them must be a goal and the others become constraints. That is what Elkington found in his review of 25 years of corporate attempts to "chase" Profit, People, and Planet goals simultaneously. Wired for profits, the executives implicitly chased this goal, the social and the environmental ones becoming constraints – the costs of doing business. The latest example of this is OpenAI, the prominent leader in generative AI development.

Founded in 2015, OpenAI was originally created as a company with a mission "to benefit humanity as a whole, unconstrained by a need to generate financial return," funded through philanthropy. However, as OpenAI and its financial needs grew, it launched a branch in 2019 backed by business investors, with capped dividends – any excess profits directed toward financing the original social mission (this governance model echoed the approach of New Lanark Mills' final round of investors discussed in Chapter 1).

Yet, investors such as SoftBank and Microsoft soon grew impatient, and by the end of 2024, OpenAI announced a restructuring plan that substantially expanded business investors' governance rights and expressed an intention to adopt Benefit Corporation status – a balancing approach. As of today, the battle over the final shape of this restructuring is still unfolding, but it increasingly resembles yet another instance of the "catch me if you can" game, underscoring the impossibility of balancing financial and social goals.

Despite being developed in the 1940s and taught for decades in business schools as part of Operational Research classes, the fundamental linear programming finding – succinctly captured in the popular wisdom of "chasing two rabbits" – is largely ignored by businesses. If taken into consideration, however, it can open up a path to changing the business mindset away from the focus on profit and in favor of another goal. Following the 2009 financial crisis, Roger Martin, a leading business thinker, proposed the idea of focusing on customers at fair profit.[53] James Cash Penney, the founder of the JCPenney chain, had this conviction even earlier, saying to the shop manager who outperformed everyone by marking up his products much more than others: "This isn't the way we do things in the JCPenney. We owe our community the service of merchandise at fair profit. We can't ever allow ourselves to make too much of a profit."[54] As the company expanded, it gradually departed from Penney's principle of fair profitability, opting instead for an aggressive pursuit of maximum profit and revenue growth.

This book will expand on this fundamental idea of having one goal to focus on, which is not profits, profits becoming both a constraint and a consequence of reaching this goal. As we bring this chapter to a close, we want to return to Dee Hock, former president of VISA International, whose quote opened this chapter.

We know how monetized corporations were. We know how they are. We know what they are becoming, and it is not a happy prospect for the vast majority of people. It is far past time to examine how such corporations ought to be and find ways in which they can evolve into a more constructive order of things.[55]

Throughout the history of modern capitalism, in the vast landscape of possibilities that free-market societies open, some entrepreneurs – mavericks and others – have made significant efforts to do good and to build companies as they "ought to be." In Chapter 4, we'll delve into these efforts to understand why they were genuinely effective. But first, in Chapter 3, we need to understand why the most celebrated approaches – especially those rooted in philanthropy – were not.

CHAPTER THREE

DOING GOOD FACE-TO-FACE OR THROUGH PHILANTHROPY?

How many are in love with humankind and not with man.
— René Char[1]

S cience shows us that humans are built to prefer the local and familiar to the remote and exotic. While many philanthropy programs
have abstract or remote goals such as "alleviating poverty" or
"combatting global warming," paradoxically, companies can achieve more
by lowering their ambitions. This chapter will examine why that is so and
why it works so much better than spending corporate money on grand
designs, as we saw in Chapter 2.

Without doubt, business philanthropy has helped alleviate numerous problems that would otherwise have remained unaddressed. It has also been subjected to many criticisms. The most traditional of them is exemplified by the critique of the nineteenth-century robber barons' philanthropy. Thus, Andrew Carnegie would harshly suppress worker unrest, remaining deaf to their demands, but later on contributed lavishly to the network of municipal libraries throughout America.

However, the great Russian novelist Leo Tolstoy (1828–1910) formulated an entirely different criticism. His mid-nineteenth century short story "Lucerne" revolves around an event described in the following way by Prince Nekhliudof, its main character and narrator:

> On the 19th of July, 1857, before the Schweitzerhof Hotel, in which very opulent people were lodging, a wandering beggar minstrel sang for half an hour his songs, and played his guitar. About a hundred people listened to him. The minstrel thrice asked you all to give him something. Not one person gave him a thing, and many made sport of him.[2]

The story goes on to recount how the protagonist manages to find the poor musician and spends an evening with him. However, it concludes with the narrator's thoughts on the deeper significance of the event, which seems to him like "something entirely novel and strange, not connected with the everlastingly ugly side of human nature, but rather with … progress and civilization." He then poses the question:

> Why is it that this inhuman fact … is … possible [in Lucerne] where civilization, freedom, and equality are carried to the highest degree of development, where there are gathered together the most civilized travelers from the most civilized nations? Why is it that these cultivated human beings, generally capable of every honorable human action, had no hearty, human feeling for one good deed? Why is it that these people who in their palaces, their meetings, and their societies, labor warmly [about] India, about the spread of Christianity and culture in Africa, about the formation of societies

for attaining all perfection – why is it that they should not find in their souls the simple, primitive feeling of human sympathy?

And he concludes with this question:

> Has the spreading of that reasonable, egotistical association of people, which we call civilization, destroyed and rendered nugatory the desire for instinctive and loving association?[3]

Tolstoy seems to have identified an evolution that began when Europe's wealthy citizens became increasingly concerned with "progress and civilization." To advance these ideals, many engaged with grand, remote causes like those he cites in Asia or Africa. Yet, these same individuals, when directly encountering a poor gifted musician, not only failed to offer a token of help but even mocked him. In other words, Tolstoy is puzzled and condemns these wealthy individuals contributing – often lavishly – to distant and grand causes while failing to contribute – even minimally – to the local and immediate one.

The question of whether Tolstoy is right or wrong in his critique leads us to discuss not only the effectiveness of philanthropy, but also the importance of business leaders' direct involvement in the social innovation in their company – the WHO effectiveness factor.

CAN PHILANTHROPY BE EFFECTIVE?

There is a long history of entrepreneurs – from nineteenth century industrialists to modern tech billionaires – who have sought to give back to society in various ways. Such giving back has also been criticized for following the whims of the givers, sometimes flattering their ego or social status, instead of solving serious challenges. In the nineteenth century, Jeremy Bentham and John Stuart Mill elaborated a philosophy of utilitarianism, which was supposed to help guide better giving. It assumes that an action is better if it maximizes net benefits – happiness minus pain – for the greatest number. Lately promoted by thinkers like Peter Singer and called "effective altruism," it emphasizes high-impact giving, urging donors to direct their resources to where they will lead to the highest estimated net benefits for the greatest numbers. Among the champions of this data-driven philanthropic movement are prominent Silicon Valley entrepreneurs, such as Facebook co-founder Dustin Moskovitz, Skype co-founder Jaan Tallinn, and Sam Bankman-Fried, founder of the cryptocurrency exchange FTX, who would later commit the largest corporate fraud in US history.[4]

You may believe that entrepreneurs have finally found a method to do good effectively. However, the empirical research casts a shadow on such a belief.

In fact, the real-world philanthropic behavior of most people rarely adheres to utilitarian standards, even if they have all the data. Studies in evolutionary psychology confirm effective altruism's claim that people are largely unaware of which donations have the greatest impact. But there is more. The vast majority of people don't seek information on the effectiveness of charities and often favor less-effective causes over more impactful ones, even when data on effectiveness are available. And they behave like that not because they are irrational or don't care, but because evolution has shaped philanthropic behavior in specific ways.

People Give for Parochial, Status, and Conformity Reasons

Though many philanthropists say that they contribute in order to benefit others – and to as many others as possible – the research in evolutionary psychology paints a different picture of philanthropists' motives. Two Dutch researchers, Jaeger and Van Vugt, summarize these findings:

> People are generally unaware of where their donations would have the largest impact. They do not search for information on charities' impact and often prefer less effective over more effective charities. In general, donation decisions are surprisingly unaffected by charities' effectiveness even when this information is explicitly provided.[5]

The last finding is particularly damaging to utilitarianism and its latest incarnation as effective altruism, which holds that if only philanthropists knew which charities provide the greatest net benefit, they would prefer them.

In fact, research rather shows that a person prefers to donate to the local charity buying dogs for blind people at the cost of $40,000 each, rather than to a global charity that can, for the same amount of money, buy anti-malaria nets to save a thousand lives in Africa. Similar findings show that people prefer to help one identified individual rather than many anonymous ones.[6]

Evolutionary psychology explains nonutilitarian behaviors as the product of natural selection. Jaeger and Van Vugt list three evolutionary reasons why people don't behave as utilitarians.

The first reason is called parochialism, from the Greek *paroikia* meaning neighborhood. For more than three million years, humans lived in small groups and developed empathy for the members of their own group, as opposed to those outside of it. That is why donating to distant causes evokes less empathy and is felt as less obligatory to us than donating locally and to charities to which we are personally connected. One study has shown that people will donate more if it saves five persons rather than one, but only if they are family members.[7] Yet, people will not donate more in order to save more strangers.

The second reason evolution provides for nonutilitarian philanthropic behavior is reputation and status. Through evolution, the group members enjoying the highest reputation and status would also enjoy such benefits as privileged access to desirable mates. Today, research shows altruists are preferred as social and romantic partners and selected as leaders.[8] Surprisingly, the research also shows that one's philanthropic reputation is not related to how beneficial their contributions were for the recipient, but only to how costly they were for the philanthropist. Moreover, a reputation for generous philanthropy will persist even if the donations have not produced any benefit at all. Furthermore, the cost-benefit-based decision-making advocated by utilitarianism is not praised socially. Worse, such utilitarian philanthropists are rated as less moral individuals and less desirable partners. People view emotions such as empathy, rather than cost-benefit reasoning, as proof of altruistic intentions.

The final reason for nonutilitarian philanthropic behavior is conformity. For the benefit of evolution, conformity is not negative. On the contrary, it provides evolutionary benefits since following others in deciding what to eat, what tool to use, or where to live increases one's survival prospects. In philanthropy, people tend to give to charities to which others are giving – even if this charity is ineffective.

Only a small proportion of individuals – such as the Silicon Valley tech entrepreneurs mentioned earlier – use cost-benefit utilitarian reasoning in philanthropic behavior.[9] The vast majority of philanthropists give for motives rooted in human evolution: parochialism, reputation, and conformity.

Even though people are not behaving in utilitarian ways, you might still conclude that such behavior might be good for their group survival but ineffective for humankind. The following archeological and primatological evidence describing the basis for the research on evolution may alter your conclusion.

OUR CARING ANCESTORS

Evolutionary psychology, and in particular, its studies of philanthropic behavior, are based on anthropological evidence on how and why our ancestors started to care about each other.

Between three million and one million years ago, archeologists found cases of old, ill, and disabled early humans who had clearly been cared for. A bit later they found the first burials – proof of care for the dead. These cases are puzzling. Indeed, in purely mercenary terms it doesn't make sense for caregivers to expend efforts with no hope of being paid back by the old, disabled, and of course, the dead. But even if there is no direct material benefit for such caring, there is a social one. By engaging in these caring acts, group members increase and maintain their reputation as trustworthy, and so increase their acceptance into trust-based group activities, such as protecting others, carrying the meat that others give you, or giving one's share to another's child or parent. Inversely, not being involved in caring acts lowers one's reputation for trustworthiness and potentially leads to being shamed, ostracized, and perhaps exiled. Groups with the behavioral norm of caring have highly increased their survival chances as compared to the groups where caring has not been the norm.

Even so, these research findings about caring as an evolutionary advantage seem to contradict the commonly accepted idea of the survival of the fittest. This idea paints the fittest as being selfish and violent, like those alpha males who get priority in mating and in transmitting their genes. Here is what British evolutionary scholar Penny Spikins writes about it:

> Evidence for care is found both earlier in our evolutionary past than evidence for interpersonal violence and is more widespread. However, such evidence receives remarkably little acknowledgement

or attention … Why this should be so is difficult to understand – we might think we should be proud of a willingness to help others. The only explanation seems to be that care and compassion feel like a *weakness*. In our modern cultures the deep-seated concept that success, and by implication evolutionary success, lies with selfish competition makes both the vulnerability of our ancestors, and their willingness to care for others, a strangely disturbing concept, one which is challenging to who we think we are.[10]

Seeking, sharing, and enforcing a behavioral norm such as caring for those who can't care for themselves is part of what turns a mere group into a community. Thus, we might reasonably suppose that in these early periods, for the first time in history, groups of individuals formed communities – but not just any type of community. An interesting question is whether these communities grew in size or on the contrary, were somehow capped. British anthropologist Robin Dunbar provides the answer.[11]

His evolutionary and neurophysiological research shows that the maximal size of a (caring) community is 150 individuals. Scientists call this *Dunbar's number*. Dunbar describes this 150-member community as based on bilateral relationships of obligation and reciprocity. It is very distinct from the 500-member circle "consisting of everyone we could count as acquaintances," and from the 1,500-member circle that includes "everyone whose face we can put a name to."[12] Dunbar has also explored the neurophysiological basis for these limits. Indeed, humans' 150 member communities of mutual care are the largest among living organisms. It is posited that such large groups are made possible by the fact that our neocortex represents some 70–80% of the overall volume of our brains. For chimpanzees, it is 50–60%, and their caring groups are limited to 50. For monkeys, it is between 30% and 50%, and their caring groups are limited to 20–50 members.

TO CARE DESPITE EVERYTHING

The preceding section strongly suggests that caring for members of our close community is innate. Yet, as Spikins pointed out, we often struggle to recognize these findings. He attributes this difficulty to modern cultures, which equate care with weakness and promote instead competition and dominance.

We believe this inability to acknowledge care as innate stems from an even darker interpretation of the human condition – one that sees humanity through the lens of a "war of every man against every man." This vision, coined by Hobbes in *Leviathan* (1651), persists because it resonates deeply with the foundational texts of modern culture – from the biblical story of Cain's murder of Abel, to Tacitus' and Flavius Josephus' accounts of Roman history as a sequence of civil and imperial wars, and to the tragedies written in ancient Greece and Rome. In fact, it was the Roman playwright Plautus who first coined the phrase: *Homo homine lupus* (man is a wolf to man).[13]

Hobbes' bleak view of human nature also persists because of the apparent omnipresence of violence throughout history – from the medieval wars of Europe and the British Civil War of Hobbes' own time, to the two World Wars and our current era, marked by terrorism and ongoing conflicts. We say "apparent" intentionally: though violence has been tragically real, most people throughout history lived in relative peace. The perception of constant violence stems from what psychological research identifies as cognitive biases, such as the "availability heuristic." For instance, because airplane crashes are extensively reported in the media, people often overestimate the dangers of flying and underestimate the far deadlier – but underreported – risks of driving. Like airplane crashes, wars, terrorism, and acts of violence are highly visible in writings and the media and thus perceived as pervasive, even when they are not. As is often said, the journalist's job isn't to report that trains arrive on time.

Hobbes' grim assessment also dovetails with the modern economic view of human nature – one that prizes self-interest and ruthless competition, encapsulated in phrases like "zero-sum game" or "winner takes all."

Finally, his vision also reflects the popular image of contemporary society as a maze of self-absorbed individuals competing endlessly in the pursuit of consumption and status.

Within these cultural, historical, economic, and social frameworks, care and empathy may appear out of place – something Tolstoy already observed in the mid-nineteenth century. But before accepting this bleak vision as truth and dismissing the idea that care and empathy are innate, we invite you to reflect on the extreme conditions in which cruelty, tragedy, war, exploitation, and the fight for daily survival were pushed to their absolute limits: the Nazi tyranny and the concentration camps.

For personal reasons linked to his family's history, one of us – Isaac – developed a deep interest in this period, conducting extensive research and listening to numerous camps' survivors. Among the many insights he gathered, two stand out.

First, when survivors spoke of the most horrific atrocities they endured, they often did so in a detached or neutral tone. Their typical comment was not directed at their tormentors but at themselves: "Humans have the capacity to adapt to anything." Listeners are frequently struck by the emotional restraint survivors display when recounting the deaths of children, the elderly, or the sick – whether in cattle cars or on the path to gas chambers.

But there was one type of memory that consistently provoked their strong emotion: recollections of someone showing them care and empathy. One such account comes from Isaac's conversation with Hermann Spiegel, who was an 11-year-old boy living in a Central-European region of Carpathian Ruthenia when WWII broke. He changed his name to Haim Sheffi when he came to Israel after the war.[14]

Sheffi fled his native town to Budapest. But in March 1944, Nazi Germany invaded Hungary, and he was deported – with nearly half a million Hungarian Jews – to Auschwitz.[15] There, he survived three times the infamous "selection" process personally conducted by Dr. Josef Mengele. Later, in mid-January 1945, with the Russian army approaching Auschwitz in Poland, the SS forced the remaining prisoners onto a brutal death march toward the camps in Germany. Sheffi ended up in Dachau – the very camp where Isaac's grandfather had also been imprisoned and killed.

Like all inmates, Sheffi was subjected to brutal forced labor, surviving on little more than a daily slice of bread. One day, as Sheffi clutched his meager ration of 150 grams, a fellow inmate – a Russian prisoner of war – snatched it away. Already weakened, Sheffi knew that losing his bread could mean death.

Devastated, he left the barracks, sat down outside, and wept. After some time, a "Dutch Jew" approached and asked why he was crying. Then, the man reached into his pocket, handed Sheffi his own bread, and said, "Take it. I don't need it anymore." Moments later, the man collapsed and died. "Alone, you're doomed," Sheffi said reflecting on his survival.

Until this moment in our conversation, Sheffi had recounted the most horrific atrocities he had endured or witnessed – always with a calm, if slightly sorrowful, demeanor. But now, as he recalled this singular act of compassion, tears streamed down his face.

As we would later read, whenever Sheffi retold this story – this moment when another human being had shown him empathy and affirmed his existence – he could never hold back his tears.

It can be argued that survivors' testimonies are inherently biased – after all, they survived partly because they encountered individuals who showed care and empathy. Conversely, those who never did, perished. Yet such caring individuals were far from rare.

Take France, for example. When it was invaded by Germany, its Jewish population numbered close to 330,000. Despite the roundups, arrests, and deportations, about 260,000 – 79% – survived. French policemen warned buildings that sheltered Jews of impending raids; foster families and religious institutions hid children; both rural and urban residents provided food and shelter to those fleeing; smugglers helped Jews cross borders – from the occupied to the free zone, or across into Spain, Switzerland, or Italy. By 2023, Yad Vashem museum had recognized 4,255 individuals from France as Righteous Among the Nations – those who risked their lives to save Jews during the Holocaust. One such savior was the Capuchin Franciscan friar Marie-Benoît, who played a pivotal role in smuggling nearly 4,000 Jews to safety from southern France.

You might think that it wasn't an innate capacity for care and empathy that drove these individuals, but rather the moral values – religious or secular – instilled through their upbringing. This argument is further strengthened when we consider that most of the Jews they helped were not part of their local community, on which innate care typically focuses.

Psychological research offers deeper insight into the motivations behind such acts. According to leading scholars of human motivation, Edward Deci and Richard Ryan, caring for others – and being cared for – is one of three innate psychological needs that all humans strive to fulfill.[16] Yet beyond this universal need, the saviors possessed distinct personal traits that set them apart: high empathy (the ability to empathize beyond one's immediate community), nonconformism (the capacity to resist social or authoritarian pressure), and a greater tolerance for risk, in contrast to the majority, who tend to be risk-averse. Furthermore, although they had been exposed to the same moral education as their peers, they possessed an ability to internalize these values more deeply – to the point of feeling morally compelled to uphold them, even at the cost of their own lives.

Another way to approach the innate versus acquired debate stems from the contemporary definition of innateness. According to the American cognitive scientist Gary Marcus, innate behaviors are not strictly hardwired but rather prewired and develop through the unique experiences of each individual.[17] Thus, humans are prewired to care for their kin, and in particular, their children. However, their upbringing – whether through education that promotes "love thy neighbor" or through Kant's imperative that every moral principle, including care, be applied universally – may extend this innate need to care to a broader population. Conversely, certain forms of upbringing may suppress or even eradicate this prewired need to care. The German filmmaker Michael Haneke explored this idea in his Cannes Film Festival Palme d'Or-winning film *The White Ribbon*. He depicted how the atmosphere of early twentieth-century rural Prussia – marked by humiliation, violence, and blind obedience – shaped the minds of children who would later become the very generation of adults in Nazi Germany.

Thus, the innate need to care for those close to us, reinforced by moral education and specific individual traits, helps explain why some individuals cared for persecuted Jews when faced with their suffering – despite the danger. At the same time, the innate need to be cared for helps explain why those rescued engraved these rare acts of care – rather than the abuse they endured – into their emotional memory. Trauma specialists often remind us that trauma is not defined by the event itself, but by the disconnection from the self and the suppression of emotion that emerge as mechanisms of sheer survival. In this light, acts of care can be seen as signals – powerful affirmations to the self – that reassert its presence and vitality, even amid the rupture caused by external events. Viewed through this lens, emotional memory is more than recollection; it is the ongoing process of reconnection.[18]

A more general question, however, lies outside the scope of psychological research: Why were most people in the West educated in moral principles – religious or secular – in the first place? Put more simply: Why were they taught the Ten Commandments or Kant's categorical imperative rather than moral codes inspired by Plautus' "man is a wolf to man," or Hobbes' vision of a "war of every man against every man"? Our answer is that the former resonates with the innate prewired human need to care and be cared for, while the latter do not. Put differently, extending the prewired innate need to care for others within one's local community to a broader population is a natural process. In contrast, suppressing this need typically requires an individual to develop within an especially humiliating and violent environment.

Yet, as Tolstoy observed, despite all forms of moral education, acts of care – especially toward strangers – are far from automatic.

BACK TO TOLSTOY AND BEYOND

Tolstoy believed that simply encountering a fellow human in need – even a stranger – should be enough to evoke empathy. Like him, caring for a few concrete people close to us, rather than for many remote and anonymous people, has its defenders among major moral philosophers, writers, and artists.

The epigraph at the beginning of this chapter is from the renowned French poet René Char (1907–1988) and expresses his preference for the concrete individual over the abstract notion of humankind. The concrete individual, the individual face, was also the main theme of Emmanuel Levinas (1906–1995), one of the twentieth century's leading moral philosophers:

Through the face, the being is not merely enclosed within its form and offered to the hand ... The face is an irreducible mode by which a being can present itself in its identity. Things, on the other hand, are what never present themselves personally and, ultimately, lack identity. Violence applies to the thing.[19]

In other words, Levinas, who also wrote about the fate of Jews in the WWII, associates care – the hand – with the possibility of knowing the individual face. Inversely, humans are capable of violence to someone anonymous.[20] In a certain sense, Levinas provides a philosophical answer to the question posed in the preceding section: Why did the rescuers choose to save Jews they had never previously encountered? But Levinas is not the only French thinker who emphasizes the key value of one specific face, one concrete human.

In a 1957 press conference, following his Nobel Prize in Literature, French writer Albert Camus (1913–1960) declared, "I have always condemned terror … At this very moment, bombs are being thrown into the trams of Algiers. My mother could be on one of those trams. If this is what justice is, I prefer my mother."[21] Camus made this statement in the context of the war in his native Algeria, which, though an integral part of France at the time, was viewed by many as an unjust colonial possession. Like Levinas, he emphasizes that the life of a concrete innocent human being – not to mention one's mother – is more important than any grand, remote cause.

Another influential writer and philosopher who championed "just and loving attention" to individual human beings over abstract moral frameworks was British philosopher and novelist Iris Murdoch (1919–1999). In her seminal philosophical work, *The Sovereignty of Good*, she critiqued both existentialism – as represented by Sartre – and utilitarianism.[22] American writer David Brooks summarizes her moral philosophy as follows:

For Murdoch, the essential immoral act is the inability to see other people correctly … representing people to ourselves in self-serving ways, in ways that gratify our egos and serve our ends … And because we don't see people accurately, we treat them wrongly. Evil happens when people are unseeing, when they don't recognize the personhood in other human beings.[23]

The great Swiss sculptor and painter Alberto Giacometti (1901–1966) offers a striking illustration of such "seeing attention." He once said, "If there were a fire in my workshop, and I had to save either a cat or the work of my entire life, the question wouldn't even arise for a second … And [even if, for a cat, it was to sacrifice] all 'Rubens,' all 'Titian.'"[24] In a sense, Giacometti's choice is even starker than Camus', as he places a living being above his own artwork – even above masterpieces of immense aesthetic value to humankind – despite his identity as an artist.

These positions fundamentally challenge moral choices based on the cost-benefit analysis of utilitarianism or even on abstract universal principles. Such analysis justifies certain small sacrifices for the greater good, while these artists believe that no cause, however grand, justifies the sacrifice of an innocent human being or even a pet.

Even though we have quoted the above thinkers and artists, we are well aware that arguments can't settle moral philosophy debates. That said, philosophical positions can be assessed in terms of their practical implications. That's what Fodor Dostoyevsky (1821–1881), another great Russian novelist and Tolstoy's contemporary, set out to achieve. He placed the question of whether intellectual rationalization or empathy should form the basis for moral choice at the very heart of many of his novels. *Crime and Punishment*, published in 1866, is his best-known work dealing with this conflict.

Its protagonist Raskolnikov becomes obsessed with an old pawnbroker woman as he increasingly pawns his belongings to her to borrow money. Murdering the woman appears to be a way out of poverty, to build the career he believes he deserves. Yet, Raskolnikov needs an unselfish moral justification for the murder. Here is how Dostoyevsky describes it early in the novel. During this episode, Raskolnikov hears a student who happened to know the old pawnbroker and shares his idea about her:

> On one hand we have a stupid, senseless, worthless, spiteful, ailing, horrid old woman, not simply useless but doing actual mischief ... On the other hand, fresh young lives thrown away for want of help and by thousands, on every side! A hundred thousand good deeds could be done and helped, on that old woman's money ... Hundreds, thousands perhaps, might be set on the right path; dozens of families saved from destitution, from ruin, from vice, from ... hospitals ... Kill her, take her money and with the help of it devote oneself to the service of humanity and the good of all.
>
> What do you think, would not one tiny crime be wiped out by thousands of good deeds? For one life thousands would be saved from corruption and decay. One death, and a hundred lives in exchange – it's simple arithmetic! Besides, what value has the life of that sickly, stupid, ill-natured old woman in the balance of existence! No more than the life of a louse ... Kill her, take her money and with the help of it devote oneself to the service of humanity and the good of all ... Would not one tiny crime be wiped out by thousands of good deeds? ... It's simple arithmetic![25]

After listening to the student, Raskolnikov is amazed that the same idea was born in his mind a little while ago.

The second justification for this murder came from his view of himself as an extraordinary person, destined to bring good to humanity. Now it's Raskolnikov himself speaking:

> I maintain that if the discoveries of Kepler and Newton could not have been made known except by sacrificing the lives of one, a dozen, a hundred, or more men, Newton would have had the right, would indeed have been in duty bound ... to eliminate the dozen or the hundred men for the sake of making his discoveries known to the whole of humanity.[26]

Of course, it's Dostoyevsky's genius, which illustrates the moral dilemma in such a stark manner. However, his general question is whether the murder of one person can be justified by "thousands of good deeds" this person prevents. Dostoyevsky's answer is a clear "no." He further deepens it in his novel *The Possessed*, published six years later through its character Verhovenski, an advocate for the sacrifice of a "hundred million heads":

> Do you, whatever it may imply, prefer a quicker way which will at last untie your hands, and will let humanity make its own social organisation in freedom and in action, not on paper? They shout, "a hundred million heads"; that may be only a metaphor; but why be afraid of it ... ?[27]

In other words, Dostoyevsky's answer is clear: however good and grand one's ends, they don't justify evil means, the suffering of even one innocent. Moreover, according to Dostoyevsky, such an "arithmetic" of sacrifices for the greater good will inevitably lead to major crimes against humanity. Unfortunately, Dostoyevsky was prophetic. The number of innocent victims of the Nazi and Communist ideological regimes of the twentieth century reached, according to historians, "a hundred million heads," all in the name of the greater good these ideologies promised.

We can sometimes hear the argument that the horrible consequences of implementing some philosophies and ideologies do not invalidate them; rather it is the fault of the politicians who misunderstood them. Still, the historical fact that *none* of these philosophies led to the "greater good" that they promised and *all* of them led to millions of sacrificed innocent lives casts a doubt on the philosophies themselves.

In sum, although Western moral education seeks to extend the innate need to care for those nearby into a universal obligation to care for all, many moral philosophers, writers, and artists do not share this view. Moreover, they argue that striving to care for remote and anonymous humanity often leads individuals to neglect those they face in their immediate lives.

THE VIRTUES OF LOCAL GOVERNMENT

You may view this chapter as theoretical, but it sheds light on many seemingly puzzling facts about whom we trust and care about. For instance, year after year, Gallup surveys reveal that Americans report having significantly more trust and confidence in local government than in the federal government. In a 2023 survey, 67% of respondents expressed either a great deal or a fair amount of trust and confidence in "local governments in the area where you live" when it comes to handling local problems, compared to only 37% who said the same about "the federal government to handle domestic problems."[28] Furthermore, in a 2024 survey, 51% of respondents expressed trust in the police, a local institution, compared to only 9% who said the same about Congress – the lowest-ranked among 17 US institutions.[29] The same trend of significantly higher trust in local governments compared to national governments is observed across all Organisation for Economic Co-operation and Development (OECD) countries.[30]

A similar disparity applies to companies. For example, 68% of Americans report having a great deal or a fair amount of confidence in small businesses – the most trusted US institution – compared to only 16% who express confidence in big businesses, which rank as the third least trusted institution, just above Congress and television news.[31]

Although national governments and big businesses provide many important services, we are inherently inclined to notice and value the care offered by local actors. This has major implications for the type of care that may be truly effective in connecting with people. As the American philosopher Christopher Lasch (1935–1994) put it:

> We love and respect particular individuals, not humanity as a whole, and that the seductive promise of universal brotherhood is a poor

substitute for local communities in which the holders of power are immediately accountable to their neighbors.[32]

Moreover, many of today's global issues can be understood through the concept of the "tragedy of the commons," an observation first noted by Aristotle: "That which is common to the greatest number has the least care bestowed upon it. Everyone thinks chiefly of his own, hardly at all of the common interest."[33] But, as Nobel Prize winner Elinor Ostrom demonstrated, escaping this tragedy is not achieved through either privatization or strict government control of common-pool resources. According to Ostrom, local communities possess specialized local knowledge that enables them to self-govern and sustainably manage common resources through collective decision-making.[34]

To go back to the biblical warning about paradise and the eye of a needle, regular philanthropists, even though they do a lot of good, seem not to be ready to pass through yet. However, it's the utilitarian philanthropists who seem to head in the totally opposite direction of paradise. In fact, the road to paradise seems to be literally narrow, when we know that the maximum number of humans that can be truly cared about is 150 people – a figure that definitely favors leaders of small businesses or of small business units in larger decentralized corporations.

As we covered in Chapter 1, instead of pursuing abstract or remote philanthropical goals, perhaps the key is for business leaders to just focus on solving the social challenges of their own employees, their clients, their suppliers, and the host communities as ends in themselves – the WHY. Perhaps, instead of looking for a social silver bullet, they can accomplish it by implementing a bundle of mutually supportive measures – the

WHAT – systematically transforming the way their particular business operates, and how their employees, their clients, their suppliers, and their host communities work and live. Perhaps, they can lead this transformation themselves – the WHO – while at the helm of their companies. If business leaders begin applying these three assumptions in practice, we may see more and more companies contributing to solving social and environmental challenges of our times, and as their number increases – to revitalizing capitalism.

This is the way caring companies have chosen and that we will describe in the following chapters.

PART II

THE CARING COMPANY WAY

CHAPTER FOUR

RUNNING BUSINESS THROUGH CARING RELATIONSHIPS

Attention is the rarest and purest form of generosity.

– Simone Weil[1]

Since the dawn of capitalism, business has been driven by transactions. As Adam Smith pointed out, free-market transactions represented a significant advancement for humankind, but they came at a cost. Some companies, however, have chosen a different path. The caring companies have avoided paying this price – and in doing so, they have reaped substantial rewards.

On one April morning, Jasmine Johnson, a customer service representative at The FruitGuys, a fruit delivery company based in California, received the following email from a client:

> Hi Jasmine – Here's the text of a Yelp review I posted. (I've never posted one before – but did for you! Thank you for all you do for me and your clients. ☺ ❤)
>
> "Delicious and beautiful fresh fruit that I look forward to receiving each week, and absolutely incredible client service! I live in the Central Valley – an area in which there are few good delivery services for The FruitGuys to utilize. I had some issues receiving my deliveries regularly, and after a couple of missed deliveries, called to cancel my service. A customer service representative, Jasmine, took it upon herself to ensure that I received my fruit in a timely manner. She contacts me each week to make sure my fruit has arrived and that I'm satisfied with my order. Recently, when she learned my fruit had not arrived, she arranged for a company representative – the director of operations! – to drive my fruit from San Francisco to Bakersfield and deliver it in person! I was truly stunned and so pleased to see his smiling face at my door. It is so rare to find a company which cares this much about its clients. I love the FruitGuys, will refer my friends and colleagues, and will be a customer as long as I live in their service area. ❤ Thank you FruitGuys!"

There are countless companies that would pay dearly to learn how to organize a customer service capable of eliciting such heartfelt reviews. The remarkable thing is that The FruitGuys receives them all the time. Before diving into its unique approach, let us first tell you how we came across this exceptional company.

UNCONDITIONAL CARE FOR YOUR CUSTOMERS

The California Gold Rush of the mid-nineteenth century didn't just attract gold seekers. It spurred the growth of countless industries and commercial ventures that thrived by serving those prospectors. Take Levi Strauss, for example. The legendary denim brand owes its origins to that era, producing durable apparel for miners who needed robust clothing to endure the rigors of their work.

Fast forward to the twenty-first century, and a new wave of prospectors has emerged: high-tech entrepreneurs. On the day we visited Silicon Valley for our research, however, we didn't find ourselves parked in front of sleek glass buildings surrounded by premium cars and lush landscaping. Instead, we arrived at an industrial site – a cluster of grey sheds and cinderblock buildings.

Yet, there's an undeniable connection between the Valley's iconic giants, located just a few dozen miles away, and the company we were there to see. Adobe, Tesla, eBay, Nasdaq, Apple, Salesforce, IDEO, and others all count themselves among the clients of The FruitGuys. In many ways, The FruitGuys may be the Levi Strauss of the modern-day gold rush.

Launching a Start-up from a Kitchen

Most Silicon Valley success stories begin in a garage. But Chris Mittelstaedt, the founder of The FruitGuys, chose a different starting point: a kitchen. After completing his studies in Pennsylvania – where he'd already dabbled in entrepreneurship – Mittelstaedt headed to the West Coast to study creative writing, dreaming of becoming a novelist. In the meantime, he supported himself with odd jobs. With a smile, he recalls being the man who received faxes in the back room of a hotel and then slipped them under guests' doors – a kind of delivery boy. It was during this time that the idea for another delivery business took root.

His inspiration came from a family surprise: his wife was expecting a baby. Suddenly, Mittelstaedt needed to feed a growing family, no easy task on $9.50 an hour. A friend working as a coffee deliveryman for a financial institution mentioned that employees often complained about gaining weight. "Why don't you try something to help people get healthier?" his friend suggested. The idea sparked something in Mittelstaedt, and he envisioned a business delivering fresh fruit to offices.

In February 1998, The FruitGuys was born. Mittelstaedt and his wife packed fruit baskets in their kitchen, and Mittelstaedt personally delivered them. The company soon outgrew their kitchen, and by 2000, sales had reached $1 million. But success was short-lived. When the dot-com bubble burst, clients slashed budgets for employee perks, causing The FruitGuys' sales to drop by half. To save his business, Mittelstaedt had to lay off employees and return to delivering fruit himself. Adding to the challenge, his family welcomed twins in October 2000 – a joyous event that only intensified the pressure to make ends meet. The California dream seemed to be slipping away.

For most Silicon Valley tech companies, recovering from the dot-com crash took years. Not so for this "low-tech" business. Mittelstaedt even describes the crisis as a "blessing in disguise." Displaced tech workers who had relocated to cities like Chicago and Dallas missed their beloved fresh fruit and reached out to The FruitGuys to ask if deliveries were available in their new locations. True to Silicon Valley's entrepreneurial spirit, the company replied, "Not at the moment, but we'll get back to you soon," and quickly began opening branches. Today, The FruitGuys delivers nationwide, carving out a unique niche as one of the Valley's leading "food-tech" companies.

Yet, there's something intriguing about this success story. Modern distribution networks already make fruit accessible across the United States, and nationwide food deliveries are a standard service. So why do Silicon Valley expats insist on calling The FruitGuys? The answer lies in the customer service philosophy that Chris Mittelstaedt has cultivated and implemented over the years – a philosophy that has set his company apart from the competition.

From a Middle Finger to Unconditional Customer Service

In 1999, about a year after he started his business, Mittelstaedt got a call from a customer.

"Your driver just made a delivery and gave me the middle finger and left," the woman said over the phone.

"I'm so sorry, let me look into this. I'll get back to you. We want to make sure you're taken care of. I'm so sorry it was offensive to you." Mittelstaedt apologized. Then he called Louis, his delivery man.

"Louis, I got a really strange call this morning from our client," Mittelstaedt said. "What happened?"

"Well, you know, ... I was late and ... I was ... upset because I knew I was getting behind in my deliveries because traffic was very bad. I get into the office and the woman who normally greets me and who always tells me to put the fruit on the table in the kitchen, she was not there. And this other woman came up to me and in a very hurried manner said, 'No no no no no, don't put the fruit in the kitchen, put it in the conference room. We have a meeting starting now. Hurry! Hurry! Hurry!' and she started yelling at me. And so, I just put the fruit where I've normally been told to always put it, and she was yelling at me and I threw up my hands and I left the kitchen," Louis explained.

"Well, even if that was the case and somebody was telling you and asking you to do something, why wouldn't you listen to that person and honor their request?" Mittelstaedt asked.

"[She] was disrespectful to me and my dad taught me … that if somebody disrespects you then you're supposed to disrespect them back," Louis replied.

As Mittelstaedt commented later:

All of a sudden, it was like my world changed and I realized that my vision of customer service that came from … the way I was raised, the experience I had with my first venture as an entrepreneur, the people I surrounded myself – [my] mentors … – that other[s] didn't have that cultural [references to] what my vision of customer service was. So, I knew that I could talk about customer experience all the time, but if I didn't have a system to actually manage people to that level of customer service, if I didn't turn that into a discipline and a way … to actually manage, correct … or teach behavior, then I wouldn't be able to ever impart the vision of customer service that I want to impart on the people.

Mittelstaedt then began to develop his customer philosophy, regularly jotting down his ideas in the small notebook he carries with him everywhere. A year later, this philosophy took shape as the *5Rs of Customer Service*: Respect, Realism, Responsibility, Responsiveness, and Being Remembered Positively.

Transaction or Caring Relationship?

In Mittelstaedt's philosophy, the story of the Bakersfield, California, delivery that opened this chapter exemplifies the "R" of Responsibility. At first glance, it may seem ordinary to follow up closely after a mistake to avoid losing a client. And we would agree with you – except this story stands out for two remarkable reasons.

First, the writer of the email wasn't a large corporate client of The FruitGuys but a private individual. If she had been mistreated and decided to stop using the company's services, the financial impact on the business would have been negligible. Devoting significant effort to a small client, from a purely economic perspective, doesn't make sense.

Second, the delivery itself involved extraordinary effort. Driving from The FruitGuys' warehouse to Bakersfield takes at least three hours each way, making it a six-hour round trip. To add to this, the driver wasn't a junior employee but the company's director of operations. For any profit-focused company, this decision would seem downright irrational.

To understand why The FruitGuys operates in this way, we need to revisit one fundamental assumption of free-market capitalism. Much of the criticism of capitalism was captured early on by Karl Marx. He argued that capitalists, driven by the pursuit of profit, seek to minimize wages, thereby perpetuating the "exploitation of man by man." We saw earlier how Robert Owen's fellow industrialists resisted his attempts to raise wages and reduce working hours. Marx, however, did not believe in the possibility of persuading capitalists to abandon "exploitation of man by man"; he called instead for their overthrow.

Yet, there is a less examined upstream phenomenon within free markets – a kind of breeding ground for exploitation – that deserves our attention. This phenomenon is the transactional relationship between economic agents.

Transactions are typically viewed in a positive light, and not without reason. Classical economics teaches us that wages and prices are set through contracts based on calculation. These calculations determine the economic value of a product or service, and the aggregation of countless rational transactions in a free market establishes equilibrium of wages and prices. This process assumes that all parties possess the necessary information to make rational decisions.

Furthermore, transactions are often seen as expressions of two free and equal wills, a notion rooted in the Enlightenment. Philosophers of the time celebrated market transactions as a leap forward for human progress. Adam Smith, for instance, extolled the emancipation that trade and burgeoning industry brought to society:

> Commerce and manufactures, gradually introduced order and good government, and with them, the liberty and security of individuals, among the inhabitants of the country, who had before lived almost in a continual state of war with their neighbors and of servile dependency upon their superiors.[2]

Servile dependency is typical of feudal order and of any "collectivist" society. In contrast, market transactions brought free and equal individuals into being and contributed to modern economic development – first in the protestant countries and in America in particular. According to the nineteenth century French philosopher Alexis de Tocqueville:

> America … exhibits in her social state an extraordinary phenomenon. Men are there seen on a greater equality in point of fortune and intellect, or, in other words, more equal in their strength, than in any other country of the world, or in any age of which history has preserved the remembrance.[3]

So, if free-market transactions have contributed to setting "free" prices and liberating the majority of people from servile dependency, why should we now consider liberating ourselves from this "transactional" approach? The FruitGuys offers us a clue.

The company's employees don't seem to act according to a cost-benefit analysis typical of transactional relationships. Instead, their actions appear to be guided by a genuine desire to maintain positive relationships with any client who crosses their path – sometimes at considerable expense. Indeed:

> While economic transactions enable gainful activities, authentic relationships allow gratuitous acts.

In other words, The FruitGuys employees deliberately avoid purely transactional interactions, choosing instead to cultivate caring relationships with their clients. This principle might sound impractical. Yet, as we've discovered, it forms the foundation of a pragmatic and highly rational – albeit unconventional – approach to business.

The FruitGuys shows us that this approach can redefine the client relationship, even in a sector as seemingly straightforward as fruit delivery. But can it function when your service has the potential to influence a client's reputation or the outcome of a critical event? To explore this, let's leave the orchards of California and step into the refined world of high-end corporate hospitality in France, where another caring company, Châteauform, has reimagined service excellence in its own, equally radical way.

Welcome to the Bathroom!

Daniel Abittan is a serial entrepreneur. In all his companies, he communicates his *utmost commandment* to all employees:

> I give you free rein to satisfy our clients, whatever the cost, and without asking anyone's permission.

Châteauform, a company Abittan co-founded in 1996, is a European leader in hospitality for high-end business seminars.[4] One day at a seminar venue in a posh Parisian neighborhood, Abittan washed his hands in the bathroom and was surprised to find that the pretty crystal soap dispenser that had always been here had disappeared. In its place, there was a sad plastic one. He asked the person in charge, "Fannie, can we get the nice dispenser back?"

"Daniel, I'm fed up! People keep stealing it!" she replied. "I'm not buying it anymore. I'm just going to leave them that ugly plastic thing in there. Enough is enough."

"No, no, and no! Which means No!" Abittan replied. At Châteauform, employees are used to a great deal of freedom, including freedom of speech, so Fannie shot back: "Very well Daniel, but it's not OK for a client to abuse the system in this way!"

To which Abittan replied: "Well, I'm sorry, but it *is* OK."

You may find this scene surreal: A business owner thinking that it's OK to have his business property stolen. But bear with us.

Châteauform's employees usually follow Abittan's utmost commandment. Sometimes, however, their instinct to defend the company's interests takes over. Most often, Abittan's veto of actions that do not respect his utmost commandment is enough. But sometimes he is forced to bring out the big guns: numbers. The following exchange is a regular occurrence at Châteauform, giving Abittan's "daily battle" the air of a military exercise with live ammunition.

"The average seminar involves a group of 23 participants who spend $8,300, approximately $360 per person; that's an average, because some groups stay two full days and others just come for half a day," he explains to a group of coworkers. Then he asks a question: "If you don't satisfy one person, how much money do you lose?"

An employee dares an answer: "$360, Daniel."

"Wrong," Abittan replies. "If one person in the group is unhappy, she'll make sure everyone knows about it: 'Did you hear the way they talked to me?' 'Did you see that thing?' And the others will start to agree! So, if you don't satisfy that one client, you don't lose $360, you lose $8,300! You put one rotten apple in the barrel, and the whole barrel is a write-off! Then, if, because of something you did, one single person in this group of 23 is unhappy because of something you've done ... we're dead."

Abittan then lists some potentially deadly pitfalls: "If someone asks for writing paper and he doesn't get paper, we're dead. If another one wants to show a presentation but our projector doesn't work, we're dead. If they ask for wine and there's no more wine, we're dead. Every time someone asks for something, it's a deadly risk! The work you do every day to satisfy all 23 people in the group is a miracle. But you have to satisfy all 23 of them!"

"You're right, Daniel," his employees say, cowed by this onslaught.

At this point, Abittan could be satisfied and end his demonstration. But he keeps charging: "Alright then. Now, if you have a dissatisfied group, how many other groups will they tell?" he asks.

Silence.

Abittan answers his own question: "10!" "I have lost $8,300. And potentially I could lose $8,300 times 10. But that's not all."

The big blow is coming.

"How many times do clients come back on average?"

More silence.

"The average client comes back seven times over 10 years. Multiply that figure by seven to get the value of a group over their life cycle. That's seven times $83,000. That's more than $580,000 lost because you didn't satisfy one request. They're gone! We're not talking about $300, $400, or $500. I don't want to hear, 'He wanted to go horseback riding but now he doesn't want to pay.' I don't care if they don't pay for the horse ride. We're talking about $580,000! Remember: 'I give you free rein to satisfy our clients, whatever the cost, and without asking anyone's permission.'"

And he walks away.

Whatever you think of Abittan's calculation, you have to admit that, while unconventional, it is undeniably rational. Yet, despite its internal logic, it diverges significantly from the typical Excel spreadsheet. It includes cost-benefit calculations, but the costs are almost disregarded, and the benefits – or the absence of them – are largely speculative. You must believe in it – and this, perhaps, is the key to understanding how caring companies operate.

Caring companies don't rely on formulas or analytical business models; instead, they operate on a bet.

They are not alone in this approach.

Analytical business models are also based on bets – they gamble that their assumptions about the future will hold true. However, caring companies take a different kind of bet. They don't gamble on future projections; they bet on a universal principle: people who are cared for will, in turn, be caring. When your clients, your suppliers, and the local community feel valued and cared for, they reciprocate, creating a network of mutual support. This dramatically increases the likelihood that the company's bet will pay off economically. This principle is an example of the obliquity we discussed in Chapter 1, brought to life in practice. The story of Châteauform is a perfect illustration.

Abittan's utmost commandment is far from naive. He is a shrewd businessman, deeply invested in the economic success of his enterprises. However, his pursuit of profit is indirect, or oblique. For Abittan, prosperity is a consequence – a result of his and his team's relentless care for Châteauform's clients.

If he were guided solely by the logic of immediate profit, he might replace luxury soap dispensers with unattractive, theft-proof alternatives to prevent losses. But as Abittan's example shows, this kind of reasoning is fundamentally flawed. It's flawed, but also widespread.

In practice, Abittan's approach has proven highly effective. Châteauform is his third multinational enterprise, following the successful development of a photography services chain and an optical retail business. Each of these ventures was managed as a caring company, adhering to his utmost commandment. Today, Abittan is not only one of France's most successful entrepreneurs but also among its wealthiest individuals.

SERVING ALL YOUR COUNTERPARTS, NOT ONLY CLIENTS

At this point, you might be thinking, "Isn't this just about taking care of your client so that your client will take care of your business?" In a sense, yes – but it's not as straightforward as it sounds. Taking good care of clients is no easy feat, as evidenced by the constant wave of customer-centric initiatives that many companies struggle to implement effectively.

Perhaps caring companies have simply mastered a higher degree of customer care compared to their more traditional counterparts. However, the following stories of unconditional care will challenge this perspective – and possibly take you deeper.

Of Owls and Gophers

Does your company have an employee whose job is "detective"? The FruitGuys does. Rebecca North, a former punk rock musician, holds the unique title of "fruit detective." In corporate terms, her role could be described as "sourcing officer" – identifying the best fruit producers for The FruitGuys. But Rebecca's duties go far beyond simple procurement.

Take Ed Magee, for example – a supplier she managed to track down. Ed is no ordinary small farmer. By day, he works at the legendary Lawrence Livermore National Laboratory (LLNL), a top US security research center focused on counterterrorism, intelligence, nonproliferation, and preventing biological attacks. At LLNL, Ed is a mechanical engineer specializing in spectroscopes used to study positron generation from ultra-intense laser-matter interactions (don't ask). But in his spare time, Ed grows peaches – with the same scientific precision he applies to his research. He grows only peaches – scientists are always specialists – but what peaches they are!

Rebecca was stunned by Ed's extraordinary produce. "Oh my, his peaches are absolutely amazing," she beamed. "They're so juicy, you need a shower after eating one!" True to the second of The FruitGuys' 5Rs – Responsiveness – Rebecca eagerly brought Ed into the fold, delighting her clients with his magnificent fruit.

But one day, Ed encountered a problem even his scientific expertise couldn't solve. In desperation, he called the "fruit detective" for help.

Rebecca drove out to Vernalis, about 60 miles east of San Francisco. There, in the middle of Ed's stunning peach orchard, she asked:

"Oh! what are all those tunnels under the peach trees?"

"Gophers! They've been getting into my orchard for weeks now. And they're eating the roots of my trees. I don't know what to do," Ed said, referring to the rapacious rodents.

Clearly, Ed still has plenty to learn about ecology. But not Rebecca. She has retained her do-it-yourself mentality since her punk-rock days, and she was also a pioneering activist in the Ecological Farming Association.

"Do you know what preys on them?" Rebecca the detective asked.

"Well, yes, of course, barn owls," Ed said.

"So why don't we try to get some to live here?"

"Do you think that's possible? How can we do that?" Ed wondered.

"We can help you if you want," Rebecca said confidently.

Rebecca's confidence came from her network. Wasting no time, she consulted an owl expert. A few months later, four nesting boxes were installed on Ed's property, and the owls took up residence. Ed was thrilled with the results. A single barn owl can eat up to six rodents in one night – a game changer for pest control.

Thanks to this intervention, Ed could continue producing his extraordinary peaches – the kind that require a shower after eating – to the delight of The FruitGuys' clients. When customers are happy, they buy more, and the company enjoys the "collateral benefits" of Rebecca's actions – yet another example of obliquity in practice.

Despite these benefits to customers and the company, Rebecca's actions weren't motivated by their interests. She acted purely for the benefit of a supplier, driven by a desire to leave a positive and lasting impression. Perhaps that's exactly what happens every morning when Ed surveys his orchard, appreciating the nocturnal accomplishments of his four owls: up to 24 fewer rodents in his magical peach grove.

It's common sense that taking care of clients can encourage them to purchase more, boosting a company's long-term economic success. But taking care of suppliers? On the surface, unconditionally supporting suppliers might not seem conducive to a company's self-interest. And yet, this unconventional approach raises compelling questions. Let's explore this further.

On Marriage, Adam Smith, and Mutual Sympathy

With the title of this section, we don't mean to imply that the previous story ended in a happy marriage between the former rocker-turned-environmental activist and the scientist-farmer. But Rebecca does speak of marriage – albeit in a different sense.

As part of her role, Rebecca trains other FruitGuys employees on how to interact with farmers. She sums up the company's philosophy this way:

> Real face-to-face interactions [with farmers] are one of the things I teach the team the most because they are [critical to] the relationship. We want long-term relationships here [and] not just one date or two. We're looking for a lasting marriage!

A lasting marriage with a supplier? It's a metaphor of course, but it illuminates the nature of relationships between economic actors in caring companies. In traditional companies, relationships often follow a one-way dynamic, where the buyer wields all the power, forcing the supplier to accept their terms – far from Smithian view of transactions among equals. This is hardly a modern marriage. It's more akin to unions of the past – or those in certain cultures today – where a bride is coerced into accepting her husband under duress or even threats.

For a lasting "marriage" between two economic actors, both parties must enter the union freely, without domination. The relationship must be based on mutual respect, appreciation, and care rather than conflict or exploitation. You might wonder if we're stretching the marriage metaphor too far. And perhaps we are. But if an economic relationship built on mutual appreciation and care resembles a stable marriage, we leave it to you to imagine what a one-off economic transaction based purely on give-and-take might resemble.

Though not literally married, Rebecca's unconditional care for her company's suppliers challenges one of the most entrenched assumptions in economics: that people act solely in their own self-interest. A brief detour into the history of ideas will shed light on whether this assumption truly holds up.

You have probably heard this phrase before:

It is not from the benevolence of the butcher, the brewer, or the baker that we expect our dinner, but from their regard to their own interest.[5]

This famous adage originates with Adam Smith, the founder of modern economics. The traditional interpretation of Smith's words suggests that each economic agent makes decisions based on a calculation of self-interest. Furthermore, the cumulative effect of these self-interested decisions is said to result in the best possible outcome for society as a whole. This is often attributed to the operation of an "invisible hand" – another Smithian concept – guiding the economy toward collective prosperity.

However, there are several reasons to question this interpretation.

First, Adam Smith was not the inventor of the idea that self-interest can produce positive societal effects. This notion predates him and is found in *The Fable of the Bees* by Anglo-Dutch writer Bernard de Mandeville, published in 1714. In this thought experiment, Mandeville imagines what would happen if people – the bees in the *Grumbling Hive* – suddenly began behaving honestly. His conclusion? Society would collapse because so many human activities are devoted to managing its vices. For example, consider how many lawyers are employed to address dishonesty in relationships or how many specialists work to ensure no party exploits another. Mandeville famously concluded that societal vices contribute to the general welfare.

This perspective is deeply cynical. It implies that addressing harmful corporate behavior, such as environmental degradation or exploitation of the poor, risks triggering economic crises or mass unemployment. But this interpretation is far removed from Smith's philosophy. For Smith, self-interest was a positive and natural quality of human beings, not a vice, and he explicitly condemns greed in his writings.[6]

Second, reducing Adam Smith's view of humanity to mere self-interest is an oversimplification. The famous quote above comes from *The Wealth of Nations* (1776), his economic magnum opus, but it doesn't represent the entirety of his thought. Smith was, first and foremost, a moral philosopher. In 1759, he published his other major work, *The Theory of Moral Sentiments*, the central concept of which is "mutual sympathy." Smith argued that the foundation of social life is the shared resonance of emotions among individuals. He believed that humans derive pleasure from observing and empathizing with the emotions of others – a view Leo Tolstoy, as mentioned in Chapter 3, shared wholeheartedly.

For Smith, this emotional connection is the root of social cohesion, standing in stark contrast to the indifference implied by pure self-interest. In *The Theory of Moral Sentiments*, he wrote:

> To feel much for others and little for ourselves, that is to restrain our selfish, and to indulge our benevolent affections, constitutes the perfection of human nature.[7]

Notably, Smith uses the pejorative term "selfish" instead of the neutral "self-interest," and contrasts it with the positive term "benevolent." This distinction underscores his belief that while self-interest is important, it is far from the entirety, much less the apex, of human nature.

Third, while the concept of the "invisible hand" is synonymous with Adam Smith, it is worth noting that he used the term sparingly – just twice in more than 3,500 pages of writings. Its outsized influence may say more about modern economic thought than it does about Smith himself.

Finally, in the same paragraph as the famous "benevolence of the butcher" quote, Smith proposed another way to explain our tendency to exchange, that is, to engage in business:

> In civilized society [man] stands at all times in need of the co-operation and assistance of great multitudes, while his whole life is scarce sufficient to gain the friendship of a few persons.[8]

From this argument, Smith concludes that unlike in other human realms, the economic exchange cannot rely on friendship, benevolence, mutual sympathy, or humanity – terms he references in his work – but rather on self-interest, a notion very close to *amoris sui* ("self-love" in English) in Thomas Aquinas' work.

This raises an important question:

Must businesses and their actors frame their relationships with clients, suppliers, and local communities through the lens of self-interest or can they base these relationships on – much more fundamental and common to humans – lens of mutual sympathy?

Rebecca's actions at The FruitGuys suggest the second. They demonstrate that businesses can operate on a different principle – unconditional care.

Moreover, they demonstrate that businesses can provide such a care not to "few persons" but to all the members of its business ecosystem who need it.

Mutual Sympathy and Charles Darwin

Rebecca's unconditional care for her company's suppliers also challenges another famous expression often embraced by businesses: the "struggle for existence." One of us – Laurent – recalls being deeply disturbed 30 years ago – while a young recruit at a large consultancy firm – by a slide in a partners' presentation during an annual meeting. It boldly declared: "Dominate or die."

The phrase "struggle for existence" originates with Charles Darwin and holds a far more central place in his work than "self-interest" or the "invisible hand" do in Adam Smith's writings. Darwin employs the term about 40 times in his seminal work, *On the Origin of Species*, including in the title of its third chapter.

However, much like Smith's concepts, Darwin's "struggle for existence" has often been oversimplified and misinterpreted in popular and business contexts. The following considerations may prompt you to question its application to the realities of the business world.

First, Darwin's "struggle for existence" is frequently reduced to the notion of competition. Yet Darwin himself explicitly described this expression as a metaphor, and his concept encompasses three distinct forms of struggle:

- Cooperation between individuals within the same species as well as between different species
- Competition between individuals within the same species or of one species against another
- Strategies to adapt to harsh environments

Competition is thus only one way to survive. In fact, it is not even the most important one.

Indeed, science, and in particular evolutionary science, has been telling us quite another story about the importance of cooperation. In Chapter 3, we discussed the key role that caring and trusting behaviors played in the survival of our species. Recent research also illuminates the ways in which cooperation – and not competition – is the main fabric of life.[9] From symbiosis to supportive behaviors within and between species, nature offers ample evidence of that view. In fact, its true laws are rooted in care and cooperation – not in competition, as the business world often assumes. In other words, it is caring and cooperation that were the true "laws of the jungle" or of the savanna that allowed human survival.[10]

As with Smith's "self-interest" and "invisible hand," the widespread popularity of Darwin's "struggle for existence" may reveal more about prevailing business thinking than about Darwin's actual ideas. It raises the question:

Must businesses continue to adopt traditional economic paradigm that views relationships – with peer companies, clients, suppliers, and local communities – solely through the lens of competing self-interests?

The enduring influence of Smithian self-interest and Darwinian struggle for existence in the business mindset highlights the challenges of transforming how businesses operate – a theme we will delve into further in Chapter 8.

Caring companies such as The FruitGuys, LSDH, Châteauform, and others, embody Smith's concept of mutual sympathy and Darwin's emphasis on cooperation. They do so in an unconditional way, without calculating immediate returns. Yet, you might question whether this approach can be generalized. After all, the examples we've discussed so far may seem to involve relatively low costs for these companies. To some, they might even resemble typical CSR activities found in many businesses today.

This skepticism is understandable. However, caring companies distinguish themselves by being ready to lose money in their pursuit of unconditional care. The following examples may dispel your doubts.

CARING AS A BET ON LIFE

Torrey Olsen is a fruit farmer in Sevastopol, in the heart of Sonoma Valley. He supplies The FruitGuys with Asian pears. Like his Danish ancestors, Torrey resents being told what to do. In 2015, the CCOF (California Certified Organic Farmers) – one of the first organic certifiers in the United States – changed its rules on how to protect trees from fire blight, a disease to which Asian pears are highly susceptible.

The day Rebecca visited Torrey's orchard, he seemed glum.

"What are you doing, Torrey?"

"We're pruning," Torrey replied.

"What do you mean, we're pruning? Its springtime!" Rebecca said, surprised.

"Yes, I know that, but the CCOF is now prohibiting us from using the fire blight treatment," Torrey told her. "And yet we've been hit by the disease. As a result, any affected branches already bearing fruit will have to be removed."

"One by one? And there are a lot of them?" Rebecca inquired in amazement.

"Yes, we're talking about several tons of loss," replied a distraught Torrey.

Rebecca grasped the magnitude of the catastrophe. She embraced Torrey in compassion. "This is his whole life, his job," she told us later. "He has a son. And he takes organic farming so seriously. He does such good work. He's really a good person! And he's sharing his pain with me like this, without even thinking that we can help him in any way."

Determined to find a solution for him, Rebecca began searching for answers. However, this time, even her trusted network of ecological experts was unable to help. Organic farming in California has become a victim of its own success, entangled in bureaucracy that even a fearless activist like Rebecca can't overcome. Still, she refused to abandon Torrey. When your marriage partner is in trouble, you don't let them down – you stand by them and help.

During their conversation, more bad news emerged. Because of the early pruning, the remaining pears would grow to twice their normal size. These oversized pears were likely to be rejected by all distributors and clients. For The FruitGuys, they presented a logistical problem: the pears were too large to fit in the company's standard crates. But Rebecca wouldn't abandon Torrey. She cared deeply about him and his despair, so she pushed herself to find a creative solution. Then, inspiration struck.

"We'll work this out. We'll buy these pears from you," Rebecca told Torrey, who could hardly believe what he was hearing.

Rebecca's solution had two dimensions. First, she decided that The FruitGuys would adapt its crates to fit Torrey's oversized pears. This adjustment would incur some costs, but as we've seen, The FruitGuys' philosophy is not driven by cost considerations but by the 5R principles of unconditional care.

The second part of Rebecca's plan was even more unconventional – and far costlier. Recognizing that the double-sized pears had no market value and were unsellable to any other client, Rebecca ensured that The FruitGuys wouldn't negotiate down the price with Torrey. Moreover, the company agreed not only to fulfill its original order but to buy all of Torrey's pear production for the season, knowing full well that no other buyer would.

We don't know if Torrey felt like Christmas had come early that year, but for Rebecca North, this decision made perfect sense. She was determined to do whatever it took to help her supplier – even at a significant cost to The FruitGuys.

The FruitGuys isn't the only company willing to sacrifice money and resources to build caring relationships. You may recall this book's opening story about the Truckers' House of the dairy company LSDH. Here's another example.

Unlike the low-tech food company The FruitGuys, Radica Games – originally based in Nevada – was a high-tech company. In the early 1990s, it became a world's leading manufacturer of electronic games. When Radica was seeking a major supplier for its new factory in China, Bob Davids, the company's CEO at the time, had an eye-opening encounter with one of its oldest suppliers.

The purchasing manager had convinced this supplier to offer a price barely covering costs. But as the meeting began, Davids surprised everyone by stating: "We won't be able to work with you anymore because your price is too low." This declaration shocked everyone in the room, especially the supplier – because at this time, in China, prices were rarely considered "too low."

Davids explained that, at the proposed price, the supplier was operating at break-even, with no profit margin. If Radica Games started doubling its production every six months as expected, the supplier's situation would inevitably become financially unsustainable. Instead, Davids suggested that the supplier raise its price to ensure a 9% profit margin, enabling it to sustain a long-term relationship with Radica.

As Davids predicted, Radica's product became a massive success, and the supplier's improved pricing ensured his financial stability. The resulting long-term partnership proved critical to Radica's success. The relationship grew so strong that Davids was the only Westerner invited to the supplier's daughter's wedding in China – a profound mark of respect and esteem in Chinese culture, signifying that Davids was now considered part of the supplier's extended family.

A larger and more institutionalized example of caring relationships with suppliers comes from Toyota. Didier Leroy, who oversaw the construction of Toyota's French plant in the early 2000s and later became the first non-Japanese member of Toyota's executive board, shared this insight: "The supplier's problem is not their problem; it's our problem."[11]

Leroy explained that whenever a Toyota supplier encountered an issue, the company would send its best engineers immediately to assist the supplier in finding a solution – rather than threatening or penalizing them.

While this approach might be seen as self-interested, it stands apart from the behavior of Toyota's competitors, who rarely, if ever, deploy their top engineers to help struggling suppliers. Toyota's approach goes far beyond addressing isolated problems. The company's *keiretsu* – a network of interdependent and cooperative supplier relationships – epitomizes a deeper philosophy of mutual care and respect.

Although traditional business thinking frames client-supplier relationships as transactional and self-interested, Toyota or Radica Games demonstrate a different path: one grounded in unconditional care. These companies have shown a willingness to sacrifice money and resources to support their suppliers, proving the sincerity of their commitment.

In essence, these companies don't view their suppliers as anonymous members of an ecosystem but as "significant others" within a shared community.

Ecosystem, Community, and the Significant Other

Many corporations have embraced the term "ecosystem," but few genuinely embody its essence. In business, the term is often used to describe a network of transactional relationships rather than true long-term interdependence. However, there is a fundamental difference between these two concepts.

In his 1924 book *The Gift*, French sociologist Marcel Mauss – nephew of Émile Durkheim, widely regarded as the founder of sociology – argued that the structure of every society is rooted in reciprocity. For Mauss, communities and the relationships between them are built and sustained through the continuous flow of gifts and counter-gifts.

Mauss' insights were drawn from his observations of traditional societies in Melanesia, where customs such as the *kula ring* exemplify this principle. The kula ring involves the exchange of ceremonial gifts – shell necklaces and armbands – between tribes, not for economic gain but to demonstrate a desire to establish or maintain alliances. These gifts serve as tokens of mutual respect, trust, and connection, creating a network of interdependence that binds communities together over time.[12] It's crucial to emphasize that this act of giving does not obligate the recipient to immediately give back, as it would in a transaction. The reciprocity here is not direct or immediate. Instead, the act of giving initiates a relationship – a connection that implicitly calls for a counter-gift, which may arrive at an undetermined time and in an unexpected form.

When you participate in this cycle of gift and counter-gift to foster a community or an ecosystem, you commit to a purpose beyond immediate gain. Your ultimate goal becomes the creation of a lasting relationship, much like in a marriage. In this dynamic, the "when" and "how" of eventual benefits are not your primary concern. Instead, you embrace the idea of a larger, more profound game – one that transcends the transactional mindset.

This is a game of trust: trust in life, in Providence, in God, or in what some might call the Field of Possibility. It is a game in which the focus shifts from individual gain to collective flourishing, grounded in the belief that the act of giving will ultimately lead to mutual prosperity, even if the path is not immediately visible. Life, or whatever you want to name it, will reward you in one way or another – will take care of you – at some stage. But of course, such a game is also a bet.[13]

Now, you may wonder why not everyone acts on the basis of such a universal principle. First, it is because of our fears. If you trust someone, you can be cheated. In other words, you are vulnerable. This is why – as you'll see in the next chapter – becoming a caring company requires an inner transformation by leaders, including the overcoming of such fears.

The second reason resides in individualism. Luigino Bruni, an Italian economist and philosopher, analyzed the roots of modern individualism.[14] He shows that when we moved from societies without "individuals" (when everyone was enclosed in the community) to the advent of the individual, the "other" started to be a threat, instead of a source of unconditional support. Individualism created people scared to be touched, to be wounded by the other, building fences to avoid this risk. This created societies where loneliness is pervasive. According to David Brooks:

> The percentage of Americans who said they have no close friends quadrupled between 1990 and 2020, [while] 36 percent of Americans reported that they felt lonely frequently or almost all of the time, including 61 percent of young adults and 51 percent of young mothers.[15]

And he concludes: "The thing we need most is relationships. The thing we seem to suck at most is relationships."[16]

The final reason lies in what Iris Murdoch, mentioned in Chapter 3, described as "attention" – or the absence of it. The act of giving or offering genuine care is fundamentally a moral choice. Yet, as Murdoch observes, we are conditioned to perceive moral decisions as "a grandiose leaping about, unimpeded at important moments."[17] In contrast, she argues that the "work of attention" to the reality of others is central to the moral life, a process that should be continuous rather than "switched off between the occurrence of explicit moral choices."[18]

In practical terms, this means maintaining constant attentiveness to others' subtlest reactions – often unspoken emotional cues or "body language," to nuanced psychological or physical states – such as appearing withdrawn, unusually tired, or to changes in typical behavior. Many of us engage in this work of attention with our family and friends. Often without realizing it, this habit of attention shapes our values, which explains why, as Murdoch puts it, "at crucial moments of moral choice, most of the business of choosing is already over."

Yet, somehow, we frequently disengage this attentiveness while at workplace, assuming that moral choices arise only sporadically there – such as when reprimanding or dismissing someone. As a result, we make most business decisions involving others – employees, clients, suppliers, and members of the local community – on a purely transactional basis.

Altogether, the fear of being cheated, the prevalence of individualism, and the neglect of attention to others' realities create significant barriers to building caring relationships within many organizations – let alone between them. But while difficult, it is not impossible. There exists a type of individual who excels at building meaningful connections, and more often than not, these individuals are richly rewarded in the long run.

To uncover the secret of their success, we must take a detour into the realm of workplace relationships, exploring how colleagues relate to one another and the dynamics that enable trust and collaboration to flourish.

Givers Protected from Takers

Is it possible to build a professional relationship grounded in genuine care for others – and achieve success as a result? Adam Grant, a professor at Wharton, University of Pennsylvania, decided to examine this very question.[19]

Grant identified two psychological profiles of people working in organizations: "takers" and "givers." Takers view relationships as opportunities to extract what they need from others while fiercely guarding their own time, expertise, and resources. They take. In contrast, givers are continuously attentive to others' realities and seek opportunities to assist them, doing so without expectations of reciprocity. They give.

After categorizing these profiles, Grant investigated which group faced the most difficulty achieving professional success. If you guessed givers, you'd be correct – but only to a certain extent. Their propensity to help others often comes at the expense of their own time and resources, making them vulnerable. However, Grant also discovered something surprising: the most professionally successful individuals were not takers, but givers. Here's why.

Grant observed that givers who fail professionally were frequently exploited by takers, who monopolize their time, energy, and competencies. He labeled these individuals "self-sacrificing" givers. Successful givers, by contrast, adopted what Grant called a "discriminating approach to generosity." They were deliberate about *whom*, *when*, and *how* they helped.

- **Whom:** Givers serve everyone unconditionally – except takers. When faced with exploitation, they're quick to demand reciprocation or set boundaries.
- **When:** Successful givers establish and communicate generous yet defined time slots for helping others, maintaining control over their availability.
- **How:** They encourage colleagues to become givers themselves, leveraging their generosity to amplify its impact. Notably, they often ask others to help third parties, rather than themselves, making it easier for people to say yes.

Critics might argue that this "discriminating approach to generosity" undermines the notion of unconditional care. However, these givers are not attaching conditions to their generosity or demanding something in return. Instead, they are setting boundaries to prevent future exploitation, striking a balance between selflessness and self-protection. Unlike those who withdraw entirely after being exploited, successful givers remain other-focused. They strive to avoid further exploitation but do not "punish" new partners by withholding trust or assistance.

Grant's research shows that people respect givers who set boundaries. These individuals develop reputations as altruistic, selfless contributors, making them highly sought after. This is why requests to them often begin with, "I know you're busy, but …" Their perceived busyness reinforces their reputation as reliable and valued professionals.

This reputation for serving others unconditionally fosters trust and goodwill over time, creating a virtuous cycle. Givers attract opportunities and winning projects because they've earned the respect, trust, and gratitude of their colleagues. Their extensive networks and positive reputations make it easier to assemble the right team for any project, further enhancing their success.

Grant's findings on the professional benefits of serving others align closely with evolutionary research discussed in Chapter 3, which highlights the role of mutual care in human communities over the past three million years. These principles also apply to the way caring companies interact with their ecosystem members.

Caring companies adopt a similar approach to individual givers. While they strive to care unconditionally for everyone within their ecosystem, they protect themselves – when they can – from takers who could exploit this generosity. By doing so, they avoid the pitfalls of self-sacrificing givers and instead build the kind of positive "halo" Grant described for successful individuals. This reputation for care attracts trust, goodwill, and opportunities, enabling these companies to thrive.

After reading these lines, you might agree that business can indeed operate on the unconditional care of suppliers by clients – clients willing to sacrifice money and resources to support their suppliers. However, you might still harbor doubts. Is it truly possible to sacrifice money and resources for a supplier – or any member of your business ecosystem – during a crisis, when it's not just self-interest at stake, but the very survival of your company?

CRISES THAT REINFORCE THE CARING COMPANIES

On March 24, 2020, just one week after the start of the COVID-19 lockdown in France, Laurent Cavard, CEO of Altho, France's third-largest potato chip producer, made an extraordinary announcement: a 9% fee increase for the company's transportation suppliers who, by the company's choice, were all local. The raise was backdated by a week, and Cavard pledged to pay invoices immediately to help ease suppliers' financial struggles, caused by diminished demand for hauling during the lockdown.

That same day, Energy Vision, a Belgian company specializing in energy consumption analysis and sustainable cost-saving solutions, took a bold step by waiving energy charges for its clients for two months.

Then, a week later, MAIF – a French mutual insurer with 8,000 employees – announced it would refund $108 million to its 2.8 million car insurance clients. This decision was data-driven: MAIF's experts had observed a dramatic 75% drop in car accidents during the first two weeks of lockdown and chose to return the resulting unused premiums. Notably, none of MAIF's larger competitors in France followed suit by refunding excess premiums to their clients.

In each of these cases, the companies demonstrated a steadfast commitment to caring unconditionally for the people "on their doorsteps" – the members of their business ecosystems – despite the challenges posed by the COVID-19 crisis. Rather than retreating from their values, these caring companies allowed the crisis to reinforce them.

In his book *Antifragile,* thinker Nassim Taleb distinguishes between fragile and antifragile systems. Fragile systems – whether organizations or individuals – break down under stress and uncertainty. In contrast, antifragile systems thrive in times of volatility and chaos, emerging from shocks not merely restored but stronger than before.

We've already seen how The FruitGuys grew stronger after the 2000 dotcom crisis. A similar transformation occurred for them during the 2008 financial crisis.

As Mittelstaedt recalls:

We had to lay people off and cut expenses. I told the company very honestly: "Okay, here's our situation. We're losing revenue … My choice, as the executive in the company that has to make sure the ship doesn't sink, is: I have to either cut jobs or I have to cut wages." And I said, "I would like to put it to a vote and understand what you guys think the right decision is to do."

The employees voted to cut wages by 25% for 90 days across the entire company. They also proposed using this period to identify reductions in nonpersonnel expenses and generate new ideas to help the company survive.

That's exactly what they did. During those 90 days, they found ways to cut these expenses and developed a new line of business serving schools and institutions, which eventually boosted revenues. By the end of the period, wages were restored to their original levels. In essence, by caring for its employees – sharing full information with them and allowing them to choose a course of action – the company empowered its workforce to create a leaner, stronger, and more profitable organization. The crisis tested its capacity to care and ultimately made it more resilient.

Of course, The FruitGuys didn't escape the challenges of the COVID-19 lockdowns – the most recent crisis.

At that time, the company operated 15 hubs delivering across 48 states. Within three weeks, its revenue plummeted from $40 million to

$2 million. Founder Chris Mittelstaedt recalls being advised to "mothball" the business by laying off the workforce entirely to minimize losses. While this option made financial sense, it clashed deeply with the company's values and vision.

During the first week of the crisis, the leadership team searched for solutions that aligned with their philosophy, even if it meant incurring "triple the losses," as Mittelstaedt described. The solution: launching a home-delivery service for private clients and establishing a program to deliver fruit to people battling COVID-19 within local communities – members of the company's ecosystem.

The FruitGuys also took a principled stand against layoffs. Instead, they implemented partial furloughs while continuing to provide full healthcare benefits. Additionally, they proactively helped delivery and packaging employees find temporary work with other businesses, minimizing furloughs even further.

The pivot to home delivery proved successful. By June 2020, the company was generating $90,000 in weekly orders, enabling it to reach a rough breakeven point. This crisis-driven innovation not only ensured The FruitGuys' survival but also positioned it for future growth, expanding its home-delivery business as a key new revenue stream. Today, the company's revenues have reached $30 million – a level approaching pre-COVID-19 figures.[20]

However, crises can test caring companies in even more profound ways. Some crises are so severe that they not only challenge a company's commitment to unconditional care but also its very capacity to survive.

This reciprocal dynamic is precisely what Radica Games experienced, as discussed earlier in the chapter when the company insisted that its Chinese supplier *raise* prices to ensure sustainability. Several years later, Radica faced a sudden crisis due to a strategic error, forcing it to cut costs by a staggering 63%. Upon learning of the situation, the same supplier offered to provide products for six months without payment – a pivotal gesture that saved Radica from bankruptcy.

A similar story can be seen in the journey of LSDH, the French dairy company we introduced in Chapter 1. At school, André Vasseneix – the company's founder – befriended the Schmitlin family, who owned a large dairy factory in Alsace, France. In the late 1980s, the Schmitlins faced severe technical difficulties. When André learned of their plight, he sent his son Emmanuel to help. Emmanuel stayed in Alsace, not for days or weeks, but for six months, until the dairy's problems were fully resolved. Remarkably, LSDH charged nothing for this service.

For many years, the two dairy factories pursued separate paths – until fate brought them together again. The Vasseneix family had owned their dairy since Emmanuel's grandfather, Roger, purchased it in 1947 with just 13 employees. However, when Roger retired in 1972, he could not afford the estate taxes and was forced to sell 93% of the business to Celia, a cheese manufacturer. Losing control of their company was a bitter pill for the Vasseneix family, especially when, in 1996, Celia decided to sell LSDH to a dairy conglomerate. Faced with the prospect of their business being swallowed by a corporate giant, the family resolved to regain ownership.

Their determination was unwavering, but no bank or investor was willing to support their endeavor. No one, that is, besides the Schmitlins. Drawing on the bond formed years earlier, the Schmitlins provided the financial support needed for the Vasseneix family to buy back 50% of LSDH, and eventually the entire company.

This wasn't simply a business transaction driven by cost-benefit analysis. Recall that no bank had deemed the loan a safe bet. It's more plausible that the Schmitlins' decision stemmed from the mutual caring relationship forged when Emmanuel spent six months helping them overcome their crisis. As we've discussed, this kind of relationship is built on trust and care, often without any guarantee of return.

Thanks to this support, the Vasseneix family regained full ownership of LSDH. Under their leadership, the company not only reinforced its commitment to care but also achieved remarkable growth. Between 2007 and 2023, LSDH grew organically from $200 million in revenue to $985 million, with a workforce of 2,000 employees. It was even recognized as the best food company in France.

These examples illustrate that during crises, caring companies not only uphold their commitment to their ecosystem – employees, suppliers, partners, and the host community – but often seize these exceptional moments to strengthen those bonds. Crises also test and reveal the resilience of these relationships, as ecosystem members frequently care back, sometimes becoming the very factor that saves the caring company in its time of need. We will see more examples of caring companies' resilience in Chapter 7 and discuss the paradigm shift that allows to achieve it in Chapter 8.

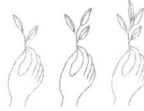

Building and maintaining a caring relationship with the members of your business ecosystem, day in and day out, is undeniably a powerful path to business success. Yet, as we will explore in the following chapters, most companies avoid this path. More importantly, we will examine what must be *unlearned* for a company to truly transform into a caring organization.

The French philosopher Edgar Morin once remarked, "We don't *have* ideas, but our ideas have us." In many ways, business leaders and thinkers are "possessed" by ingrained habits and beliefs. Becoming a caring company demands not only the acquisition of new skills and approaches but more crucially, the willingness to unlearn outdated practices and mindsets.

This process of self-transformation – affecting leaders and employees alike – is the focus of next chapter.

CHAPTER FIVE

THE HEARTSET SHIFT: ON SELF-TRANSFORMATION

Walk through the dark night with a raised lantern. There is no use in worrying about the pitch-black path; just trust the light of the lantern you hold up high.

– Issai Sato[1]

The journey from transactional to caring business is not merely an organizational transformation – it is a personal one. As we suggested in the previous chapter, becoming a caring company requires more than adopting new practices; it demands the unlearning of deeply embedded habits and beliefs. This is no easy path. It's often painful and counterintuitive – much like walking a dark trail with only a single lantern to illuminate the way. The story of Eisai and its CEO, Haruo Naito, brings this metaphor vividly to life. It illustrates how a leader's inner shift can catalyze an entire organizational transformation.

You may not be familiar with the Japanese pharmaceutical firm Eisai, but you almost certainly know some of its patients. Eisai is a global leader in the treatment of dementia, including Alzheimer's disease. It is Eisai that, in the 1980s, developed Aricept, one of the world's most effective and widely used drugs for slowing the progression of Alzheimer's. By 2002, Aricept accounted for around 40% of the firm's revenue. That year, when CEO Haruo Naito addressed an audience of newly appointed managers, he mentioned the drug but in an unusual way:

> When one of our products becomes no longer effective, that is when our true value shall be tested.[2]

This striking statement was not an isolated remark. It follows a series of similarly unusual declarations, such as: "If, for instance, Aricept should become completely ineffective, we would still have to provide our patients with the best information they would need [regarding alternative treatments]." And a bit later, Naito elaborated, saying: "In reality, people would rather not have to take medicine or even go to see a doctor. They just want to live a normal life." And to ensure his audience clearly grasped his message, he added: "Here at Eisai, we must mentally extricate ourselves from the mere manufacture and sale of pharmaceutical products."

At this point, one might wonder if some of the managers in the room had begun questioning whether they had joined the wrong company – or perhaps suspected that Eisai was preparing to diversify beyond its core pharmaceutical business into the service sector. On the latter, they wouldn't have been entirely wrong. Eisai had, in fact, branched out into services. However, Naito's words carry far deeper significance. To fully grasp his vision, we need to delve into the company's evolution.

EISAI PHARMACEUTICAL

Eisai was founded in the early 1940s by Toyoji Naito, a businessman with considerable experience in the pharmaceutical sector. Noticing that his competitors were seemingly content to import drugs produced overseas, he made the bold decision to invest in the creation of a dedicated R&D division. Eisai soon began producing its own range of medicines, including treatments for strokes, ulcers, and gastritis, as well as various neurological disorders.

Toyoji's son, Yuji, became the company's second CEO and spearheaded another strategic move that set the firm apart from its Japanese competitors: international expansion. By entering Asian and US markets, Eisai propelled itself into the world's top 30 pharmaceutical companies. However, it was only when Yuji's son, Haruo Naito – who took over as CEO in June 1988 – that Eisai would turn into a truly exceptional company.

Unlike his father and grandfather, Haruo Naito began by focusing not on what the company should do, but on what it shouldn't do – or rather, on what it shouldn't think. As early as April 1989, he delivered a following message to newly recruited Eisai managers: "The main focus of any medical treatment is the patient, their family, and the public at large. Those are the people we need to serve."

Naito aimed to challenge the expectations of the new hires. Some of them might have been delighted to hear that their company had set itself such a noble mission. Others, especially those with more professional experience, might have questioned how much these lofty ideals would impact their daily work. Such skepticism was understandable.

Yet by 1990, Haruo Naito's proclamations were not mere rhetoric. They became institutionalized as the foundation of Eisai's new business philosophy of *hhc* – human health care: "The defining characteristic of an *hhc* company is its capacity for empathy with those suffering from illness."[3]

It took Haruo Naito two years to fully develop this new vision for himself and for Eisai.[4] Realizing it, however, took much longer, requiring a profound transformation in the way employees approach their business activities – as we will see shortly.

An intriguing question arises: Why would a CEO stepping into a company founded by his grandfather and expanded by his father choose to radically transform it? Why didn't he simply continue running Eisai in line with his ancestors, particularly in Japan, where tradition holds such importance?

The *hhc* Imperative

When we met Naito in his Tokyo office, the very first thing he said to us is: "Every decision consists of choosing the option which works best for you. We like to choose the option which works best for our patients."[5] This was our second visit to Eisai, and as we delved deeper into the *hhc* concept, we asked Naito how it guides him in making the right decisions. Naito explained that *hhc* is much more than a business philosophy. For him, it is an imperative that shapes every concrete decision: to always choose what is best for patients and their families. He provided a concrete example. "If you encounter side effects, how do you handle that information?" he asked. He then elaborated, explaining that Eisai chooses the option that best serves its patients, announcing, "We experienced these side effects, and we'd like to inform you of what is happening. After thorough analysis, we will report back to you."

We wondered how traditional pharmaceutical firms might respond in a similar situation. Naito suggested that such firms would likely conduct additional analyses, wait for the results, and only then consider making an announcement.

And herein lies the critical difference between Eisai and its competitors: the former provides patients with all the information they could need, even if it means raising concerns that might later prove unfounded. At first, we assumed that Naito's choice of side effects as an example was hypothetical, but it wasn't.

In 1988, shortly after Naito's appointment as CEO, Eisai was shaken by a series of noncompliance scandals. It wasn't just the company that was affected. Naito himself bore the brunt of the crisis – losing 44 pounds and enduring significant psychological strain. "Mentally, I was very weak. I was at the top of the company, but I couldn't make good decisions." Naito became aware that if another scandal of this nature occurred under his leadership, he would be unable to function as CEO. This awareness spurred not one but two transformative decisions. The first was: "I decided to change myself." The second was to radically transform Eisai, ensuring that no one in the company would ever take an action that he, as CEO, would be ashamed of. *hhc* became both the name and philosophy that guided this transformation.

Hearing this tale of a CEO wracked with shame, one might picture the familiar image of a Japanese business leader bowing apologetically before an audience. Japanese culture undoubtedly played a role in such behavior, and Naito was unequivocal on this point: "You should never do anything that brings shame upon your name." This imperative, he explained, stems from the Bushido way, a code of honor governing the conduct of the noble warriors known as samurai.

The 1968 Samurai

The core principles and precepts of Bushido first appeared orally between the eleventh and thirteenth centuries. In the seventeenth century, during the Edo period, these ideals were codified in writing, profoundly influencing the moral fabric of Japanese society. Naito outlines this historical connection.

During the Edo period, also known as the Tokugawa shogunate, Japan experienced a prolonged era of peace. In this context, the samurai assumed new roles as civil administrators. Bushido, originally a warrior's code, evolved to encompass values suited to civil society. Samurai were now expected to demonstrate compassion for those of lower status, uphold their reputation, and act with integrity. As Naito explained, the samurai "had an obligation to society: to make people happy. If they failed to do so, they brought shame upon their name."[6] He concludes that the Bushido code is fundamentally about the public good and asserts that it is ingrained in the DNA of the Japanese people – a deep-seated sense of responsibility to society as a whole. That is why, he explains, "we should never do something that would bring shame to ourselves … nor to our shareholders."

By hearing the word "shareholders," you may wonder whether all of Naito's declarations ultimately serve the goal of satisfying this group. The answer is both yes and no. Shareholders are undoubtedly on Naito's mind; as the CEO of a publicly traded company, they must be. However, the way he and Eisai choose to serve their shareholders – and, by extension, the public and society – is not through the relentless maximization of shareholder value. That said, Eisai's shareholder value has increased significantly during Naito's tenure, a result that aligns with the earlier discussed principle of obliquity: achieving results indirectly. We will discuss how they have been achieved, but first, let us return to 1989 to understand how Naito launched Eisai's transformation.

In 1989, Naito was searching for a way to ensure that neither he nor Eisai would ever feel ashamed again. He concluded that Eisai's focus on profits was the root cause of past failings. Determined to transform the company, he began asking employees a simple but profound question: "What is Eisai's purpose?" Most replied predictably, stating that it is to develop and sell drugs. Then, one employee offered an answer that deeply resonated with Naito: "To relieve patients from suffering."

You may think that the difference between "developing and selling drugs for patients" and "relieving them from suffering" is purely semantic. The rest of Eisai's story will show you how decisive this realization was both for Naito and for the company.

This response struck a chord with Naito because of its alignment with the Bushido code, as prioritizing patients inherently serves the public good. But there is more to the story. When we asked Naito about the influences behind his decision to adopt the *hhc* vision, his answer had less to do with Japan's cultural traditions than one might expect. First, he laughed, then confided that what he was about to share was something he had never discussed publicly before. And then he began to speak about the Vietnam War, the opposition to which was at its height in 1968 when Naito was in high school.

He recalled participating in demonstrations, not out of any particular ideology but because he and his peers were grappling with profound questions: "We were at a very sensitive age, asking ourselves, 'what is the socially right thing to do? ... what is the right direction for the country?'" Without pausing, Naito transitioned to describing how these youthful experiences inspired him to reflect on the decisions Eisai had made in the past – particularly its focus on sales and on profits – and to question whether these priorities truly served the best interests of society and business. "We are not denying profit-making," he explained. "At the end of the day, we want to achieve good results, but those profits are the results, not the objectives. The goal is the betterment of people and society, achieved through our business activities."

Later in this chapter, we explore how the vision Naito uncovered became the foundation for Eisai's transformation, driving societal betterment and, indirectly, exceptional business performance. But before we do so, it is worth considering whether Naito is a truly unique leader.

Special and Not

Eisai's internal *Blue Book*, which documents the company's transformation, concludes with a thought-provoking musing:

> Some might wonder whether Haruo Naito, the originator of *hhc*, is some sort of exceptional human being. Others may wonder if he was uniquely gifted to recognize the genius and potential of *hhc*.[7]

It then emphasizes that the spirit of *hhc* is shared by everyone at Eisai, even though it was Naito who has first launched the concept.

You might have heard this age-old question of whether exceptional leaders are truly extraordinary human beings. From Alexander the Great to the Founding Fathers of the United States or Churchill, many have sought to pinpoint their unique qualities – whether charisma, integrity, or something else entirely. But equally compelling is the hypothesis that certain situations demand specific qualities. After all, Churchill, hailed as an exceptional leader during World War II, lost the general election immediately afterward. This interplay between individual traits and circumstances, a concept scholars term "situational leadership," is a fascinating lens through which to explore leadership dynamics.

Naito is certainly not unique in adhering to the principles of the Bushido code. Observing the Japanese – marked by their respect, trust, and care – it becomes clear why Naito asserts that the Bushido code permeates Japanese culture. Yet, we know of only a few Japanese CEOs who have successfully harnessed the Bushido code to inspire their companies' vision and daily behavior.

Naito's experiences at antiwar demonstrations may have played a role in his alignment with the public good – specifically, prioritizing the well-being of patients and their families over profits as the purpose of a corporation. However, even here, other CEOs might share similar experiences of youthful social or political activism without channeling those into a focus on the public good at their companies.

Thus, despite sharing certain biographical elements with other Japanese CEOs, Naito appears to possess something that sets him apart. The same observation applies to other leaders we have studied. For instance, Chris Mittelstadt and Daniel Abittan share aspects of their biographies with other CEOs, yet they have developed distinctive personal and corporate visions that few others have elaborated. They seem to possess a "magical touch" that allowed them to become exceptional leaders.

But while these leaders may seem exceptional, we do not want to create the impression that their achievements are the result of some enigmatic or unattainable force. These leaders are human, performing roles much like your own. Like Naito, they transformed themselves. Moreover, their leadership is neither magical nor innate; it has been cultivated. Yes, it has required time, effort, and introspection, but understanding the essence of this "magical touch" and the deliberate steps they took to develop it can provide valuable insights. These lessons can help you uncover and refine your own unique leadership approach.

THE MAGICAL TOUCH AND HOW YOU CAN FIND YOUR OWN

Perhaps you've experienced a similar situation. One weekday morning, passengers are gathered at an airport gate, waiting to board their flight. Many are professionals, deeply engrossed in their laptops or making calls to clients and colleagues. Suddenly, an announcement blares over the speakers: the flight is delayed indefinitely due to severe weather.

After a brief moment of processing the news, most passengers spring into action – calling clients, rearranging meetings, or notifying family members, all while juggling their schedules to minimize disruption. Their focus is clear: keeping the delay from derailing their plans – a completely logical reaction.

Now, picture the person sitting next to you. After a quiet moment of reflection, she picks up her phone and says, "Please, cancel the client meeting. Actually, cancel all my meetings. You know what? I think I'm done with this job. It's not for me anymore. I'm quitting. I'll stay in the business world, but I don't know yet what I'll do exactly. I need some time to figure it out."

At the very least, you'd be taken aback. But this scenario mirrors the experiences of the leaders we have studied. In this moment, they are your neighbor at the airport gate.

Gordon Forward, freshly armed with a PhD from MIT, joined the research and development department of a major Canadian steel company.[8] One day, his boss called him into the office and said, "You've done well in research … I just wanted to tell you where you'll be in 20 years if you stay with this company." The executive then pointed to the top of a three-story research center: "You'll be up there, heading the research department for the entire company."

Forward later reflected that his manager likely believed this would motivate him. Indeed, such a conversation – with an executive expressing appreciation for your work and promising a brilliant career – could seem like a positive moment. But not for Forward. Leaving his manager's office, he thought, "I don't want to know where I'll be in the next 20 years. I want to make a difference, enjoy my work, and be successful at it." That very evening, he resigned. He later became the CEO of Chaparral Steel, building it in line with his vision and values. By the 1990s, he was celebrated as one of America's most transformative business leaders.

The same kind of awakening is reported by Anne-Laure Le Cunff, a former successful Google employee, now neuroscientist and founder of Ness Labs. She recalls a holiday back in her family, when she did not know how to answer really to the question "How is life?":

> How *was* life, really? I hadn't ever asked myself this … I was so consumed by the routine, the rubric, and the next rung on the ladder that I had lost the ability to notice anything else … While I had spent my younger life guided by a genuine yearning to learn and grow, I was now following a prescribed path trodden by so many colleagues before me. Realizing how I felt was like an electric shock … On my first day back in the office after the holiday, I quit[9]

Here is one more case.

Prior to becoming a CEO of Poult, a European leader in private-label biscuits, Mehdi Berrada felt he had two "selves." On the one hand, there was his professional self – his identity in the demanding world of high finance. On the other was his personal self – shaped by deeply held values and aspirations.

At first glance, nothing suggested he was destined to lead this medium-sized company. After graduating from a top-tier business school in Paris, Berrada was recruited by Rothschild, where he built a promising career in investment banking. Yet the growing rift between his two "selves" drove him to explore ways to bridge it. Drawn to issues surrounding the North-South economic divide, he began engaging with various nongovernmental organizations (NGOs) in his spare time – an endeavor that ultimately left him unfulfilled. All the while, his banking career continued apace.

In 2005, he inherited the Poult account, tasked with overseeing the sale of the biscuit company. But after its sale, Berrada made an unexpected decision: instead of moving on to another project within Rothschild, he resigned. He chose to join Poult.

While working on the sale, Berrada was inspired by the company's bold and caring vision, spearheaded by Carlos Verkaeren – a former private equity banker turned CEO. The opportunity to join Poult offered Berrada a chance to align his professional ambitions with his personal values, reconciling the "selves" that had long been in conflict.

His leap of faith was rewarded. Poult garnered widespread recognition in the early 2010s for its pioneering social innovation, earning multiple awards and becoming the focus of a case study in a prestigious INSEAD Business School collection.[10] For Berrada, this journey wasn't just transformative – it was life-defining, leaving a profound and lasting imprint on his identity.

In our research, we have encountered dozens of persons who, at different stages of their professional lives, experienced an event – unfortunate, accidental, or even fortunate, like Forward's, Le Cunff's or Berrada's – that effectively "grounded their airplane."

It happened to one of us – Isaac – too. Six months into his first job as a software engineer, he was having lunch in the company cafeteria with his friend, an engineer from another department, and that department's manager. At some point, the manager looked at Isaac and said, "I've been hearing great feedback about your work. If you keep this up, in 15 years, you could be a manager like me." He clearly meant to be encouraging, but Isaac knew something about him – every afternoon, this manager would lock himself in his office with Isaac's friend and play chess for two hours. Though Isaac loved software engineering, something about that moment made him question his professional path. Before long, it led him away from software engineering altogether and onto a completely different trajectory.

Here are the events that "grounded the airplane" for some of the leaders we studied. For Bob Koski, who went on to found Sun Hydraulics, an industrial company in Florida, and Harry Quadracci, who established the commercial printing giant QuadGraphics, it was the profound deterioration of labor relations within the companies where they had previously served as executives. For Chris Mittelstaedt of The FruitGuys, it was an employee giving a middle finger to a customer. For Roger Pinard, a Cognac producer in France, it was his young son's severe breathing trouble caused by pesticides used in their vineyard. Pinard would later become Cognac's first organic producer.

Still, many leaders and aspiring leaders encounter similar events without "refusing to board another flight." Why? One explanation is rooted in the ideals people adopt in their youth. Many develop values in opposition to the world around them, often acting to embody those ideals. But then comes "the age of reason." Professional demands, followed by the responsibilities of family life, create a new normal – leaving less room for those youthful ideals. As the French maxim inspired by the events of 1968 suggests, "A firestarter at 20 becomes a firefighter at 40."

This insight offers a plausible resolution to the enigma. Perhaps, in a minority of individuals, these ideals and values are more deeply ingrained – their nature predisposing them to greater sensitivity to their inner lives.[11] For such individuals, when their "airplane" is grounded, they refuse to wait for another flight. Then, they face the question of what to do next.

Where Do I Go

A popular adage says, "If you don't know where you're going, all roads lead there." Leaders like Naito, Mittelstaedt, and Berrada realized they did not want to continue on their existing paths.

They paused and took the time to discover where they truly wanted to go – crafting an inspiring vision rooted in their values and beliefs. This vision provided these leaders with both direction and a pattern for their thoughts and actions.

As the philosopher Ralph Ellis puts it, "the way we choose to advance from one state of consciousness to another … defines us as who we are."[12]

You might think that the traditional vision of becoming the most profitable company in its industry could also provide clear direction and pattern for its leaders. However, examining the facts closely may challenge this assumption. Most publicly listed companies aim to maximize profits, yet it's nearly impossible to predict how their CEOs will act after a quarterly report. Depending on the results, the same CEO might pursue an acquisition or initiate a spin-off, open a new plant or close an existing one, hire additional employees or announce layoffs. When unexpected external events – such as market fluctuations or global crises – occur, their actions often become utterly unpredictable. In other words, we can't discern who they truly are – what their self is.

This unpredictability, however, does not apply to CEOs guided by an inspiring vision. Recall the actions of Laurent Cavard, CEO of Altho, and Pascal Demurger, CEO of MAIF, mentioned in Chapter 4. During the onset of the COVID-19 lockdowns, Cavard raised transportation suppliers' fees to support struggling partners, while Demurger refunded millions to MAIF's car insurance customers. These decisions may seem irrational when evaluated through the lens of profit maximization but make perfect sense within the framework of their companies' visions. What's more, these decisions – though exceptional – were also predictable because they were aligned with the visions of these CEOs and their companies.

> When leaders lack an inspiring vision, they often default to short-term, reactive, and oscillating decisions. In such cases, their actions resemble the swings of a pendulum – investment or disinvestment, expansion or retrenchment, cost increases or reductions.

Their unspoken mantra becomes, "If you don't know where you're going, any open door will do." Despite all the movement, the organization remains in a state of fundamental stasis.

But let's be clear: Leaders with an inspiring vision are not closed to business opportunities. Their decisions, however, are not driven by profit maximization or conventional cost/benefit analysis. Instead, they ask themselves, "Will this opportunity allow us to stay true to our vision?"

Take the example of Handelsbanken, a leading Swedish bank that we discuss in Chapter 6. Unlike its rivals, Handelsbanken consistently eschewed seemingly lucrative strategies during the real-estate bubble of the 1990s and the rush into Eastern Europe in the early 2000s. While financial markets punished the bank for its restraint, its CEOs stood firm, explaining that taking opportunities where the bank could neither add value nor uphold its vision was not an option. Instead, in the early 2000s, the bank made the surprising decision to expand into the UK retail banking market – one of the most challenging to penetrate – and achieved remarkable success.

Another example is FAVI, a parts supplier for the automotive industry, transformed into a liberated company by Jean-François Zobrist, as mentioned in the Introduction. Its vision was to sustain and develop the company in the rural region where it was founded. When FAVI's major client, Renault, asked it to build a plant close to Renault's new facilities in Romania, Zobrist replied: "No, we won't follow you there because it's not our dream." Renault threatened to cut ties with FAVI if Zobrist persisted, and it carried out its threat. Yet, FAVI stayed true to its vision. Employees of vision-driven companies often say: "This company and its CEO are doing what is right for our vision, not merely chasing the opportunity of the moment." This sentiment contrasts sharply with the disillusionment employees feel when their CEO embarks on yet another pendulum swing, draining morale and motivation.

At this point, consider another variation of the adage that begins with, "If you don't know where you're going." This version comes from Bob Davids, already mentioned in Chapter 4, a transformative leader who headed six companies, including one listed on the NASDAQ: "If you don't know where you're going, you're already there." It's a common phenomenon. Many leaders believe their role is simply to maintain their companies as they are.

Gordon Forward recounted how one president of a steel company told him, "Gordon, I've always admired what you do, but I'd never do it. I feel uncomfortable with radical change. I just want to run the company." Reflecting on this, Forward remarks, "I'm comfortable with change, I love it! I don't want to [just] run the company."

Perhaps you're a leader, weary of the frequent pendulum swings, of merely running your company. Like the protagonist in the airport story, you may be ready to pause, reassess, and search for your path. This might involve replacing the uninspiring goal of pure profit maximization with a balanced approach – integrating profit with people and planet goals. Or, if no meaningful corporate purpose resonates with you, you may even consider a radical shift: pursuing a nonprofit career or launching a passion-driven venture, such as a vineyard or a restaurant. We understand the discomfort of being stuck at a crossroads. We also recognize that the habits driving your past success may push you to act immediately. Yet this impulse – the habit of solving problems head-on – may be the first behavior you need to change. Instead, consider embracing the void that a problem creates.[13]

The void created by a problem is a fertile space in which creativity can flourish.[14] Creativity research refers to this as the *incubation phase*, in which the problem rests while you remain open to new thoughts and experiences. Techniques such as asking, "If money was not an obstacle, how would my life and work change?" can also help uncover the vision of the life you deeply aspire to lead.

This process is less like painting on a blank canvas and more like what Michelangelo described as his creative process: sculpting marble by chipping away patiently to reveal a vision that was always within you. Once it emerges, this vision will feel authentic and give you the assurance that you have deeply aligned with your true self. For some, this process feels natural, and the result comes quickly – a long-awaited promise to live fully. For others, it requires significant time and effort, complicated by personal, family, or professional constraints. Yet, embracing the problem's void – rather than rushing to fill it – demands patience and perseverance.

Eventually, your inspiring vision will emerge, perhaps sooner than you anticipate. As the saying goes, "When the going gets tough, the tough get going."

But let's assume you've uncovered your inspiring vision. The next challenge lies in how to get there.

How Do I Get There

Having successfully led numerous projects in your professional life, your instinct might be to roll up your sleeves, rally your team, step onto the stage, and unveil your grand vision – a dream destination where your reality, the reality of your coworkers, and your company's trajectory will be transformed into a bright future. This instinct is understandable, but you should resist it. And not because people won't believe you.

Yes, some will think you've just returned from yet another off-site with a management guru, and that soon enough you will attend another one and return with a new, shiny idea. Such employees will try to wait out their leaders. But the majority will believe you – and it is precisely there that the greatest danger lies.[15] There are two reasons for it.

First, how can a leader be certain that their vision truly aligns with employees' aspirations for the company's future – and with how they envision their role within it? From our experience, when leaders articulate authentic visions that reflect their own core values and aspirations, such narratives often strike a chord with many employees. However, this is far from guaranteed. More critically, a leader who fails to engage employees in shaping the corporate vision may be perceived as *uncaring*. As French business philosopher Jean-Christian Fauvet aptly observed, "To fully harness the aspirations of the members of the social body, the common good must reflect their private happiness."[16] Even the most well-intentioned speech, if delivered unilaterally from a podium, risks overlooking employees' perspectives on what constitutes their "private happiness" within the organization. Capturing this requires a deliberate process grounded in authentic dialogue – one that often unfolds over months, if not years. For example, at Harley-Davidson under CEO Rich Teerlink's guidance, it took two years of participative effort to develop their "Joint Vision Statement." Or, as Canadian CEO Dominique Tremblay – whom we will meet in Chapter 9 – explains, in order "to build shared meaning ... a compass to refer back to, reminding us where we are headed and offering a common ground for alignment," each individual must first answer the question: "What story do I want to be part of?" The common vision emerges then "from the unique stories and realities of each individual within the group."[17]

Second, such a speech will ignite hope in their hearts – hope they will be eager to see realized. However, most leaders won't be able to meet these expectations, not in two weeks, nor even in two months. Transforming reality – whether it's fixing a broken air-conditioning system, streamlining a process such as reducing the five signatures required to purchase a computer mouse, let alone eliminating profit as the foundation of client relationships – takes time.

Inevitably, when the employees see that nothing has changed in their daily professional lives, they will feel disillusioned – even betrayed. Anger and frustration will mount among the very people whom you set out to inspire. Unfortunately, the "get it done" habit has driven many leaders to fall into this trap.[18] By kicking off a corporate transformation with fanfare, you risk sabotaging the very possibility of building a better future – for yourself, your coworkers, your company, and your business ecosystem.

The "get it done" habit is widespread. Many professionals, perhaps you, have acquired this habit because it works for daily tasks. The inventory of the "to do list" only gets bigger every day if things are not done right away. Yet when the problems are serious, you need to do the opposite – let it rest. We saw in Chapter 1 how this bad habit led leaders in Netflix and Gravity Payments to take ineffective one-off social measures. Rushing it will drive you to use conventional or one-off solutions, which were perhaps the reason why the problem became serious to begin with. Creative solutions need time to emerge. Moreover, "revolutions" require patience. According to French philosopher Emmanuel Levinas (Chapter 3), "rapid and efficient action, where everything is at stake all at once" is violent by nature. He adds:

> We must recall [the] virtues of patience, not to preach resignation in the face of the revolutionary spirit, but to make one feel the essential bond that links true revolution to the spirit of patience. True revolution is born of great compassion.[19]

This spirit of patience was clearly embodied by Zobrist in the transformation he led at FAVI (Chapter 1). As Fauvet reflected on Zobrist, "You were quick to find that balance because you progressed through small steps, minor reforms always guided by events, and by consistently fostering consensus [with employees] directly on the ground."[20]

Now, imagine you acknowledge that transforming the current reality into an envisioned future takes time, and you commit to address the impulses behind the "get it done" habit. Even so, the greater challenge lies in another habit, ingrained in the belief that you can drive such a transformation – or any other company-wide project – entirely on your own. The reality is, you can inspire it, guide it, but you cannot implement it – only your people can.

Your team members are the ones who truly understand what hinders their activities and what changes are needed to improve their work environment. However, they won't share their insights with you – or take meaningful initiative – unless they believe you genuinely care about them. As John Wooden wisely observed, "Care, concern, and sincere consideration for those on your team is a mark of a good leader."[21] This applies not only to people's willingness to hear what *you* know, but even more so to their willingness to tell *you* what *they* know.

In one of our previous research projects, we studied several dozen companies to understand what makes their employees come up with initiatives on how to improve and innovate in their work.[22] Here is one case in point.

Delphi's French plant – then a world-leading American auto parts supplier – specialized in manufacturing diesel fuel injectors. Didier Gaudin, an operator responsible for a boring machine that enlarges preexisting cylindrical surfaces for the injectors, was deeply frustrated. His machine broke down as often as 10 times a day.

The cause was cylinders arriving at his station with a diameter smaller than 0.5 inches. This manufacturing defect meant the cylinders could not be tightly held in his machine, causing them to tear loose during drilling and damage the machine's interior.

For months, engineers and technicians worked tirelessly to eliminate this defect at earlier manufacturing stages. The problem, however, was complex and resistant to their efforts. Gaudin, determined to minimize the frequent disruptions, approached the issue differently – not by attempting to fix the defect itself, but by ensuring it never reached his machine. And then came his "Eureka" moment.

Observing that robotic tongs were used to pick up the cylinders from a box and place them in his machine, Gaudin devised a simple yet ingenious solution: he adjusted the tongs to prevent them from gripping any cylinder with a diameter smaller than 0.5 inches. By adding a small piece of metal that restricted the tongs' range, defective cylinders remained in their boxes, never entering his machine.

When Delphi introduced its new employee involvement program – designed to value and implement employee-driven improvements – Gaudin was the first to share his idea. The initiative proved extraordinary. Given that there were three machines like Gaudin's, calculations revealed that his idea saved the company $3.6 million annually by eliminating stoppages and the costs associated with damaged equipment. It was rightfully recognized as the "Idea of the Month."

Impressed, we asked Gaudin: "When did you find this solution?"

"Four years earlier," he replied.

"But why didn't you share your solution earlier?" we asked, surprised.

"Because the program for employee ideas was only launched last year," replied Gaudin. And sensing our astonishment, he explained, "Before that, we weren't allowed to touch the machines or suggest how to fix them."

In other words, Didier Gaudin had known for four years how to save his company $3.6 million per year, but the company's indifference to its frontline employees' ideas in Gaudin's case alone cost them $14.4 million over four years.

While Gaudin immediately trusted the company's good intentions, convincing most employees that their ideas are truly valued typically requires years of consistent leadership. Such leaders actively seek employee initiatives that touch every corner of the organizational environment and not only their immediate perimeter – from executive parking privileges to outdated reporting systems. Just as Naito encouraged employees to "rethink their activities" to align with the company's *hhc* vision, leaders such as Robert Townsend, Avis Rent A Car CEO in the early 1960s, didn't hesitate to ask employees, "What was the cause of any complaints today?", "What took too long?", or even "What's just plain silly?" to align with Avis' vision: "We are No. 2, but we try harder."[23]

However, simply asking these questions isn't enough. Few employees are likely to respond, as they may not yet believe that their input matters – or that they can trust you. Their hesitation is understandable. For years, they may have seen you and other managers as the sole decision-makers, leaving them to simply execute orders. Ironically, this very dynamic created the reality you now seek to transform.

To earn their trust, you'll need to prove that you've changed the habits and behaviors that once led them to think their ideas weren't valued.

BECOMING A CARING LEADER

The question of whether our beliefs shape our habits or if our habits shape our beliefs is indeed timeless – a classic "chicken-and-egg" dilemma. What we know with certainty is that our core beliefs are formed very early in life, influenced by perinatal and early childhood experiences. Equally well-documented is the idea that these beliefs shape how we experience the world: two individuals might face the same event but take radically different courses of action based on their lived experiences and underlying beliefs.

We will set aside this broader debate. For the sake of clarity, let us examine the transformation of a leader's habits and beliefs as if they were distinct processes. Of course, this simplification does not fully capture the intricate internal dynamics of a person. With that context in mind, we can begin by exploring habits.

Changing Habits

Leaders may have heard that the habit of giving solutions to their subordinates when they bring them a problem is counterproductive. By offering a solution, they are essentially taking the proverbial monkey – the problem – off their employee's shoulder and placing it on their own. The one who provides the solution ultimately owns the problem. Moreover, this habit deprives them of the valuable insights their coworkers could offer, reducing the latter to mere implementers of the leader's ideas rather than contributors of their own.

But changing the habit of offering solutions is far from easy. There's a good chance leaders have risen to their current position *because* of their ability to find effective solutions in the past. On top of that, offering solutions can be personally gratifying. It's a way to demonstrate their expertise and affirm why they hold the top position – and not their associate. Such a habit can even turn into a sort of addiction, providing a short-term reward, but jeopardizing their long-term performance and well-being: it becomes hard to get rid of it. But unless they break this habit, they'll struggle to convince their associates that they genuinely value their ideas and intelligence.

The "taking the monkey" habit is only one of the habits in need of change. Table 5.1 lists other examples of habits practiced by caring leaders.

Table 5.1   Some Habits of Ordinary vs. Caring Leaders

	Ordinary leaders	Caring leaders
Decisions	Jumping to them	Left to those who own the problem
Actions	Getting them done	Trusting coworkers to carry them out
Task priority	Important and urgent	Important and not urgent
Physical presence	Executive office	Up to one hour per day on the frontline
Communication style	Providing answers	Asking questions
Reaction mode	Advising	Suggesting/telling stories
Sharing information	Need-to-know basis	Lavishly
Attention to others' reality	Limited, sporadic	Full and continuous
Crediting	Mostly themselves	Mostly the people
Error management	Finger-pointing or blaming themselves	No blaming, seeking opportunity to learn

This list is not exhaustive; our goal is to highlight the traditional habits that may need to be changed. If you already possess some of the habits common to caring leaders, they are a significant asset in your transformational journey. By all means, continue to leverage them.

That said, some of your existing habits may reflect those of ordinary leaders. As the renowned executive coach and thinker Marshall Goldsmith puts it: "What got you here won't get you there."[24] Transforming these habits will require both time and effort. Even a leader as caring and accomplished as John Wooden continuously worked to improve his own habits and cautioned against neglecting this ongoing process:

If you are a lazy leader; if you are not willing to pay the price to go to clinics, conferences and seminars; if you don't read all that you can; if you don't seek information from all sources; if you don't analyze those under your supervision as well as yourself (and then let yourself be governed by that analysis) – if you are not willing to do all these things … no one else may know … Nevertheless, you … are not doing your job to your fullest ability.[25]

As a leader, you must be a lifelong learner … A leader who is through learning is through. And so is the team such a leader leads.[26]

His parenthetical comment, "let yourself be governed by that analysis," indicates that the goal of learning is very much about changing leader's habits. It isn't easy. We know that it is already hard for bad habits, such as smoking or eating unhealthy snacks. It's even harder to change habits that we believe have proven beneficial to us. Moreover, this work of changing your current habits into new ones has to be carried out while you are running your company.

Because of the need to make all these changes, many executives who aspired to become caring leaders worked with executive coaches. For example, Hubert Joly, while the CEO of Carlson, worked with Goldsmith on the habits of always trying to add value and to be right, needing to win too much, and passing judgment.[27] These kinds of habits are quite hard to change, since they have often been at the heart of a winning strategy. We all have this little voice inside us that tells us not to change anything, even the beliefs that may damage us. This "immunity to change" prevents us from touching some deeply ingrained habits or beliefs – whatever they are.[28] This immunity can be greater for leaders with power. Understandably, they may avoid digging into their own vulnerability not only to protect themselves – like most of us do – but also because they fear the consequences it can have on the organization they are responsible for.

Working with a skilled coach or mentor can lead to significant changes in a leader's habits within just a few months. However, there are times when leaders' challenges run deeper, requiring the support of a psychoanalyst or similar professional. We know of several CEOs and presidents who have taken this approach. Perhaps the most notable example is Douglas McGregor, the MIT professor who, in 1960, conceived *Theory Y*. Earlier, from 1948 to 1954, McGregor served as president of Antioch College in Indiana, where his leadership played a transformative role in the organization. McGregor openly credited psychoanalysis with helping him become an effective leader.

These examples suggest that while some leaders can develop caring habits independently, others may need professional support, with the time required for this transformation ranging from a few months to several years.

So how do leaders know they have successfully developed caring habits? A practical approach is to assess your current habits, set a clear target for change, and measure your progress. For instance, as the head of your organization, you might recognize that you make approximately two decisions per day – about 10 per week and 500 per year. On reflection, you may realize this volume stems from a habit of "taking others' monkeys" or an ingrained tendency to always try to add value. You could decide to replace this with a caring habit, such as saying: "I trust that if you take a bit of time, you will find a solution." Finally, to measure your progress, you might set a target to reduce your decision-making to no more than one decision per week – about 50 per year.

At first, such a goal may feel unachievable, but as you practice and progress, you may even surpass it. Consider Xavier Huillard, CEO of Vinci, a global leader in construction, energy, and highway and airport operations. In 2018, Huillard noted that he had made just four decisions over the entire year – and still considered it too many.[29] He explained to his surprised corporate audience that Vinci's thousands of business units must make their own decisions, informed by those who have local knowledge.

Changing Beliefs

Another way to look at caring leaders is to observe what kinds of beliefs they hold about themselves, their actions, and other people. Our beliefs greatly influence our perception of reality. This is how, for instance, the placebo effect can be explained: if you believe that a pill *can* alleviate your pain (even if it contains no active ingredient), the probability that it *will* alleviate it is estimated between 30% and 50%.

So, if beliefs can somehow create new realities, it's worth contrasting beliefs of "caring leaders" with those of "ordinary leaders." As with habits earlier, Table 5.2 is not a systematic review, but provides a flavor of what we have observed in the caring leaders we have studied.

Table 5.2   Some Beliefs of Ordinary vs. Caring Leaders

	Ordinary leaders	Caring leaders
Mode of action	Strategizing	Power of intention
Relationship between actions and results	Control	Detached commitment
Relationship to the future	Planning	Synchronicity
Main resource for decision making	Rationality	Intuition
Relationship with others (including Nature)	Separateness	Deep connection (you are me; I am you)

Many of the techniques we have just discussed – such as executive coaching – can also work to change the beliefs of leaders in their quest to become caring leaders. In addition to these, new experiences can also change one's beliefs. These experiences can come from outside – as happened with Naito or Forward – and can be unpredictable, "a blessing in disguise" as Chris Mittelstaedt would say. But these experiences can also be deliberately designed.

Harvard researchers Kegan and Lahey describe such a therapeutic practice in their book *Immunity to Change*.[30] They first suggest a specific process to identify the core belief that produces a gap between what a person says they care for and their actual behavior, between the "talk" and the "walk." For example, an executive says she's committed to being a team player, but she realizes that, in practice, she frequently makes unilateral decisions. By digging deeper with their client, Kegan and Lahey help the executive to uncover a belief behind this tendency to make unilateral decisions: "I assume that no one will appreciate me if I am not seen as the source of success." After uncovering this, Kegan and Lahey encourage the executive to design concrete experiences that would help her confirm or rebut the validity of her belief about being seen as the source of success. The executive could, for instance, design an experience where she would simply assist a colleague with his idea without appearing "on the radar" and check whether she is still valued despite him and not her being recognized as the source.[31]

We come back to this type of process in Chapter 8, when we discuss how a company as a whole or even an entire social system – like modern-day capitalism – may be transformed if its actors modify some of their core beliefs. The conclusion to be drawn here is that, whether through changing their habits or their beliefs, caring leaders have not merely transformed themselves. They have also helped to transform their coworkers and companies.

Becoming a Caring Leader Works

Hubert Joly, who transitioned from serving as CEO of Carlson to leading a struggling Best Buy, drove the company to five consecutive years of growth. John Wooden's extraordinary leadership at UCLA, where he guided the team to 10 championships in 12 years, earned him the title of ESPN's Coach of the twentieth century. Douglas McGregor, during his tenure as president of Antioch College, transformed the institution into a hub of innovative practices, fostering collaboration among faculty, staff, and students in decision-making on nearly every aspect of the academic environment. Notably, McGregor's leadership experience at Antioch profoundly influenced development of his groundbreaking *Theory Y* approach to leadership. Finally, Xavier Huillard, as CEO of Vinci, expanded the company from $35.3 billion in revenue in 2010 to $72.7 billion in 2023 – achieving this remarkable growth both organically and through strategic locally initiated acquisitions.

These are just a few examples. But caring leadership isn't only validated by anecdotes; it is backed by science. Evolutionary psychologists Hardy and Van Vugt, in their empirical study aptly titled "Nice guys finish first: The competitive altruism hypothesis," found that caring individuals are preferred as interaction partners and as leaders (as mentioned in Chapter 3, they're also preferred as romantic partners).[32] The researchers conclude that while altruistic, caring behavior may be costly in the short run, it pays off in the long run, "because in a world where people can choose with whom they want to interact, altruists create more opportunities for themselves than do selfish people."[33] In other words, caring leaders attract many more followers, which is what a leader wants.

Indeed, acquiring caring habits and allowing those around you to experience them will make people more willing to do just that: listen to your inspiring vision, hear your appeal for initiatives, contribute their ideas, and implement them. This outcome is not magic; it is backed by science.

Actually, leaders who cultivate caring habits meet relatedness, one of three universal human needs along competence and autonomy. As mentioned in Chapter 3, according to Edward Deci and Richard Ryan, two leading psychologists in intrinsic motivation, to care for and be cared for – what they call relatedness – is one of the three fundamental human needs.[34] When people feel their leader cares for them, they are more likely to care about their company's vision. As wise saying goes, "Nobody cares how much you know until they know how much you care."[35] Moreover, the caring leader's habits also meet people's needs for competence and autonomy – for example, when they search for their own solution and implement it by themselves. This produces employees who are intrinsically motivated to take initiatives that can transform their company.

As the adage says, "People don't resist change. They resist being changed." This is what happened in Eisai. The company didn't push its employees to change, but instead created a caring environment for them. As a result, employees changed and started to care.

CARING EMPLOYEES

Soichi Matsuno heard about *hhc* for the first time just after Naito came up with this vision. Matsuno worked in sales and was perplexed, as his way of thinking differed significantly. "We want[ed] to be evaluated based on the volume of our sales and … profit we [brought] in," he recalls.[36] "I wondered why we need this new slogan … Incorporating *hhc* into my everyday work activities and actually having to be directly involved with patients just didn't make any sense to me at the time." Matsuno saw his colleagues feeling the same way. To him, it all seemed like another case of lofty leadership visions tangling up the daily grind of business operations.

When Matsuno was transferred to the United States and tasked with introducing Aricept – freshly approved by the FDA – to the American market, *hhc* was far from his mind. His immediate priority was recruiting about 100 top American medical representatives and sales managers. Matsuno believed he knew exactly what would motivate them to switch jobs: higher compensation.

Initially, the interviews went as expected, with most candidates focusing on compensation. But as the conversations progressed, candidates began asking questions Matsuno wasn't prepared for: "What exactly does your company do?", "What direction is your company going in the future?", "How will my experience contribute to your company?" Matsuno was caught off guard.

These questions led him to reflect on Eisai's identity and corporate purpose. That's when he recalled the *hhc* vision. From this point onward,

Matsuno began answering directly from the *hhc* playbook. To his surprise, he was met with a "barrage of enthusiasm" from candidates. Responses ranged from "That's exactly what I was looking for!" to "Getting a great salary and being successful has been great ... but I've always felt dissatisfied somehow. What you're describing with *hhc* might be the solution!" Many would later say that they joined Eisai not for the compensation but because of *hhc*.

Matsuno's experience reflects that of many employees who are initially skeptical of such lofty visions. It took him seven years to rethink his activities through the lens of *hhc*. But for the self-selected American sales professionals he hired, the process may have been much shorter – they joined Eisai precisely because of its *hhc* vision. This is remarkable as sales professionals are widely assumed – not just by Matsuno – to be primarily motivated by compensation. Deci and Ryan's findings about intrinsic motivation seem to apply here: relatedness, competence, and autonomy can be powerful motivators, even for sales professionals.

Thousands of Eisai employees, from R&D scientists to managers, have similarly transformed their activities. However, unlike the US sales professionals, most took years rather than months to align their work with *hhc*. One significant obstacle was their limited interaction with patients, which made it challenging to see and empathize with their reality just as Iris Murdoch argued (see Chapter 4). Recognizing this, Eisai introduced a process inspired by Japanese management thinker Ikujiro Nonaka's knowledge creation model.

The first step of the model – socialization – encourages every employee to spend time in nursing homes and interact with elderly patients. The goal is to empathize with patients' concerns, understand their experiences, and reflect on what employees could do to help.

Take the case of Tsutomu Harada, an R&D expert tasked with creating "good medicine": formulations that are not only chemically effective but also easy for patients to take. While developing alternatives to Aricept tablets, Harada realized that many elderly patients struggle to swallow pills. One evening, when his son refused to take a bitter-tasting powdered medicine dissolved in water, it sparked an idea: instead of a liquid solution, a sweet jelly formulation could be ideal for elderly patients. He was further encouraged by the fact that no competitor offered such a solution – presenting a clear opportunity for innovation.

Paradoxically, when Harada proposed the jelly project, Eisai rejected it, arguing that since no competitor offered jelly formulations, there was no market for it. Frustrated, Harada considered leaving the company, thinking, "*hhc* is nothing more than a double standard!"

But in 1998, Harada decided to challenge *hhc,* reframing the project as an *hhc* initiative focused on patient needs. He began working directly with physicians to gather patient feedback on jellied medication. To his surprise, many physicians were indifferent to whether medications are easy for patients to take. Determined, Harada decided to visit nursing homes himself. However, compliance issues prevented him from bringing jelly samples – even nondrug versions – for testing. "If a food supplier brings jelly, it's fine," he noted, "but if a pharmaceutical company does, it's a placebo and raises compliance issues."

Despite these challenges, Harada persisted. He commuted daily to a nursing home, observing patients. During meal preparation, he had a breakthrough idea: to have the nursing home itself prepare jelly desserts. This allowed him to gather data demonstrating that jelly is safe and convenient for elderly patients with Alzheimer's.

In 2009, the jelly formulation of Aricept was launched by Eisai.

Matsuno and Harada are just two of thousands of Eisai employees who – inspired by *hhc* in their own ways – transformed their activities. They succeeded because Eisai's leaders cared for them, creating an environment in which they in turn could care for patients and express that care through their work. While Harada experienced challenges, he reflects positively on his journey:

> I had finally discovered an area where my own personal life meaning, existential significance, and value had overlapped with the core mission of *hhc*.

CARING FOR THE PUBLIC GOOD AND STILL MAKING PROFITS

Harada approached the Aricept jelly project as a business activity aimed at improving patients' lives – not at increasing profits. In fact, producing the honey-lemon-flavored jelly cups costs five times as much as manufacturing tablets. Yet the jellies were sold at the same price as the tablets, meaning Eisai was actually losing money on the jelly version.

Even so, as a business activity, Eisai, like many Japanese companies, continuously sought ways to reduce manufacturing costs through *kaizen* (continuous improvement) – and managed in considerably reducing the cost of jelly. While its production remained more expensive than tablets, this was beside the point for Eisai. The project succeeded because it improved patients' lives, achieving its primary goal.

Eisai has undertaken numerous business initiatives since the early 1990s that focus on benefits to patients rather than on profits. For example, in 1992, the company launched a toll-free phone service to answer questions not only about its products but also about medical science, pharmacology, and everyday health. This hotline is accessible to everyone, including patients, their families, physicians, and pharmacists. Eisai introduced this service because it viewed providing information and alleviating patients' anxieties as a critical benefit aligned with its *hhc* vision.

These practices reflect exactly what Naito meant when he said Eisai's purpose is not profits but the betterment of people and society through business activities. To drive the point home, he doubles down:

We completely deny the concept of corporate social responsibility. There is nothing [in Eisai] called Corporate Social Responsibility ... There is no border between social and business at all, for us. All business is social and all social is business.

Eisai's stand deserves a pause, particularly when considered alongside our earlier description of the "catch me if you can" game that many companies play. Recall that CSR typically encompasses activities such as corporate philanthropy and environmental or social projects – initiatives often designed to enhance corporate or brand reputation. These projects are typically overseen by dedicated CSR departments, and very few are integrated into core business activities, such integration requiring their transformation.

Eisai, however, does not have a CSR department. It *cannot* have one, because its goal is for all of its business activities to contribute directly to society. This is why Naito asks every employee to transform their activities with *hhc* in mind. Yet, Eisai undertook projects that might superficially resemble CSR – or even pure corporate philanthropy. One such initiative aimed to eradicate lymphatic filariasis.

In 2011, Eisai began providing the World Health Organization (WHO) with free medication to combat this mosquito-borne tropical disease. Lymphatic filariasis, also called elephantiasis, affects 120 million people worldwide, with 40 million suffering severe disabilities that cause their lower extremities to swell, resembling an elephant's.[37]

As of May 2022, Eisai manufactured and delivered more than two billion tablets to between 170.8 million and 341.7 million at-risk individuals in 29 countries.[38] This initiative has cost Eisai $13.1 million. Many companies might label such efforts as philanthropy or CSR – but not Eisai. Naito comments:

> We have contracts with WHO to provide 2.2 billion tablets. We explain that this project is not a donation, this is not social responsibility but a business investment. Because once we overcome the difficulty of filariasis, people can get back to productive activities and ... become middle class in the future. So, this is an investment in that.

We asked Naito to whom Eisai explained that initiatives like the lymphatic filariasis project were investments rather than philanthropy or CSR. "To shareholders," he replied, adding that they are "not cash-oriented people at all." Naturally, we asked for proof of such a sweeping statement, and Naito readily provided one.

In 2005, 15 years after the launch of *hhc*, Naito and Eisai's board proposed a significant change at Eisai's annual shareholder meeting: a modification to the company's corporate statutes. Instead of the original profit-focused first paragraph, Naito proposed replacing it with two new ones:

1. The Company's corporate concept is to give first thought to the emotions (joy, anger, sorrow, and pleasure) of patients and their families, and to increase the benefits that health care provides. Under this concept, the Company endeavors to become a human health care (*hhc*) company.
2. The Company's mission is the enhancement of patient satisfaction. The Company believes that revenues and earnings will be generated as a consequence of the fulfillment of the mission. The Company places importance on this positive sequence of the mission and the ensuing results.

Naito recalls being "somewhat thrilled" to propose the modification for a vote by 2,000 shareholders. Questions were asked and answered, but there was little opposition, with the majority approving the change. This marked the first time a publicly traded company removed shareholder value as its primary goal – not only in Japan but perhaps globally.

It is worth examining whether it's true that revenues and profits would follow as a consequence of *hhc*. Indeed, since Naito became CEO in 1989, Eisai's sales have steadily grown, earning the company a spot among the world's top 20 pharmaceutical firms in 2001. Between 2010 and 2023, revenues oscillated between $4.69 and $9.39 billion, driven primarily by organic growth, with profits oscillating between $0.4 billion and $1.3 billion.[39] In 2024, Eisai was named to *Time Magazine's 100 Most Influential Companies*, a global list based on the criteria of impact, innovation, ambition, and success.

WALK WITH A RAISED LANTERN

We began this chapter with a quote from a late Edo-period Confucianist. Haruo Naito often refers to this quote to illustrate his posture since his "heartset" shifted – not only his mindset. The lantern symbolizes this new heartset, focusing on the suffering of patients and their families. Initially, only Naito was aware of it, and darkness surrounded him. So, he raised the lantern, walking the talk, hoping others will notice. More than simply joining his walk, he hoped they would light their own lanterns and forge their own paths.

Of course, corporate reality is far from a bucolic walk in the woods. Naito was keenly aware of Eisai's realities. As we've seen, for employees to feel intrinsically motivated to embrace *hhc*, their needs for care, growth, and autonomy had to be met.

This is why Naito had championed numerous programs to enable employee involvement in *hhc*. In 1992, 103 managers from across Eisai departments participated in on-site sessions at nursing homes to understand patients' emotional experiences. Afterward, these managers would contribute to the change in mindset and practice of Eisai employees in their own workplaces. In 1996, Eisai committed to producing only "barrier-free" drugs – medications designed to be easy to take for all types of patients. This decision required extensive collaboration among R&D, sales, and manufacturing teams, necessitating the transformation of many company processes.

Yet, a 1997 survey revealed that while employees recognized there was energetic action within Eisai, they still perceived the company as somewhat bureaucratic. The jelly formulation case highlighted how a patient-centered project could be obstructed by traditional R&D processes.

That year, Eisai founded the Knowledge Creation Department to provide tools for transforming business processes in line with *hhc*. The department also significantly scaled up employee engagement with patients' emotional experiences. By the mid-2000s, nearly 3,000 employees had spent time in nursing homes. They also participated in simulations of elderly patients' experiences, wearing weights, leg-movement-restricting knee pads, and blurred eyeglasses. During our visit to Eisai, we experienced these simulations ourselves and must admit they profoundly changed our understanding of the elderly experience. Caring for someone often starts with understanding their unique point of view.[40]

By the mid-2010s, Eisai was initiating between 500 and 600 *hhc* projects annually, each involving 10 to 20 participants. When asked how many employees were engaged in these projects, Dr. Takayama, head of the Knowledge Creation Department, replied resoundingly: "All!" This was true for roughly 3,000 employees in Japan, with additional participation from Eisai's divisions in the United States, Europe, and Asia.

Yet, despite these significant achievements, Eisai believed further transformation is necessary. In 2009, rather than indulging in self-congratulation, Eisai decided to transform its business model. The new model shifted away from a hierarchical, siloed structure focused on the economies of scale and outsourcing to one emphasizing autonomy, demand-driven innovation, talent, and value-chain orientation.

When we asked Naito how far Eisai was from realizing its *hhc* ideal, he paused and said: "Not over 50 percent yet." He then added:

We are at the very base of the mountain. We can see the peak, but in the clouds, not clearly. We think we have found out how to climb up [the peak] but maybe [the real path] is different. So, the plan is evolving.

It seems that Naito has succeeded in guiding his coworkers to the base of the mountain, illuminating the pitch-black path with his raised lantern. Now, they can begin the journey to the top and determine the best route to ascend.

While the leader's inner transformation is essential, it is only the beginning. Without a corresponding organizational transformation, even the most authentic leader's actions and inspiring vision can be swiftly undermined by entrenched systems of control and inertia. Just as a new mindset and heartset must take root within the leader, so too a new managerial framework must be co-constructed to reflect and reinforce them. In the next chapter, we turn to the story of Handelsbanken, where the leader's convictions were brought to life through a radical organizational transformation.

CHAPTER SIX

BUILDING THE CARING COMPANY

The preoccupation with rules is the death of action ... It is futile to keep ready-made rules which will never be exactly adjusted to the conditions in which we will have to apply them. There is no action that does not presuppose a preparation [of] certain means [and] that does not aim at certain ends. But when it is carried out, it is no longer a slave to these means or ends ... It is a new creation that overcomes all models and becomes its own model.
— Louis Lavelle[1]

A CEO's personal transformation is essential to leading a corporate shift toward a caring company. However, it is not sufficient on its own. Just being an authentic and visionary leader can even be counterproductive. Indeed, if the vision that the CEO proposes is not aligned with the existing – typically traditional – managerial framework, not only will it fail to drive transformation within the company, but it will also lead employees to conclude that the CEO doesn't "walk the talk."

In this chapter, we explore the principles and key elements of building a caring company, drawing on lessons from a financial institution and from several other businesses.

Imagine the following bank:

- Has no sales targets
- Doesn't practice cross-selling, such as offering to sell you insurance after you take out a mortgage
- Has no budgeting process
- Calls it a promotion when a head office executive becomes a local branch manager
- Obliges corporate IT and marketing to pitch their new projects to the assembly of branch managers to get their approval

You may think that such a bank does not exist. But it does. Its name is Handelsbanken. If it is unfamiliar to you, you might think that it is one of those new internet-based banks that recently rattled the brick-and-mortar banking incumbents. But Handelsbanken is as brick-and-mortar as it gets. A top Swedish retail bank, it has more than 200 branches in the country, more than 140 in the United Kingdom, and a few dozen branches in Norway and the Netherlands. Nor is this bank new. Established in 1871, it was a mainstream conservative bank until something happened to it in 1970.

THE POWER SHIFT

In 1970, Jan Wallander, a former researcher with a PhD in economics, took office as CEO. The bank was in serious financial trouble, and a currency scandal had recently tarnished its reputation. In the previous decade, Wallander had successfully overhauled a regional bank in northern Sweden, and so Handelsbanken's board hoped he could do it again.

Wallander quickly analyzed Handelsbanken's difficulties and attributed their root causes to the bank's managerial framework. He compared it to "a heavy freight train roaring through the night," noting that "the driving force behind this train was the activities of the head office departments." Convinced that the train was heading in the wrong direction, Wallander quite logically decided to stop it.

Here are the brakes that he pulled:
- Central departments were no longer allowed to send memos to the branches, except for those related to day-to-day operations or government regulations (previously, an average of 12 memos *per day* were sent to each branch from Marketing, Sales, Finance, Purchasing, Human Resources, Legal, Business Development, Planning & Strategy, etc.).
- All budgeting and reporting activities were eliminated.
- Head office committees and workgroups dedicated to business development were asked to summarize on a single sheet of paper the results they had achieved to date and were then disbanded (110 committees and workgroups were affected).
- Work on a new information-technology system was stopped (involving several hundred people).
- The long-term planning and strategy department's activities were terminated.
- The marketing department's work on preparing a new campaign was stopped (at that time, Handelsbanken was one of the country's largest advertisers; the department of 40 people would be soon reduced to one person).

You might think that a bank cannot abolish its corporate support departments without disappearing the next day. But Wallander had different ideas. He wasn't convinced that he'd stopped the train yet, so he took another measure that resonated far beyond the head office.

A centenary is a date celebrated with great pride in every company. Understandably so: research shows that only 1% of companies survive 40 years.[2] Moreover, the bank's longest-serving employees still remembered the pomp with which the bank celebrated its 75th anniversary. Preparations were in full swing, employees placing bets on the amount of the centenary bonus. Imagine their shock when Wallander cancelled all the celebrations. With a tremendous squeal, the train came to a halt, giving Wallander, as he puts it, the space and time to set up the bank's new managerial framework.

It took him five years to build it. And Wallander's framework is still in place today.

The Branch Is King

Many organizations declare that their customer is a king, and few question management thinker Peter Drucker's motto that "Marketing is everything," meaning that caring for their customers should be the ultimate company's concern. But one CEO, Vineet Nayar, disagreed, titling his 2010 book *Employees First, Customers Second*. Based on his own experience of transformation at HCL Technologies, an IT services company with more than 200,000 employees, he argued that employees would only take care of the customers to the extent that employees themselves were taken care of by their managers. Wallander thought along similar lines: if the branch had the maximum power for making decisions and provided employees with an environment that met their human needs, these employees would be motivated to care for customers.

"Decentralization," as Wallander called it, started by dividing the bank into eight regions for Sweden. More than 50 years later, whilst regions have been replaced by smaller geographical entities – reflecting Handelsbanken's desire to be ever-closer to the customer – they still operate in this decentralized and autonomous manner. The same is true for other countries in which Handelsbanken operates. A "county" – or "district" as they're known in the UK – encompasses all the branches within a specific territory, with each branch typically consisting of 10 people and serving as the entity that makes practically all business decisions.

The mantra "Branch is king" has a very practical meaning when it comes to decision-making. In financial services, making loans is at the core of the relationship between customers and their bank. It is often when you need a loan that you start to compare your bank with others. If your bank is not responsive enough or not cost-effective, it can drive you to a competitor. At Handelsbanken, 75% of loan decisions are made promptly at the branch level, with no intervention from the central or regional level. In the same spirit, each branch decides which clients they wish to acquire or to get rid of, which products to propose, and how to market the bank locally.

The freedom and responsibility of the branch and its advisors are made possible thanks to an accounting system that allows branch managers to know exactly how their local entity is doing. In fact, unlike in most other banks, in Handelsbanken each branch has a separate P&L. And the bank's corporate financial department is not devoted to controlling branches, but to serving them.

As Michael Green, the current CEO of Handelsbanken, points out:

> Our bank has two main categories of job descriptions: You either do business or you support those who do business. If you look at it from this angle, it is relatively simple to identify what needs to be done.[3]

Concretely, the branch managers decide what corporate services and products to accept and at what cost. Moreover, a special committee, mostly composed of branch managers, reviews projects and the costs of head office services for the coming year and decides whether to use them, to develop those services themselves, or buy them from outside suppliers.

Yet, you may doubt whether local branches can really handle the corporate finance function. After all, someone must do corporate budgeting, right? Wallander disagreed:

> In a market economy, budgeting produces either a result that is trivial and uninteresting and does not need the whole apparatus for its production, or one that is dangerous because it can be an obstacle to making changes. In other words, I believe that this type of activity should be given up.[4]

Since Wallander estimated that "in modern companies the management devotes 20% to 30% of its time to the budget and planning process," he decided to give up on budgeting, the finances being tracked by a trust-based "beyond budgeting" approach.[5] Instead of tracking dozens of metrics, it looks at just one: relative profitability.

Fine for budgeting. But you may still question whether a bank can boost revenues and profits without a corporate business development or strategy department. Unsurprisingly, Handelsbanken proves that it can. The bank has no growth targets and takes the time it needs for robust organic growth. But here too Handelsbanken does it differently from most companies. Instead of aiming at profit maximization, the bank aims at a profitability *higher than the market average*. Despite its apparent simplicity, this is a highly sophisticated approach.

Overall, it requires Handelsbanken to achieve a higher return on equity (ROE) than its average competitors. Within the bank, a similar principle also applies: each county or district must, in turn, aim for a higher ROE than the other regions. Finally, within each county or district, each branch must aim for a cost/income ratio (costs divided by net banking income) better than the average of the other branches in its region. While this may seem a simple metric, this relative profitability principle completely overturned the way the bank was organized from the moment Wallander introduced it.

Overnight, budgeting and internal reporting became useless. Indeed, as Wallander liked to explain, at any given moment and everywhere, the profitability of half the regions was below average. They did everything in their power to be in the top half. At the same time, those who were already there had to redouble their efforts, feeling the breath of others close behind. As a result, the bank's overall profitability was rising steadily without it being a goal, but a mere constraint. Corporate headquarters had not given the branches self-direction in order to maximize profits, but to pursue the bank's real goal: to provide outstanding care for all the bank's customers.

You may wonder what remains of the head office if all the activities of these branches are run without it. In fact, Wallander has not replaced Handelsbanken's heavy managerial framework with a vacuum. What he did was replace formal, mechanistic links with human relationships. Thus, every month he would have a meeting with all the regional managers, sometimes in Stockholm and sometimes in one of the regions. The meeting would begin in the afternoon and continue through dinner. No decisions were taken at them and no minutes were kept. The purpose of these meetings was different: to have conversations, informing each other and agreeing on common principles with which to resolve the bank's problems.

Every month, following these conversations, Wallander would write a letter to *all* employees in which he gave his personal viewpoint on current issues and provided information on various developments taking place within the bank. All the regional managers did the same, writing to the branches in their area. Wallander called this way of coordinating the bank's activities "steering through conversations," a practice that the CEOs who succeeded him have continued.

Full Availability of Advisors for Caring

Revamping the bank's managerial framework freed advisors to be fully available to care for the customers. In Wallander's words, "[Handelsbanken's way] means getting close to the customer and being able to suit local conditions and match decisions and action to the customers' needs and wishes."[6]

The fact that branch employees have no sales target is key to their availability to customers. Said otherwise, conversations between advisors and clients aren't contaminated by the (not so) hidden agenda of pursuing a sale. As a result, in contrast with other banks, where customers shifted – or should we say, "were shifted" – online, Handelsbanken's customers appreciated one-on-one in-person meetings. As Michael Green, CEO of Handelsbanken, says:

> At Handelsbanken, customers don't talk to machines. On the contrary, our personal meetings are our principal competitive advantage. Our customers shouldn't have to deal with chatbots or endless touch-tone choices.[7]

And the bank's annual report stresses "value in each customer meeting":

> For us, long-term relationships start with meetings between people. Customer meetings are therefore at the core of everything Handelsbanken does … In every meeting, we listen and learn, to ensure that our offering matches our customer's needs. This leads to better decisions and more satisfied customers.[8]

Many banks would agree that it is impossible to truly care for their customers if they never meet with them face to face. However, unlike Handelsbanken, they have never revamped their managerial framework to free their branch advisors to meet every customer who seeks it, understand their needs, and promptly make decisions to take care of them. The results of this full availability had already showed up in 1973 and continues to show up to the present day.

Lasting Results

For 50 consecutive years Handelsbanken has demonstrated a better return on equity than all of its competitors (see Figure 6.1).

Figure 6.1   Return on equity of Handelsbanken compared with peer banks (1973–2023).
Source: [9]/Handelsbanken.

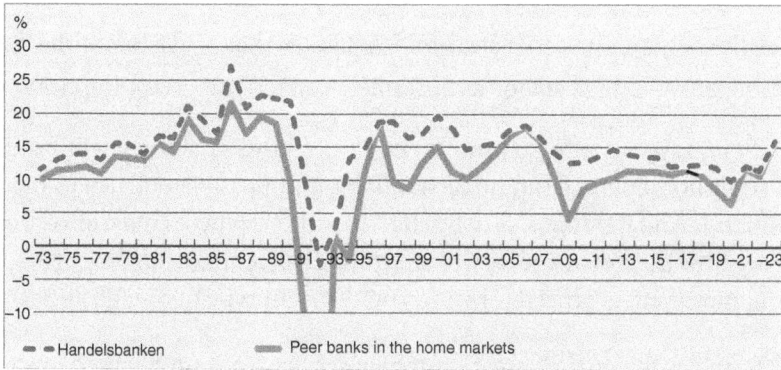

Moreover, Handelsbanken:

- Was named Sweden's "Bank of the Year 2023"[9]
- Was ranked top for customer satisfaction in the UK for 16 consecutive years (2009–2024)[10]
- Was ranked Europe's safest bank in 2024[11]
- Has the world's highest combined credit rating from S&P and Moody's and Fitch[12]

And here is one final metric of Handelsbanken's performance. A study by Björn Wilke and researchers, based on data collected by London Business School, compared the stock prices of tens of thousands of listed companies since 1900. Handelsbanken's shares multiplied in value by 1.9 million times – more than any other company in the world over this period.[13]

As impressive as Handelsbanken's record is, you may wonder whether the revamp of Handelsbanken's managerial framework is relevant to other companies. To answer this question, we need to understand Wallander's thinking about the right type of organization.

ON THE RIGHT TYPE OF ORGANIZATION

Since the beginning, it was clear for Wallander that his vision of the bank offering unwavering care for its customers carried important implications:

> If employees are to commit themselves to this goal, they will need to see it not only as clear, understandable and possible but also as meaningful. And if this goal is to be effective, the employees must also clearly see how their own efforts will affect the chances of attaining it. This last requirement is crucial for choosing the right type of organization.[14]

To make the goal of great customer service both understandable and meaningful for employees, Wallander employed a healthcare metaphor:

People's financial situation is [nearly as] important as their health. A good banker should have the same sort of qualities as a good general practitioner or district nurse.[15]

Doing your best for the financial health of your customer – and certainly, like doctors, doing no harm – is a vision that every employee could grasp and find significant. However, Wallander didn't assume that simply because employees understood and valued their company's vision that they would naturally act to fulfill it. On the contrary, he believed that the type of organization he inherited at Handelsbanken hindered such efforts and needed fundamental revamping.

But what, then, is the right type of organization?

To delve into this, Wallander posed an even deeper question: What drives employees to feel motivated, "to think it is a pleasure to go to work every morning"?[16] Wallander's experience as a researcher made him well-versed in many psychological theories of motivation, with a particular focus on the humanistic approaches developed by Abraham Maslow and Douglas McGregor. From Maslow's hierarchy of human needs, he concluded that while employees require a "fair and reasonable" salary and good physical working conditions, their "higher" needs centered on "harmonious relations to others in the group and ... a desire for self-fulfillment."[17]

From McGregor – whose *Theory Y* was itself inspired by Maslow's work – Wallander deduced that the satisfaction of employees' "higher" needs, such as belonging and self-fulfillment, depends profoundly on management's attitude toward them. If management perceives employees as lazy, unambitious, irresponsible, and reliant on direction – the essence of *Theory X* – it will create a managerial framework rooted in subordination and control. Conversely, if management sees employees as individuals who enjoy work, seek responsibility, possess creativity, and are capable of self-control and self-direction when committed to meaningful goals – *Theory Y* – it will establish a managerial framework based on trust and autonomy.[18]

Wallander shared *Theory Y*, and he believed that many managers shared it too. However, he cautioned against overlooking its implications:

If ... one takes this attitude seriously, it will have very great and often overlooked consequences for a company's organization. If one looks upon staff in this way, the logical conclusion is that they should be given the opportunities to utilize the abilities one has such faith in. Otherwise, the picture that one has painted does not agree with the reality the staff will meet – which is a conflict that frustrates and disappoints them. If one is really serious, the result will be a decentralization of decision-making in the company. Managers throughout the whole hierarchy must relinquish power to their subordinates, and this should take place from top to toe.[19]

The "top" refers to the head office, and since Wallander was committed to his attitude toward employees, he led a comprehensive revamp of Handelsbanken's managerial framework, which was restricting the autonomy of branches and limiting the decision-making power of their advisors.

He was a firm believer in the latter, saying that "people in small towns all over the Scandinavian countryside can produce better solutions that those at the head office in Stockholm."[20]

To Revamp or Not to Revamp

In light of Wallander's arguments for revamping the traditional managerial framework, you may wonder why Haruo Naito, described in Chapter 5, did not do the same at Eisai. In other words, you may wonder whether Handelsbanken's lessons about revamping the managerial framework are universal or particular to its case. It's an important question.

From our observation of several dozen caring companies, we have found that Wallander's fundamental logic applies to all of them: a *Theory Y* attitude toward employees implies building a managerial framework that allows them to fully contribute to the company's vision. However, to what extent and at what pace you build it depends on the unique context of the company.

We all know of organizational revamps that went awry. And they almost all went awry because the CEO and others did not consider their company's unique cultural, human, and historical context. Handelsbanken's context of an underperforming, century-old, large Swedish bank is not the same as Eisai's context of a family-led, successfully growing global Japanese pharmaceutical. It's not only about a company's geography, or its industry, or whether it's young or old. In fact, every company's context is unique and complex, composed of a myriad of elements. Ignoring that context and trying to apply one-size-fits-all recipes is what gets so many revamp efforts into trouble.

To stick to the intention while respecting the constraints requires a high level of transformational leadership. On the one hand, disregarding the context may create resistance, slow down and even halt any transformation intent. On the other hand, if revamping is too slow, the employees will get frustrated and conclude that "it is all for show."

In the context of Handelsbanken, Wallander opted for a radical and rapid revamp. He weighed the danger of employee frustration to be greater than the potential resistance from the head office. And when he anticipated important resistance, for example, to shutting down the executive board, he didn't abolish it but simply stopped it from meeting.

At the other end of the continuum, in the context of Eisai, Naito chose a gradual and slow revamp because he weighed the inertia and resistance from the head office and managers as a bigger obstacle than potential employee frustration. To help alleviate the latter, he continued to affirm the importance of employee efforts to realize Eisai's *hhc* vision, while he trained Eisai's managers and provided them with the knowledge and skills to facilitate employee initiatives. The later replacement of profit maximization with the *hhc* vision in the corporate statutes was also a potent signal for employees. In addition, it provided leverage to revamp head office controls and metrics of employee performance.

In sum – unless a company is already a *Theory Y* organization – the answer to the question "to revamp or not to revamp" while building a caring company is definitely to revamp. But to what extent and at what pace both depend on the company's unique context.

Why Revamp Administrative Bodies?

Even before the work of motivational psychologists, a pioneering thinker who delved into human needs and the type of organizations required to address them was the prominent twentieth-century French philosopher Simone Weil.

In 1942, fleeing persecution from the Vichy French government, Weil departed for New York. Five months later, she joined Général de Gaulle's staff in London, tasked with conducting studies to establish a philosophical foundation for reforming the principles of the French state. Her focus turned to the French constitution's *Declaration of the Rights of Man and of the Citizen*, which she deemed a failure. In its place, she began working on the *Declaration of the Duties Toward the Human Being*.

It was during this project, completed in May 1943, that Weil introduced the concept of the State's duties as rooted in the fundamental needs of human beings. Remarkably, her ideas bear a striking resemblance to Maslow's theory, published just two months later. Weil categorized these needs into physical needs and needs of the soul. She argued that deprivation of the former leads to the death of the body, while deprivation of the latter reduces life to a vegetative existence.

Altogether, Weil identified 15 "needs of the soul," including freedom, responsibility (initiative), honor (respect), and risk-taking. She also linked these needs to the obligations of the State. For instance, when addressing freedom, she wrote:

> An essential nourishment for the human soul is freedom. Freedom, in the practical sense of the word, consists of a real possibility of choice. Wherever there is communal life, it is inevitable that rules, imposed by common interest, will limit choice.
> … Rules must be reasonable enough and simple enough that anyone who wishes to and possesses an average capacity for attention can understand them … They must not emanate from an authority that is seen as foreign or hostile but rather be loved as belonging to those they govern. They must be sufficiently stable, sufficiently few, and sufficiently general so that the mind can internalize them once and for all, rather than clashing against them every time a decision must be made.[21]

Our regular "clashing" against a complex government's rule or form proves that Simone Weil's warnings about bureaucracy potentially depriving citizens of their freedom remain strikingly relevant. However, Weil didn't confine her ideas to the obligations of the State alone.

Having spent eight months as an assembly-line worker in a factory, she also reflected on the responsibilities of business administrative bodies in addressing human needs. Regarding the human need for responsibility and initiative, she observed that the unemployed are the most deprived of its fulfillment, followed closely by assembly-line workers:

> The satisfaction of this need requires that a man often has to make decisions, whether about major or minor issues, affecting his own interests, but also that he must continuously make efforts, and, finally, that he can intellectually own the entirety of the work of the community to which he belongs, including in areas where he has never had any decision to make or opinion to give. For this, he must be encouraged to take an interest in them, made aware of their value, utility, and, if applicable, their significance, and clearly shown the part he plays in them.[22]

And Weil follows with this implication:

> Any [administrative body] that does not provide these satisfactions to its members is flawed and must be revamped.

So, just like her contemporary Maslow, Simone Weil believed in the universal higher needs that must be satisfied for individuals to thrive. And much like McGregor would do later, she criticized traditional administrative bodies – business included – for failing to meet these needs. However, unlike McGregor, who trusted that his ideas were self-evident enough to inspire organizations to revamp voluntarily, Weil was more skeptical. She argued that we must revamp administrative bodies – whether in government or business – from the top down to ensure they meet human needs.

Revamping Managerial Framework Allows Building a Caring Company

About 30 years later, Wallander echoed Simone Weil's belief and revamped his managerial framework from the top down. The decentralized organization he established – designed to meet employees' human needs and encourage them to make customer decisions aligned with the company's vision – remains intact, upheld by all subsequent CEOs except one.

In the mid-2010s, a newly appointed CEO wanted to introduce an additional hierarchical layer within the head office. This move was swiftly met with resistance, resulting in his prompt dismissal. The bank's chairman, Pär Boman, explained the decision with the following statement:

> All managers at Handelsbanken – and especially the branch managers – must possess a very high degree of autonomy. As a consequence, being the CEO of this bank requires a special kind of leadership, which is much more complex than that found in traditional management.[23]

But that was an exception. Asked about Handelsbanken philosophy, the new CEO Anders Bouvin said:

> The absolute basic foundation of Handelsbanken is the humanistic outlook that we have … that the vast majority of people want to do a good job if the head office allows them. If you don't believe that, if you think people are, generally speaking, risks and, given the opportunity, they will do bad things then, of course, you should control them. [But] in Handelsbanken we say that we work with human nature, not against human nature.[24]

The bank continues to uphold its "right type of organization," a managerial framework that fulfills employees' needs and fosters the "pleasure of going to work every morning." However, while this motivation drives any type of action, Handelsbanken also took additional steps to allow employees to take actions contributing to the bank's vision of unconditional customer care.

When Wallander inherited Handelsbanken, he not only faced a bloated and centralized head office but also a transaction-based operational model. Granting decision-making power to the branches was a critical step, but it wasn't enough. If financial "doctors and nurses" merely handled transactions with branch customers instead of unconditionally caring for their financial health, the bank's vision could never be fully realized.

As discussed in Chapter 4, for a company to care unconditionally for the members of its business ecosystem, it must transform its activities from being based on self-interested transactions to being based on authentic relationships. And as discussed in Chapters 3 and 5, motivated employees are willing to play an active role in this vital transformation, since people are quite naturally interested in caring for others.

WHEN EMPLOYEES TRANSFORM CORE PROCESSES

You won't be surprised – or perhaps you will – to learn that Handelsbanken, unlike its competitors, does not spend a single Swedish krona on mass-market advertising or marketing. There is marketing "intended to raise awareness of the kind of bank we are," according to Simon Alderson, Head of Corporate and Customer.[25] But these actions are always connected with branches' local marketing, such as sponsoring a local event or meeting in which customers are involved. For a long time, the bank tried to avoid the media too. It has changed its approach somewhat, but – as usual – with a difference. The case of one subsidiary is worth telling.

In 2000, Handelsbanken decided to enter the UK market – not exactly a banking desert. Any other bank would have a rollout plan based on a prepared standard process of opening new branches. Not Handelsbanken. For three years, it didn't open any branches at all – and not due to a lack of ambition, but because it insisted on the right conditions for expansion.

Its small UK corporate team had identified a town in northern England that they thought would be a propitious location for its first branch. Then they set out to find the ideal local candidate to become the branch manager. It was out of the question to bring in someone with no relationship to the local business community. And to make things harder, following Handelsbanken's approach when hiring from outside, competence and network accounted only for 5% of the process. The other 95% was dedicated to understanding the values of the person and whether they fit with Handelsbanken's philosophy.

After some time, a rare ideal candidate was identified and offered a position, but he did not want to leave his bank to join Handelsbanken. So, the head of the Northern Region, Anders Bouvin – who would later become CEO of the UK business and, eventually, of the entire bank – decided to wait. No other candidate was found until, one day, Bouvin learned that the initial candidate's situation had changed and that he was now ready to commit to Handelsbanken.

Since the incoming branch manager shared Handelsbanken's philosophy, the bank entrusted him to invent how to open, and later to run, his branch. Specifically, he had to decide on its location and opening date, hire his staff, and choose the products it would offer.

You might think that after that experience, the UK corporate office would use this successful opening experience to standardize its branch-opening process. It didn't. Certainly, it became better in identifying candidates in other English towns, but every time it entrusted new branch managers with the same authority to decide on all the aspects of opening and running their branches. Focusing on transactions would lend itself to the standardization of a branch's business processes, but focusing on relationships did not. Relationships are not the same in an industrial town, in a port, or in a rural town. The physical branch location, its opening hours, and products offered are different in order to take care of the financial needs and cultural habits in each of these areas. Put differently, it was not the role of the head office but of the branch managers and their colleagues to define the activities that would best provide unconditional care for their customers.

By 2007, Handelsbanken had opened its 50th branch and, by 2011, its 100th branch in the United Kingdom. No one seemed to notice. However, it's hard to stay overlooked with a network of 100 branches. Around this time, the BBC's business department asked to meet Bouvin, the country's CEO for Handelsbanken.

How to Communicate in the United Kingdom

At any other company, such a request would be a no-brainer. But not at Handelsbanken. As we mentioned earlier, the bank only did local marketing. So, "to speak or not to speak" was a very serious question for Bouvin. If he did speak to the BBC, he ran the risk that the story would – as they often do – depict him as a brilliant executive, which would not reflect either his real contribution or the decisive role of his local colleagues. Conversely, if Bouvin refused the interview, the story would come out anyway, without him providing his perspective.

So, just as Bouvin didn't think that he knew better how to open and run the UK branches, he didn't think he knew better how to communicate with the UK business media. And just as he believed in local branch managers' competence, he believed that a local media expert might have a better idea on how to handle the challenge. Therefore, he set out to find an expert in the landscape of the UK financial sector. But, since competence weighs only 5% in a recruitment decision, he also needed someone who shared Handelsbanken's philosophy. Needless to say, it was not easy to find this rare pearl in a hurry, but Bouvin gave it a try.

Shortly afterwards, Richard Winder, then a communications consultant in the banking sector, replied to an advertisement. After a few meetings with the chief operating officer, with a branch manager, and with Bouvin, he got the job. And he got it not because he mastered the typical communication strategy of a traditional English bank. On the contrary, instead of a press release written at the head office, Winder proposed to communicate locally – in alignment with Handelsbanken's way. Specifically, he suggested to pitch the story's topic to all the branches and those who were interested could tell how they got established in their city and the kind of relationships they've built up with local customers. At the same time, they could emphasize that they are part of a retail banking network of a hundred or so branches. Put differently, Winder was able to conceive on the fly a communication process aligned with Handelsbanken's philosophy – which got him the job.

Despite his success in being recruited, Winder still retained some old reflexes. "On the morning of my first day," he recounts, "I waited for a boss to come in and say: 'We need to set the objectives and start implementing your plan. We're going to measure your performance in such and such a way, and we're going to guide you in your work.'" But the person who greeted him said something quite different:

> You're part of us now. We're confident that you share the same values with us, but have specific expertise. You're in charge. It's up to you to decide what your reasonable ambitions should be, your approach to both big challenges and everyday problems. And then act.

In this story, Richard Winder – a future colleague – was taken care of not only as a professional, but as a person. This is how, as a person and as a professional, he was able to design and implement a crucial communications process based on relationships instead of on transactions.

A Better Place to Take Care of Customers

Transforming the communication process is of course important, but – as we have discussed – Handelsbanken's core activities happen in the branches. In particular, it's the branch managers who have the autonomy to transform the way their branch is run. It sounds like a dream job.

Peter Sturesson has such a dream job, running a branch in the key Stockholm business quarter. But reading about his work habits, you might doubt that it is a dream.

Sturesson's cell phone is available on Handelsbanken's website, like the cell phone numbers of all bank advisors, and his phone is never far away. "On Saturday mornings," he explains, "my smartphone is on my bedside table. If there's water damage or a paving stone has been thrown at the branch, I prefer to know right away, because the branch is a bit like my home." The same goes for a customer who finds it urgent to contact him on a Saturday. Unlike other banks, which put many constraints on transactions with their customers, Handelsbanken puts few on the relationships with theirs.

This attitude and behavior are very well in line with Wallander's view:

Behind our concept of the great value of a network of local branches lies not only the importance of close contact with the market but also faith in the importance of trusting and personal meetings between people.[26]

In fact, removing such constraints and designing the best possible approach to face-to-face interactions is what Sturesson focused on.

It didn't seem so when we visited Sturesson's branch. To begin with, we couldn't find it. All we found was a discreet doorbell labeled "Handelsbanken" on the front door of an apartment building, alongside half a dozen other buttons. Not really the greatest way to welcome customers, we thought.

After we rang, someone waited for us at the top of the stairs and led us into a waiting lounge furnished with designer sofas in an open space. A bit further away, we could see all the advisors' desks.

Sturesson fetched us and led us to a spacious meeting room. We were curious about the unusual physical setup of this branch; Sturesson explained that it was a consensus decision of the branch's employees. Always looking to improve the physical set up for face-to-face interactions, the staff concluded that their former street-level location was not well-suited to this need. Customers coming to the branch needed privacy and personalized treatment. Moving into an entire floor of an upscale building offered a much more appropriate setup for their customers' needs. And in this new location, employees welcomed customers and treated them all the same way, whether they are the owners of a large business in the neighborhood or a private individual with a simple account in the branch. Interestingly, already in 2003, Wallander mused that it was time for bank branches to quit the street level and move upstairs. At the time, however, he was concerned with vaults, which were often underground – and too heavy to install in the upper stories of an ordinary building. With the advent of digital banking and fewer cash usage – today, cash is rarely used in Sweden – Wallander's concern became less relevant. Sturesson and his colleagues understood that customers don't want to wait on physical lines or digital lines. They want to be cared for.

This belief is still at the heart of the bank's way of doing business. Its 2023 Annual Report stresses that "Handelsbanken creates value through unique customer meetings," and the company's website states: "We believe that close relationships form the foundations for long-term value creation and financial well-being."[27]

The initiatives of Winder or Sturesson and his branch colleagues to reinvent their branch's business processes for better caring are just a few examples. Many more employees of the bank have taken such initiatives. But Handelsbanken is not the only company we studied that allowed its employees to transform their business activities from transaction-based to relationship-based.

Gas-station-building World Record

Reitan Retail is a 45,000-people company operating more than 3,600 retail outlets, such as supermarkets, convenience stores, gas stations, and newsstands in seven countries.[28]

Reitan has undergone its own organizational revamping. Currently, despite being Norway's fourth-largest corporation, its Oslo head office employs fewer than 20 people, most of them in finance. Yet, corporate finance at Reitan is far from what one might expect in a company of this size.

Partly inspired by Handelsbanken and Jan Wallander, whom the CFO Kristin Genton and the CEO Odd Reitan visited at his retirement, Reitan Retail operates without conventional control structures such as budgeting, instead relying on trust-based beyond budgeting approach. However, Genton has taken things even further by revamping the functioning of the finance department itself. To explain her approach, Genton used a compelling analogy:

> How many times have you read the user manual for your smartphone apps? Never. It's not that these apps aren't complex, but they hide that complexity to offer an intuitive and simple interface. That's what many people fail to do when providing financial information.

Guided by this approach, Genton regularly challenged her team with a simple yet powerful question: "Why is this report presented to this recipient, and why in this format?" She encouraged her colleagues to think like designers and to model their financial reports after Apple's "insane" user interfaces.[29] This mindset led to the creation of user-friendly financial tools and resources, particularly tailored to support – and coach – the franchisees of the retail group.

Reitan's trust-based managerial framework extends far beyond its finance department. It empowers employees to provide unconditional care for customers. For instance, if a store runs out of stock for an item, employees are permitted to purchase the item from a competitor's store, using cash directly from the register, to satisfy the customer's need.

More importantly, this managerial framework gives employees the freedom and autonomy to reinvent activities in ways that better care for members of the company's business ecosystem.

You might think that the manager in charge of building gas stations for Reitan's Uno-X gas distribution division would have very little opportunity to care about customers or the local community. Yet, Roger Hertzenberg – the man in charge of this process – thought otherwise.

In 2006, Reitan Retail acquired a network of gas stations formed through the merger of Norsk Hydro and Texaco, seeing it as a natural fit with the 7-Eleven chain it already owned in Norway. The merged company, branded Uno-X, focused on automatic gas stations – a concept that also aligned perfectly with Reitan's food stores, as their parking lots were often conveniently nearby. Uno-X tasked Hertzenberg with overseeing their construction.

If you were to visit Japan and pass by an urban construction site, you might be struck by the large electronic billboards displaying the decibel level. Their purpose is to show the neighborhood that the construction company cares about noise levels and is taking every measure to reduce them. Similarly, when a truck exits a site, you might notice an employee ensuring that it only pulls out when the street is empty and does not disrupt the neighborhood's traffic.

Hertzenberg felt that his own company was falling short in reducing the nuisances caused by its construction sites. The timeline for building a new Uno-X automated gas station – from the first shovel strike to the arrival of the first customer at the pump – averaged around 30 days. While this was an impressive timeline compared to competitors, which typically took about 90 days, it didn't sit well with Hertzenberg.

Soon, he discovered that a competitor held the world record for building a station, at just 10 days. If Uno-X truly cared for the local community, Hertzenberg realized, it needed to aim even higher. He set an ambitious goal: to build a gas station in just five days. To achieve this, Hertzenberg engaged his Finnish supplier. They assembled a "dream team" and approached the task with the precision and preparation of elite athletes. They redesigned the entire construction process from the ground up. Work began at dawn on a Monday, and by 4 p.m. on Friday, the first customer arrived to fill up at the pump. Result: A new world record – 4 days, 14 hours, and 21 minutes.

You may wonder whether the team relied on unsustainable measures to achieve their record-breaking performance. Such doubts are understandable – after all, you might have heard stories of Stakhanov, the Soviet coal miner celebrated for setting records in personal productivity. His achievements were famously exploited by Communist propaganda to justify unrealistic productivity demands on other miners. However, the same propaganda conveniently ignored the dozens of support workers who contributed to Stakhanov's record-breaking performance, both upstream and downstream of his efforts. In contrast, Hertzenberg readily acknowledges that special conditions – and additional costs – were necessary for his team to break the record.

But it's important to remember that Hertzenberg's goal wasn't to slash costs, but to reduce the duration of construction projects – and, by extension, the nuisances they cause to the surrounding neighborhood. In that respect, he fully realized his company's caring vision.

When CEO Odd Reitan saw a video documenting this achievement, his reaction was characteristically insightful. He first congratulated Hertzenberg but then inquired whether the operation had been more expensive than their previous approach. After all, Reitan Retail operates

Scandinavia's largest discount-store chain. Hertzenberg's response was as pragmatic as it was reassuring: "Yes, exactly. Seven days would be perfect for an optimal cost."

The CEO was reassured by the confirmation that his concern was valid. However, he did not order Hertzenberg to revert to building gas stations in seven days rather than five. Once again, the company's purpose was the caring relationships with the local community and not cost savings. Costs were only a constraint.

The Uno-X executives seem supportive of its employees' initiatives to transform their activities. But do these executives transform their own corporate activities to care better about the company's business ecosystem?

Buying Better Fuel

In 2015, Uno-X CEO Vegar Kulset needed a new leader of the gasoline Supply and Distribution business in Norway. The idea was to turn this department into a real company, a 100% subsidiary, with its own profit and loss ledger. He had recruited Alex Guindos, who had 15 years of experience in this industry's large corporations.

When Guindos arrived in his new role, Kulset welcomed him unshaven and in a T-shirt. After an hour and a half talking about cycling, children, or hobbies, Kulset got up and left. Standing in that meeting room, Guindos thought to himself: "This is my first day here, and this is my integration? So, what do I do now?" He was shocked.

Yet Guindos did remember that he left his major oil company because of the lack of confidence he felt. It dawned on him that Kulset trusted him completely from day one and gave him the keys to the store.

Thanks to this unconditional trust, Guindos soon embarked on radically transforming one core process of the company: the purchasing of fuel. At this time, Uno-X was buying biofuels made from by-products of palm-oil production. Guindos saw this as a threat to the image of Uno-X and the Reitan Retail. He believed that it should be changed, but first – and quite naturally – he wanted to involve his company's top executives in this decision. He therefore called a meeting. But the conversation didn't go exactly as Guindos had planned.

"I've invited you here to talk about an important decision we need to make concerning our supplies," began Guindos.

"Alex, for us it's a 'Yes,'" interrupted other executives.

"But wait, I haven't told you what it's about yet …" he said, surprised.

"Okay, but the decision is made: it's a 'Yes'. Now, tell us about the problem," they continued, ending the meeting almost as soon as it has begun.

Uno-X was sourcing its biofuels from a major energy group that had repeatedly demonstrated its lack of interest in alternative energy. Its fuel was made from the waste products of the palm oil industry. However, at that time, Reitan Retail had already announced it would no longer accept any new food products containing palm oil in its REMA 1000 supermarket chain. Admittedly, these were food products, not fuel, and admittedly, it was palm oil, not its derivatives, that were a concern and have never been criticized by the environmentalist NGOs. Yet Guindos saw a difficulty. He believed that Uno-X had to go beyond the expectations of NGOs and be totally consistent with the REMA 1000 brand's zero tolerance toward the palm-oil industry. The search for a biofuel supplier with no links to palm oil led him to neighboring Sweden, where he approached the leading local supplier. Their fuel was 3% to 5% more expensive than that of Uno-X's historical supplier, which meant a reduction in margin of around a third. For a low-cost distributor like Uno-X, this is huge. Despite this, Guindos broke with the old supplier and signed a long-term partnership with the Swedish one.

This story may seem secondary, but it is rich in lessons. First, many companies sincerely wish to preserve the environment of the communities in which they operate, but the implementation of concrete solutions all too often comes up against economic considerations. In other words, transactions win over relationships with the local community. Caring companies, on the contrary, do not subordinate the pursuit of such relationships to the maximization of profit, nor do they pursue both simultaneously.

Second, this history of supplier change shows us that unconditional care for your local community is impossible without revamping the company's managerial framework, just like in Handelsbanken. Hence the importance of trust. Guindos put it plainly: "In my previous company, I could never in my life have done such a thing!" Here's what Jens Haugland, CFO of Uno-X Norway, had to say:

> The concept of real trust is our backbone. If you have this trust, it's extremely strong. With it, you no longer have to defend your arguments, you no longer have to convince others. You sit down at the table and the others trust you. If you have such and such a point of view, you have good reason to have it. They trust you, and then you go for it.[30]

This is exactly how Uno-X's trust- and autonomy-based managerial framework allowed Guindos to transform, one-by-one, the company's processes for unconditional care.

BRINGING THE BOARD ONBOARD

Earlier in this chapter, we mentioned Handelsbanken's chairman dismissing the CEO who intended to introduce an additional layer of management at the head office. But imagine if the board of directors had chosen not to act. Over time, the transformation initiated by Wallander and continued by subsequent CEOs and employees would have been undermined and reversed.

This isn't a mere presumption. We have observed this pattern in several companies: When boards fail to respond to the initial actions of a new CEO that run counter to a company's nascent culture of caring, the collapse of the transformation often follows swiftly. The most committed individuals, those who had strongly contributed to the company's vision, are typically the first to become frustrated – and to leave. Others "quit quietly," remaining in their roles but ceasing to take initiatives or contributing beyond the minimum. The consequences are predictable: a vicious cycle of deteriorating results, which leads to greater reliance on controls and subordination, further disempowering employees, eroding performance, and eventually resulting in the dismissal of the CEO. Wallander warned of such dangers, which could unravel transformations, saying, "It's so easy to centralize."[31]

You may wonder why a CEO – stepping into a bank that had outperformed its competitors for 45 years and had proven that trust and autonomy work – would choose to reverse such a successful approach? And why would other CEOs we observed make similar contradictory decisions and reverse successful transformations? The explanation of this paradox is two-fold.

First, as we discussed in Chapter 5, these incoming CEOs have not developed the habits and beliefs necessary to uphold the values of trust and autonomy. While serving as executives beneath a transformational CEO, they might seem comfortable with these values. However, once they assume the role of guardians of the company's values, it becomes clear that their own mindset and behaviors are misaligned with them. It is as if they had endorsed the values because they had to, not because they chose to.

The second explanation lies in the nature of the dominant economic system in which caring companies operate. The pressure to focus on profit maximization – or, at best, to balance profits with social and environmental goals – is pervasive in society: in newspapers, in academia, in business circles. Therefore, it is very difficult for any executive to prioritize unconditional care for their business ecosystem members.

Also in Chapter 5, we showed what CEOs can do to self-transform. But they can take further steps to alleviate the pressures of the current economic system focused on profits by working with their board. The aim of such work consists in bringing their boards of directors to share and protect the company's philosophy. At Handelsbanken, this support existed from Wallander's era onward. In contrast, at Eisai, it took 15 years before CEO Haruo Naito felt confident that the board and the stakeholders' General Assembly would formally approve unconditional care as the company's singular purpose.

These examples demonstrate that it is possible to secure board-level support for unconditional care – even in publicly traded companies. The preliminary step is for the CEO to recognize the importance – and feasibility – of transforming the CEO-board relationship. In our observations, neglecting this relationship, or assuming it cannot be changed, often results in boards dismissing visionary CEOs, thus undoing years of transformation.

Once the CEO has this intent, the concrete manner of transforming her relationship with the board will depend on each company's context. Eisai and Handelsbanken are examples of publicly traded caring companies, but the same is true for private companies. For them, we have distinguished two typical governance contexts.

The first is that of the newly formed board of a privately held company. When founding CEOs seek to establish a board, their key selection criterion is ensuring that the directors share the company's vision. While this is often easier to achieve with independent directors, we also observe success with investors. As Timo Joensuu, the founder of Docrates Clinic in Finland (whom we'll meet in Chapter 8), put it, "I have realized that there are quite a few wealthy people who seek to do good, to invest in meaningful businesses."[32]

The second context is that of an existing board of a privately held company. Transformational CEOs, typically salaried and holding only a minor equity stake, often inherit traditional boards that are primarily focused on financial performance. Already busy with their transformational efforts, some CEOs try to "fly under the board radar" and avoid scrutiny of their transformational initiatives – until the extent of the transformation is discovered, as seen with Robert Owen. Others take a "show-of-strength" approach, which works as long as financial performance remains exceptional.

However, CEOs building truly caring companies adopt a different approach: they engage their boards in regular meetings about the company's vision outside of the required meetings of the board. This dialogue creates opportunities to align board members with the company's purpose of unconditional care and with its values.

As Thibaut Hyvernat, CEO of Sterimed, whom we'll meet in the next chapter, states regarding relations with a majority private equity owner:

> It's not easy, but you need to carefully choose your fund to retain control and ensure a personal and cultural alignment with its team regarding your project. In the same way that transparency with employees is essential, transparency with shareholders is equally important – and it must be absolute ... Next, an agreement must be reached on value distribution: how much for the fund and how much for the employees.[33]

These approaches are not universal formulas but types of dialogue with board members. It respects their priorities and goals within a framework of trustful conversations. Such a dialogue primarily concerns existing boards but is also relevant to newly formed ones.

Through such conversations, the CEO has an opportunity to clarify that the company is not merely an investment vehicle: its purpose is to care for the members of its business ecosystem and it operates on the belief that fulfilling this purpose will – as a consequence – lead to financial performance that exceeds industry averages.

There is another major benefit of supportive boards beyond merely opposing the actions of a new CEO that run counter to a company's ongoing transformation. In fact, boards are responsible for appointing a new CEO in the first place. If they engage in trustful conversations with the transformational CEO, there is a greater chance they will appoint a successor who upholds the company's ongoing transformation rather than undermining it. They may even be disinclined to sell the company – should a sale be necessary – to buyers who might dismantle the transformation's accomplishments.

Indeed, based on our observations of approximately one hundred transformed companies, the two primary reasons for a transformation's reversal are a new CEO or a new owner (or both) taking actions that contradict the ongoing transformation.

LESSONS IN BUILDING THE CARING COMPANY

Handelsbanken's journey toward building a caring company is unique, as are the paths of several dozen other firms we studied. Yet, despite the diversity stemming from the distinct contexts of each company, we have observed several points of commonality in their approaches.

First, companies like Handelsbanken, Eisai, The FruitGuys, Châteauform, Reitan, and others adhered to the three key factors – WHY, WHAT, and WHO – that ensure the effectiveness of their social innovations. Specifically, it was always the leader at the helm who drove the transformation (the WHO), through a bundle of mutually reinforcing measures (the WHAT), all aimed at creating a company that cares (the WHY).

Furthermore, these companies' paths to becoming caring ones tended to unfold through a series of common stages:

1. **The CEO's self-transformation.** These leaders seek to live a unified life rather than separating personal and professional selves. In other words, they decide to behave in their organizations just as they do with their friends or family – willing to serve everyone they interact with unconditionally. To achieve this, many leaders work on themselves – often with the help of coaches – to change ingrained professional habits and beliefs.

   This self-transformation demonstrates to their coworkers that their leader genuinely cares about them, creating the conditions for employees to, in turn, care deeply about the company and the members of its ecosystem.

2. **Co-constructing an inspiring vision.** Together with their coworkers, leaders invest the time to co-construct an inspiring vision for their organization. This vision centers on unconditional care for the company's customers, suppliers, and the local community and is shared by a growing proportion of employees.

3. **Revamping the managerial framework.** Leaders overhaul management systems, organizational structure, and cultural habits to foster employee initiative and responsibility. The scope and pace of this overhaul varies depending on the organizational context and are often carried out in parallel with Stage 2.

   The revamped managerial framework provides the corporate and managerial support needed for employees to actively engage and contribute to the next stage.

4. **Transforming core business activities.** Leaders at all levels encourage employees to shift their business activities from profit-centered transactions to care-focused relationships. They discourage the simultaneous pursuit of caring and profit-maximization, emphasizing that

in such cases, care would inevitably become subordinated to profits and ultimately, sacrificed.

Over time – sometimes quickly – higher profits begin to emerge as a natural byproduct of this care-focused approach, without the company directly pursuing them.

5. **Taking care of the owners.** Depending on the governance type, CEOs engage in specific dialogue with their boards to describe the unconditional care philosophy, to build the support from those who share it, and to propose a fair disinvestment path to others who don't share it.

So far, we have described the core philosophy and practices of caring companies, as well as the transformation process of a traditional business into a caring one. You may wonder, however, whether a caring company can create impact beyond its immediate business ecosystem members. The examples in Chapter 7 will show you that some caring companies can impact all of society for the better.

PART III

SHIFTING BUSINESS AND THE ECONOMY

CHAPTER SEVEN

CARING ABOUT
THE ENTIRE
SOCIETY

We should be an asset to society, not a burden on society.
– Anders Bouvin, CEO of Handelsbanken[1]

When a company's managerial framework reflects its leader's vision and values – as at Handelsbanken – its impact can extend far beyond customers, suppliers, and the local community. It can become an actor, benefiting society as a whole. In this chapter, we explore how caring companies contribute at scale – starting with a figure who redefined what it means to give back: Steve Jobs.

In a 1985 interview, Steve Jobs reflected on his net worth of $450 million and the challenges of reinvesting it "back into humanity" with this comment: "I'm convinced that to give away a dollar effectively is harder than to make a dollar."[2] At just 29 years old, he had already amassed a decade – or, as he dubbed it, "ten lifetimes" – of hard entrepreneurial experience, transforming Apple Computer, Inc. from a garage start-up into a leading US producer of personal computers. This journey, coupled with his relentless commitment to self-education and self-transformation, shaped a set of core values that he claimed guided all his actions.

One of these values was perfectionism – an uncompromising resolve to not merely accomplish tasks, but to execute them flawlessly. This value was evident when Jobs recognized that the Apple III wasn't a computer everyone would love to use and likewise doubted the potential of another product, Lisa, to express this value. In response, he initiated and led a separate project within the company to create the "perfect" computer: the Macintosh. This same perfectionism extended to his considerations about reinvesting in humanity – except this time, he struggled to envision how it could be done flawlessly.

Jobs didn't trust the government to discover such a path, nor was he convinced that philanthropy offered the solution. Drawing on his entrepreneurial experience, he believed that identifying the perfect way to reinvest in humanity required opportunities to fail – but to fail, one had to measure whether a particular approach worked:

> The problem with most philanthropy – there's no measurement system. You give somebody some money to do something and most of the time you can really never measure whether you failed or succeeded ... So if you can't succeed or fail, it's really hard to get better.[3]

Moreover, unlike many of his Silicon Valley peers, who – as highlighted in Chapter 3 – have donated significant sums to "effective altruism" causes, Steve Jobs did not subscribe to such an approach:

> Most of the time, the people who come to you with [philanthropic] ideas don't provide the best ideas. You [must] go seek the best ideas out [yourself], and that takes a lot of time.[4]

Indeed, Jobs never found a perfect philanthropic approach. After pursuing some philanthropic projects privately, he established a public foundation – only to dissolve it several years later. Beyond his dissatisfaction with philanthropy, there was another reason Jobs turned away from it. He strongly believed that he contributed far more effectively to humanity through his business endeavors than through philanthropy. Specifically, he held that making computers accessible and easy-to-use amplified human potential, fostered creativity, and connected people.

Today, there is ongoing debate about Jobs' management style, particularly his demanding approach, which at times veered into disrespect for colleagues. However, there is broad consensus that he succeeded in realizing his vision of contributing to humanity through Apple computers. While it may not qualify as a "caring company" by our definition, Apple has nonetheless made a meaningful contribution to human lives through its computers.[5] This observation raises an important question for caring companies.

Apple has undeniably benefited its users on an enormous scale, not only throughout the United States but around the globe. As Jobs remarked, Apple employees aim "to make a little dent in the universe."[6] The question is whether caring companies can achieve such large-scale impact – reaching entire countries and beyond. If they can, they could show businesses a pivotal way to shift the economy for good.

To begin exploring this question, let's leave the western shores of America for the northwestern shores of Europe.

CARING AT THE LOCAL SCALE

If you are unfamiliar with Trondheim, a picturesque Norwegian city nestled in one of the countless fjords at Iceland's latitude, you can be forgiven – unless, of course, you are Norwegian. Every schoolchild in Norway is taught that this northernmost kingdom of Europe traces its origins to a hill overlooking the Trondheim Fjord. It was there – in a small castle on a large farm known as Lade Gaard (the Lade Manor) – that the Earls of Lade made their residence between the ninth and eleventh centuries, during which time it also served as a royal seat.

For those planning a visit to this magnificently restored historical site, two surprises are in store. First, certain rooms, particularly the council room, are off-limits. Second, the manor's current owner is not a descendant of the Norwegian royal family. Instead, it belongs to Odd Reitan – a man whose domain of influence lies not within European royalty but in the realm of discount retail. Indeed, Reitan Retail – which we've already mentioned in Chapter 6 – started making its fortune in 1979 in Norway, later expanding to other Nordic countries. Its flagship division is the discount store chain REMA 1000, REMA standing for *Reitan Mat* (Reitan Food), and 1000 referring to the 1,000 products said to be available in each store (which has now grown to 2,500 items). Reitan acquired Lade Manor in 1992. It's a bit like visiting Monticello only to discover that Thomas Jefferson's mansion belongs now to Dollar General.

It all began with a modest shop in Trondheim, opened by Odd Reitan's father. When we met Odd at Lade Manor – which now serves as the headquarters of his holding company – he was quick to share the story of his family's humble origins. He also summarized for us Reitan's philosophy: "Trust and real decentralized system, real … meaning … [people] are allowed to make decisions."[7] However, this part of the conversation came later in our journey. Fittingly, our first encounter with this unique company also took place in a manor, although this time in Oslo.

At the Oslo Manor

While coordinating our visit to Reitan Retail, the CFO Kristin Genton (mentioned in Chapter 6), extended an unexpected invitation: "Upon your arrival, would you like a working dinner at Reitan's head office with the head of values training?" Naturally, we accepted, intrigued by the unusual offer. It marked the first time our field study began over dinner in the evening rather than in the CEO's office in the morning. Little did we know, the surprises were just beginning.

As our taxi made its way from Oslo Airport to Reitan Retail's head office, we passed the royal park and palace at the city's heart before turning onto a small street that led us to a gated entrance. Behind it, a stately manor and its pastoral, country-style cottages stood in stark contrast to the urban architecture we had glimpsed in Oslo's city center.

We were greeted by two women: Kristin Genton and Berit Hvalryg.

"I am principal of the School of Values," Hvalryg introduced herself.[8]

This unusual title piqued our interest.

"Our definition of value-based leadership is to build strong and great people that act based on trust," explained Hvalryg.

"[And] you have to train to give trust and also train to receive trust," added Genton.

"We want to be recognized as the most value-driven company," said Hvalryg, concluding the initial introductions.

We understood right away that their convictions were firm, and they were willing to make it clear from the start. But we sought concrete proofs.

Four years earlier, when Odd Reitan hired Berit Hvalryg, he described the "why" behind her mission rather simply: "When I go to bed each night … as an owner, I need to know that everyone understands what our vision is about." It was up to her to determine how to achieve this ambitious goal. With a corporation spanning 3,800 franchised stores and 38,000 employees at the time, we assumed Hvalryg had a large team to support her efforts. She did not.

As we learned during our visit, the Oslo head office employed at that moment just 18 people essentially dedicated to two functions: finance, led by Genton, and values training led by Hvalryg. Most of the head office employees were in finance; for her cultural mission, Hvalryg had the assistance of just one subordinate and one key external associate: the CEO himself. Indeed, Odd Reitan used to take an active role in values training, personally conducting 20–30 three-hour sessions annually to share stories that bring the company's philosophy to life. However, as the organization expanded, he recognized he couldn't manage this alone, which led to hiring Hvalryg. Together, she and her colleague now oversee onboarding values training for employees across the company. That doesn't mean Odd Reitan has stopped being involved in culture training. When we met him later, he said he spent *half of his time* on it, and that every meeting, every activity, is an opportunity for him to reinforce culture. And that's how Hvalryg explained the strategic importance of her own role:

> You can copy everything ... all the concepts ... all the products, but you can't copy the people. [That's why we build] the strong culture and people that can take decisions when they meet customer or when they're out in ... the stores.

If you are familiar with Norway, a country renowned for its trust-based and civil culture, you might assume that training Norwegian recruits in values would be a simple task. After all, Norway consistently ranks as one of the world's most ethical societies. For instance, in a 2019 study by American and Swiss economists, 17,000 wallets were intentionally dropped across 355 cities in 40 countries. Some contained cash, others were empty, but all carried contact information. Norway, along with the Netherlands and Switzerland, recorded the highest wallet-return, including all the cash when it was there – a testament to the nation's ingrained values. (Notably, in the United States, which ranked average overall, all wallets – and cash – dropped in Chicago and Salt Lake City were returned.)[9]

However, not all participants in Hvalryg's values training reflected Norwegian society as a whole.

The Pøbel Program

One day, Hvalryg was tasked with leading a values training session for a group of troubled youngsters. Unlike regular Reitan recruits, these participants came to the session through Pøbel, an NGO program with which Reitan had partnered. As the session began, Hvalryg followed her usual approach but quickly realized that her audience was not connecting with the content at all. Seeking to buy time and build a rapport, she fetched a ball and shifted the conversation to sports. It was then that she had a breakthrough.

"If you could make one tattoo on yourself saying who you are, what would it be?" she asked.

"Dignity," "pride," "honesty," came the answers.

"[Well, you] are speaking of your values," she replied, finally bridging the gap and connecting them to the concept of "values."

However, a significant challenge remained. Unlike her typical participants, these youngsters named values they had rarely, if ever, experienced in their own lives. That was because they were not merely troubled youngsters – they were petty criminals.

In fact, the name Pøbel translates to "hooligan," and the NGO's mission is to help rehabilitate convicted young people and reintegrate them into society. Among them was Travis Lyons, one of the participants in Hvalryg's session.

"Bad Boy" Turned Manager

After high school, the trajectory of Travis Lyons' life took a less-than-promising turn. With grades too low for university admission, he had to retake classes to improve his academic record. In Norway, where all young people receive an allowance to support their studies and living expenses, Travis chose instead to spend it on a trip to the United States – visiting Houston, San Francisco, and Las Vegas.

In the gambling capital, Travis and his friends gambled and – as you might expect – lost everything. Cutting their trip short, they returned to Oslo still recovering from a month of overindulgence, which included heavy drinking. But the excess didn't end there. Upon landing at 11 p.m., the group decided to hit the town for yet more alcohol.

That night, Travis ended up picking a fight – with the police. The encounter resulted in a hefty fine of more than $3,000, which the authorities gave him a month to begin paying off. In the meantime, with his bank account completely empty, his phone service was cut off. Adding to his troubles, his parents refused to bail him out, believing that a 21-year-old should take responsibility for his actions. That said, they also knew their son lived in a country he himself referred to as "socialist."

Indeed, in Norway, there's a government service called NAV – short for *Nye Arbeids- og Velferdsetaten*, or New Employment and Social Welfare Administration – that helps individuals like Travis. A woman at NAV greeted Travis with kindness, coaching and assisting him in dealing with the police, his phone company, and his job search. One day, she called to ask if he would join the Pøbel program. Thinking it was a way to help him learn job-seeking skills, Travis agreed. It turned out to be much more.

The first three weeks of the program were intense, resembling a crash course in job search training. Participants focused on essential skills such as punctuality, effective communication, and interview preparation. One day, they were asked to stand in front of the group and share three personal dreams.

When it was Travis's turn, he confidently listed his: starting his own business, becoming a coach to help others, and returning to school. As fate would have it, the founder of the Pøbel project was in the room that day.[10] He had connections at REMA 1000 and asked Travis if he might be interested in working there, with the potential to one day have his own franchised store.

For Travis, the opportunity indeed felt like a dream – almost too good to be true. But he chose to believe in it and accepted the offer.

Rising in REMA 1000

Travis's first day at work left an indelible mark.

The regional director greeted him warmly: "Hello Travis. Nice to meet you."

"I was met with so much heart and love … the big boss meeting me on the first day and giving me this chance meant a lot," Travis later reflected on that moment.

"If owning your store is your dream, we can make it happen," the regional director told him.

Starting as an entry-level employee, Travis quickly gained experience in his first store. He then joined Mehmet Teknoz, a franchisee at another location, as a mentee. Over the next three years, Teknoz mentored him in every aspect of running the business, from operations to leadership. One evening, Teknoz handed Travis the keys of the store and left for the night.

By 11 p.m., Travis was alone, locking up for the first time. That's when it dawned on him just how far he had come – from a petty criminal to someone entrusted with the full responsibility of a store.

The year we met Travis he was 27 years old and had applied for REMA 1000's Talent Program, a preparatory school for future franchisees. The program costs around $20,000, an amount the franchisees can gradually repay once their store turns profitable. His application was accepted and with it, his circumstances would soon change, allowing him to achieve two of his three dreams – returning to school and starting his own business.

Meanwhile, Travis was already actively pursuing his third dream: helping others. Every day, he saw how his care for customers and colleagues created a ripple effect. "If you greet a person really nicely and you give them a lot of love … it will spread out," he explained. "Because you will give joy to someone and he will give it to the next person that comes by."

For some customers, Travis had already become a source of comfort and connection. One woman, battling cancer, visited the store daily – not always to shop, but simply to share her thoughts and feelings about her treatment.

Local Impact
Doesn't Mean Low Impact

You might think that the Pøbel program is merely a drop in the ocean when it comes to addressing petty crime. Reitan Retail's CFO Genton, however, does not share this perspective. Regarding the impact of the Pøbel program itself, she notes the following:

> We did some research … about how much each of these troubled youngsters cost society. [These figures] show how important it is for the community and for the society … [Reitan Retail's efforts to] try to redirect them.

But there is more.

Odd Reitan, like many, was deeply affected by the September 11, 2001, attacks – an event that struck him symbolically, as it coincides with his birthday. In the aftermath, he sought to understand how such a mass murder could occur. His conclusion was stark:

> Many people view their lives as hopeless and unchangeable. In the absence of any meaningful action, they turn to supernatural forces, and once they are radicalized, they are ready to sacrifice their lives.

Reitan Retail partnered with Pøbel to take a step toward changing this. Since its start, the program has hired more than 100 youngsters into REMA 1000 stores. Still, you might question whether integrating a small number of petty criminals could truly make a difference for Norway. The following facts may help dispel that doubt.

Coincidentally, Odd Reitan's reflections on the root causes of terrorism align closely with the ideas of Hernando de Soto, a prominent Peruvian economist. De Soto has written extensively about combating terrorism through economic inclusion and has noted that "in an atmosphere of deprivation and frustration, those who make false promises easily attract adherents."[11] Starting in the late 1980s, de Soto's recommendations, implemented in his home country of Peru, enabled countless individuals and small businesses to emerge from economic illegality and poverty.

One of the consequences of these reforms was the dismantling of the *Communist Party of Peru - Shining Path*, a Maoist insurgent group – recognized as terrorists by the United States, Canada, the European Union, and many other countries – that bloodied Peru in the 1980s. Involved in attacks and drug trafficking, the Shining Path primarily recruited its members from among poor, landless peasants. However, as these individuals regained independent means of subsistence, the Shining Path faced increasing difficulties in attracting new recruits. In fact, this terrorist organization explicitly blamed Hernando de Soto for its challenges, even going so far as to carry out an attack on his research institute.

Although de Soto's recommendations have primarily been adopted in developing countries, one can see parallels with the recruitment strategies of terrorist groups in Europe. For instance, following the 2015 massacres in France and Belgium, researchers identified a common profile of the terrorists: a petty criminal who becomes radicalized while in prison.[12]

In the United States, a similar experience highlights the link between poverty and public safety, and how education can strengthen the latter.

In 2011, we visited The New American Academy (TNAA), an innovative school housed in the Public School 770 building in Brooklyn, New York. Its founder, Shimon Waronker – a graduate of the Harvard Graduate School of Education and a former US Army intelligence captain – believed that traditional school structures were not adequately preparing students for success, both academically and socially. Unlike most alternative schools, TNAA was developed in partnership with teachers' unions, ensuring collaboration rather than conflict.

As we approached the school during our visit, all we saw were dilapidated houses and massive bars covering the lower-floor windows – a clear sign of the prevailing insecurity and criminality in this neighborhood.

Inside the building, the ground floor was occupied by a traditional New York City Department of Education elementary school. We did not see a single smiling student – only vacant and disengaged expressions. The second floor, however, was a stark contrast. This was the space where Waronker implemented his bold vision for elementary education. His primary goal was to instill in students "the knowledge of power and the skills of freedom."[13] He believed:

> That this type of approach empowers our young leaders to use their heads, hearts, and hands in ways that are beneficial not only to them personally, but to society at large.[14]

The groundbreaking approach relies on teams of four teachers, a mastery-based career ladder, and six-year looping cycles, with each classroom serving as a center of educational innovation. Furthermore, teachers continually evaluate and refine their practice through daily 90-minute meetings and weekly reflection sessions. The results were steadily showing up. For example, in 2022, The New American Academy Charter School (TNAACS) – TNAA's successor since 2013 – outperformed 72% of comparable schools in English language arts, 60% in science, and 46% in mathematics.[15] But the school is not solely focused on academic achievements. As the school's principal, Lisa Parquette Silva, noted, "We didn't want to be a test prep factory because if you have children that do well academically but aren't good citizens, you have half a child."[16]

It's the school's ability to shape good citizens that drew some very unexpected visitors: several heads of the US security establishment. They clearly recognized that if the country wants to address public safety – including the threat of terrorism – it must start by targeting the root causes, where petty crime takes hold. In other words, it's the "other half of the child" – the one which, if neglected by the education system, could potentially turn into a criminal or, worse, a terrorist.

Thus, by helping individuals to change their lives and move away from delinquency, Reitan Retail, perhaps, disrupts the fertile ground on which terrorist organizations recruit – a vital public safety issue in Norway.

Doing It Through Business Activities

In the case of the Pøbel program, measuring its impact on public spending is possible, but doing that for safety is much harder. The reason is simple: the terrible negative impact of terrorism is visible in the acts that occur, but the positive impact of preventing such acts – or ensuring they never happen – remains intangible. That said, Reitan Retail contributes to its host community in many other meaningful ways.

We've already mentioned in Chapter 6 the efforts of its gas division, Uno-X, to reduce noise pollution during the construction of its gas stations and its use of biofuels free from palm derivatives. But Uno-X is also looking ahead, investing in hydrogen stations despite the limited number of hydrogen-powered vehicles currently in Norway. The company understands that this is a "chicken-and-egg" problem: gasoline distributors hesitate to invest in hydrogen infrastructure due to low demand, while consumers avoid purchasing hydrogen vehicles because of a lack of refueling stations. Aware that such investments are currently unprofitable, Uno-X has chosen to break this impasse, taking short-term losses to pave the way for decarbonized transport in Norway.

Reitan Retail's care for the local community also extends to customers and suppliers. Its discount grocery chain, REMA 1000, offers high quality products at the lowest price, sold and produced in a responsible manner. For example, as Lars Sangolt, the director of the Tollboden store in Bergen, explained: "For all our private label products, we reviewed their suppliers' manufacturing conditions and ensured that fair wages are paid."[17] He was also especially proud of the chicken sold by the company, which carries a unique story behind its sourcing and quality. A young veterinarian employed at Reitan noticed that chickens in one of the industrial poultry farms operated by the company appeared sickly. She proposed to her CEO the idea of finding a chicken breed better suited for industrial farming – a bold initiative that he approved. Her search led her to farms worldwide, ultimately identifying a more robust breed, Hubbard, in the Netherlands. The company gradually replaced its previous breed with Hubbard chickens – not just at the original farm, but across all eight poultry farms it owned. These farms were transformed into open areas that allowed for free movement of the chickens.

This project may seem a bit unconventional – and indeed, REMA 1000's CEO initially thought so too. But such bold, "crazy" initiatives are exactly what corporate CEO Odd Reitan had in mind when he asked employees "to be more crazy … be a little more different than the others."[18] That also meant pursuing the company's values, even at a loss. Indeed, replacing the chicken breed came with a cost – the production price per pound of Hubbard chicken being higher than the previous breed. Yet, REMA 1000 chose not to raise retail prices.

Interestingly, by optimizing the cutting and processing of Hubbard chickens, REMA 1000 reduced meat waste, ultimately offsetting the higher production costs – an oblique result. In 2018, REMA 1000 awarded the young veterinarian the Social Contribution of the Year prize. The jury noted that she had "contributed to a historic transformation and improvement in animal welfare in Norway."

Reitan Retail's philosophy of care doesn't stop there. By offering good, healthy food at affordable prices, REMA 1000 also supports the financial and physical health of its customers. But even without this additional contribution, Reitan demonstrates the powerful potential of a caring company across its four aspects.

First, each of these initiatives has been effective and carried out through the company's business processes rather than outsourced to NGOs. For example, Reitan supported the rehabilitation of petty criminals through its standard hiring and employee integration practices. Genton was clear on this: "We give money [to an NGO] to get knowledge and then ... to see how we can integrate ourselves into the project ..." And in an echo of Steve Jobs' search for the perfect way of giving back to society, she concluded:

> When it comes to charity, for a business to be able to spend that money over time, it should be business as well. Just to pay off your bad conscience, that's very old fashioned. You need to [conduct your social efforts] as an integrated part [of your business.]

Second, Reitan Retail facilitated these employee initiatives through a revamp of its managerial framework. As described earlier, although Reitan Retail has more than 3,600 retail outlets, its corporate finance department consists of about a dozen employees. The company has eliminated traditional budgeting and redefined the department's role as coaches for store managers, providing them with financial information through Apple-inspired "insanely simple" interfaces rather than exerting control over them. And when it comes to store management, REMA 1000 is deeply egalitarian. As employee Hassan Osman shared: "When I'm assisting a customer or restocking shelves, and a bottle accidentally falls and breaks, the store owner immediately steps in to clean it up."[19]

Third, these initiatives focused on local members of the company's ecosystem – people and causes directly connected to the communities in which the company operates rather than causes remote in space or time.

Finally, though profitability was not the primary goal, many of these initiatives have led – obliquely – to business success.

Currently, REMA 1000 – Reitan Retail's largest division – operates nearly 1,000 stores across Norway and Denmark, employing more than 30,000 people. It holds close to a quarter of the market in Norway's grocery retail sector.

But there is more. During the global rise of German deep-discount retailers like Lidl and Aldi, Reitan Retail handed them their only two defeats. When Lidl entered the Norwegian market in 2004, few believed REMA 1000 could survive. Yet by 2008, Lidl had exited Norway, selling its 50 stores to REMA 1000. Similarly, in 2023, REMA 1000 acquired 114 Aldi stores in Denmark, prevailing over yet another German discount giant. These outstanding business successes have not been achieved by Reitan Retail's superior business model but by their relentless focus on social and environmental values – rather than on profits. As Odd Reitan remarked, when times were tough and a competitor waged war against them, "The employees kept the belief in the concept and values and continued to be proud … [That's how] they won the war."

Year after year, Reitan Retail consistently generates healthy profits. The company also insists on being debt free, which is one of its corporate values, and maintains multibillion cash reserves. Yet, as Reitan Retail's CFO Genton remarked, "[Reitan Retail's founder's] goal is not to have as much money as possible. His goal is … to build great people … to whom you give trust." As we can see, when trusted people act freely, it has – as a consequence – both great social and sound economic results.

CARING AT THE NATIONAL SCALE

Reitan Retail demonstrates the power of using business processes to care for issues important to local consumers and host communities, whether it's the rehabilitation of petty criminals, noise pollution, nonuse of palm oil derivatives, transport decarbonization, health, and even animal welfare. As we noted, some of these initiatives, such as rehabilitation of petty criminals, have a potentially national impact on public spending and safety. And as Genton observed, Reitan Retail's initiatives are not "window dressing" – or as we have called them in Chapter 2, escape routes in the catch-me-if-you-can game – CSR-type activities but are all integrated with the core business processes. The multiplication of such initiatives, launched by trusted and responsible employees encouraged to follow their dreams and be "crazy," may make Reitan Retail a real force for the common good at the national level. However, some caring companies have taken initiatives that right away impacted their whole country.

In Chapter 4 we mentioned the French insurer MAIF, which refunded $108 million to MAIF's 2.8 million car-insurance customers. True, out of 39 million insurance customers in France, it is a small proportion. Yet the impact could have been much broader, as MAIF's CEO tried to sway all his fellow insurance CEOs to offer the same refund, though he didn't succeed. We can also add that with its outstanding customer service – ranked N°1 for the insurance industry 20 years in a row and N°1 or N°2 across all industries in France for the past several years – MAIF contributes to all of its customers' peace of mind.[20] As the CEO Pascal Demurger told us, "We are an insurer who enjoys paying." Those of you who have struggled to get paid by your insurer will understand what such a level of care means. Interestingly, like Handelsbanken, MAIF carried out a trust-based revamp of its managerial framework. From the removal of time clocks to granting the authority to make decisions to solve customer's problems in real time, it all contributed to employees' ability to provide outstanding care to this insurer's customers.

Handelsbanken, discussed in Chapter 6, is another financial institution providing outstanding service to all of its customers. With close to 15% of Swedish market, it is thus taking care of the financial health of an even larger proportion of its home country's citizens than MAIF. And just like MAIF, Handelsbanken took a national initiative during a crisis – in this case, the 2009 global financial crisis.

The Savior Bank

You may remember the history of countries rescuing large corporations, such the US government bailing out Chrysler in 1979 or the French government saving Areva – a world leader in nuclear technology and uranium – in 2015. But there is one sector in which a significant number of companies are not just saved occasionally, but constantly: the banking sector. The justification for this massive taxpayer expenditure is that a country – under threat of a total economic meltdown – cannot afford the failure of its systemically important banks. The problem here is that banks benefit from public money but simultaneously "shut off the taps" to the public and small and medium-sized enterprises by drastically limiting or shutting down credit during crises. In other words, taxpayers rescue banks to keep the economy running, but those banks restrict credit to economic actors at the moment they need them most. But in 2009, Handelsbanken did just the opposite of all the other banks.

It decided to continue to disburse loans to its old and new clients during the crisis, thus saving hundreds of households and small to medium-sized enterprises (SME) from bankruptcy at a time when overall demand and employment drastically declined. Moreover, unlike all the other banks in the country, Handelsbanken declined any help from the Swedish state.

When we suggested to Anders Bouvin, its CEO at the time, that his bank could be viewed as a "national savior," he chuckled and after a brief pause, elaborated:

> You're absolutely right. [During] a boom period … our branch managers tend to step aside, [since] they know that this is getting too heated. So … we contribute to the cooling off of the economy, when the economy needs to be cooled off. And [when the bubble bursts, which] always happens, when the credit dips and the other banks go into intensive care and need support from shareholders and governments, then … we take steps ahead … We should be an asset to society, not a burden on society.[21]

In other words, Handelsbanken not only helps the national economy during crises but also contributes to its stabilization to prevent them.

Characterized by its avoidance of super-profits tied to super-risks, its absence of bonuses for executives, and its attention to employees – notably by contributing the same amount for everyone to its pension fund – Handelsbanken has sometimes been labeled in Sweden as a "socialist" company.

The paradox is that the "socialist" Handelsbanken is perhaps the most capitalist of all its peers, which, because of their relentless pursuit of super-profits and their ignorance of related super-risks, had to be bailed out by taxpayers and were de-facto nationalized. Moreover, during banking crises, Handelsbanken has never asked for money from its shareholders. Consequently, it has been frugal and responsible, not only with taxpayers' money but also with its capitalist shareholders' funds. And that was the second time Handelsbanken had helped the Swedish economy: the first major crisis was the 1992 real-estate bubble, when the state bailed out all the other banks. Moreover, during the 2009 crisis, the bank dramatically helped the UK economy too, accounting for 50% of new SME lending in the country that year, even though it had 1% of the market. It's perhaps time to call the banks that chase super-profits only to be bailed out by taxpayers when the crises arrive the real socialists.

We saw the different role that Handelsbanken played during these crises. Yet you may attribute that to the particularities of Sweden, which has a history of socialist national policies with Europe's highest taxes and largest welfare state. If this is what you think, we want to present to you another "savior bank" – but this time in a European country, which by many standards has one of the most capitalist economies of all, United States included – Switzerland.

The 1929 Savior Still Alive

Certainly, the WIR Bank is not as well-known globally as the major international banks of Switzerland, but all Swiss people know it – and for good reason. It was founded following the 1929 crisis by two medium-sized

Swiss companies that couldn't secure credit from existing banks. Their idea was a highly unusual cooperative bank that would issue its own currency – backed by its own equity – and would lend to its members and facilitate transactions between them in this currency. WIR is an abbreviation of *Wirtschaft* (economy in German), but more importantly, *wir* means "we" in German, one of Switzerland's national languages.

The bank quickly attracted a large number of SMEs by offering financial solutions that were either unavailable elsewhere or more affordable than those provided by traditional banks – such as loans at below-market rates. However, WIR has played a role its founders had not anticipated: that of a stabilizer for the Swiss economy. During economic and financial crises, which often restrict credit provision by traditional banks, WIR remains entirely unaffected and, thanks to its control of its own currency, finances the working capital and other financial needs of the Swiss SMEs that are its members.

If you still think that it's a kind of socialist bank in a capitalist environment, let us give you some data. Today, its balance sheet stands at $7.2 billion, but more essentially, its equity ratio is 15.1% – five times the legal minimum requirement of 3%.[22] This makes it by far the most robust bank in Switzerland.[23] Moreover, in a highly competitive Swiss banking market, 17% of all Swiss SMEs – more than 50,000 – chose to be members of WIR (with membership fees amounting to less than a hundred dollars per year).[24] We may thus conclude that this admittedly unconventional bank not only holds its market position, but for close to one century, constitutes a major stabilizing and countercyclical factor in times of crises.

Of course, the cases of financial institutions – often viewed as villains – positively impacting entire countries are great. Yet, you may wonder if nonfinancial medium-sized companies, which represent a large proportion of all companies, can have a national impact. In fact, they can.

Replacing the Government

In mid-March 2020, COVID-19 locked down most of Europe and Asia. For Sterimed, a 900-employee maker of high-end sterile medical packaging, this development brought mixed news.[25] The sudden 40% increase in demand for its products was welcome, but ramping up production at its French plants posed a real challenge. One element was particularly thorny: caught totally unprepared, the French government was unable to supply protective masks to its population, including for Sterimed workers.

Because it refused to endanger its French employees, Sterimed had to find a solution. Though medium-sized, the company manufactures its products in France, the United States, and several other countries, while selling them to more than 100 countries, including to China. It's a huge paradox that a Western manufacturing company not only doesn't import anything from China but exports 30% of its French production to China. This export activity helped Sterimed to find a creative solution to its mask-shortage problem.

Indeed, Sterimed quickly realized that one of its Chinese clients was producing protective masks, but China had clamped down on their export. Still, using its ingenuity, this producer could always send several large boxes of "free samples" to France. Thus, Sterimed ended up with more masks than needed, and CEO Thibaut Hyvernat immediately thought he could use this surplus to benefit the local industrial community. "I started calling my friends who run manufacturing businesses and began sharing some of the spare masks," he told us.[26] Then, something struck him: "Instead of helping several dozen friends, I could help 20 million friends!" Luckily, China was lifting its export ban at around this time.

Working from his home in suburban Paris, he called an executive team Zoom meeting, and in 10 minutes the group decided to launch a totally new activity: importing medical supplies. The company leveraged its core technical, regulatory, and supply chain capabilities to put in place the needed financing and logistics. By mid-April – that is one month after the lockdown – the company had brought 25 million masks from China to France. This was approximately the same amount the whole French government – with hundreds of thousands of agents working on the problem – promised to bring to the country. But that's not all. While the price of masks had multiplied 30-fold and large quantities of them were extremely difficult to find, Sterimed sold them at cost, plus estimated transportation fees. "If air transportation costs exceed our estimations, we may well lose money. But that is not the point," Hyvernat told us in the midst of these events.

Interestingly, as with other caring companies, Sterimed also revamped its managerial framework based on trust and responsibility. As Hyvernat noticed:

> To succeed in an adventure like ours, it must be founded on human values. If employees feel trusted, and if everyone feels they are part of a shared adventure, clients sense it, and that creates success.[27]

When we asked if such a trust-based managerial framework facilitated putting in place the new-to-the-company import activity of masks from China, Hyvernat answered:

> [When we decided to start this activity,] I was quite cautious … When the [CEO] asks for something – there's always a tendency to say yes … So, I [asked employees]: "Are we capable of handling this workload? … Will it work in our warehouses? Can we manage it in terms of handling?" And all I got was, "Yes, we'll manage" … People spontaneously volunteered and said, "We'll do it, don't worry."

So, as with other caring companies, Sterimed's revamped managerial framework – inspired by the principles of "liberated companies," to be discussed in Chapter 8 – was key to empowering its employees to invent a caring business activity. In this case, an initiative that benefited the country's entire population. Also, as with other caring companies, Sterimed carried out these caring activities through its core business processes of sales, supply chain, and regulatory compliance.

And did it finally make profits while caring, as other caring companies often do? Indeed, by the end of the year, the company managed to turn some profit from its new mask-import activity. But these profits were oblique; a by-product of caring and not a goal, as Hyvernat said from the beginning:

> I don't have a problem with money or profit. That is to say, if at the end of the day we realize that we've made a profit from [importing masks], well, so much the better.

Sterimed's national impact was significant. But can caring companies have an even bigger – global – impact?

CARING AT THE GLOBAL STAGE

In Chapter 5, we described how, beginning in 2011, Eisai provided more than two billion tablets in 29 countries free of charge to combat the tropical disease elephantiasis, which affects more than 300 million at-risk individuals. We explained that Eisai does not view this initiative as philanthropy, which it rejects in principle, but rather as a caring activity conducted through its core business processes of drug manufacturing and distribution.

This example demonstrates that caring companies can have a global – beyond one country – impact. Yet, Eisai is a large corporation. The question remains whether SMEs – which are far more numerous – can also have a global impact.

From Sonoma Valley to the World

Like Eisai, Sonoma-based Traditional Medicinals is a company that prioritizes the health and well-being of its clients. It does so with medical solutions rooted in the origins of pharmacology – medicinal herbs. The story begins with Rosemary Gladstar, an Armenian-American who sought to revive the herbalist traditions of her great-grandmother. Forced into the death marches that decimated the Armenian people during the genocide of 1915–1916, her great-grandmother saved lives through her knowledge of plants, using them for both food and healing. In 1974, Rosemary and her husband, Drake Sadler, decided to share these centuries-old remedies to address the ailments of people in their neighborhood.

However, Rosemary felt disheartened – while she wanted to teach others how to use plants for health, most people were only interested in finding a quick cure. Drake, however, saw an opportunity. The couple produced 10,000 packets of herbal tea, and Drake set out in their Volkswagen van to sell the products to local grocery stores. He thought it would take nine months. Eleven days later, he called Rosemary: everything had been sold.

Nine months later, the fledgling Californian "herbal tea start-up" had achieved a turnover of half a million dollars – a success as surprising as what Steve Jobs and Steve Wozniak experienced around the same time, 80 miles south, with their Apple computer. And much like the Apple founders, they had a disagreement on what to do with their newfound success. Indeed, Rosemary was not enticed by the rapid growth or the financial rewards it brought.

"This has gotten completely out of control," she said. "It's too big; we have people working for us; this is not what we agreed to."[28]

And indeed, the couple had agreed to make just enough money in order to move to Mexico and try to live there.

"But, Rosemary, now that we sell the product, that's the way to get into everyone's home. Everyone brings this [tea] home. How about if we put information about herbs inside every bag. Why don't you start writing things? … We will educate. It's an extension of your desire to educate … Think about it that way. Don't think about it as business," Drake suggested.

Rosemary eventually agreed. Drake commented to us that in this moment they began to define their company's purpose: "educating the general public on the virtues of medicinal plants," without making it contingent on profit-seeking.

Not long after, a second turning point arose. Business was booming, and large crates of raw materials began flowing into the company's Sonoma Valley location. The labels revealed diverse origins – Ecuador, Mexico, Indonesia – that sparked Drake's curiosity. Yet he quickly realized that he knew little about the production and harvesting conditions of these plants. Rosemary, meanwhile, was primarily focused on their medicinal properties and was equally unaware.

One day, in what felt like a natural extension of their earlier Mexican dream, Drake suggested they visit some of their suppliers in these exotic countries. In Guatemala, on their way to a lemongrass plantation that supplied them, they were captivated by the vibrant, intense green of the plant's pointed shoots and the fragrant aroma that filled the air. However, they soon discovered that very young children were working in these fields.

During a subsequent conversation with the plantation owner, despite his kindness and warm hospitality, the couple came to a stark realization: the production conditions of their raw materials did not align with the values and vision they held for their company. Their healing solutions for consumers in the United States were inextricably linked to child labor and, in many cases, the farmers' exposure to hazardous pesticides.

Upon their return, Drake shared his discouragement with a friend who happened to be a medicinal plant wholesaler. The friend provided a "country-by-country" account of medicinal plant production practices, and the reality he described was even more alarming than Drake's first-hand experience in Guatemala. At the time, the situation was grim: there were four or five intermediaries between Traditional Medicinals and the impoverished farmers who harvested the plants – half of which were harvested in the wild. The farmers, and often their children, were the biggest losers in this chain.

Drake had a background of fighting poverty in rural US communities at the Office of Economic Opportunity, led by a very influential mentor to him, a certain Mrs. Sloan. Hence, the situation was deeply upsetting him.

"Rosemary, I don't think we can continue. This is completely contrary to my training. I will never be able to face my mentor again," Drake explained.

He finally decided to visit Mrs. Sloan, who curtly suggested: "If you don't like something, you change it … Go figure out how to change it. One village at a time. You're not gonna change the world."

This is how the second pillar of Traditional Medicinals' caring activities took shape: empowering the planet's impoverished indigenous communities, who cultivate and collect medicinal plants. The company began investing in projects to help these local communities become more resilient and less vulnerable. Working alongside local producers, Traditional Medicinals' experts assessed what was needed to improve their welfare. These efforts included projects ranging from building schools and water wells to enhancing farming methods – often to meet organic standards – in collaboration with local partners.

As Mrs. Sloan put it, it started with one village, but it grew. Today, Traditional Medicinals has transformed the lives and working conditions of all 160 of its suppliers and their communities across 35 countries worldwide.

Like other caring companies, Traditional Medicinals carried out these initiatives through its core business activities. The company's supply chain experts were the ones analyzing farmers' welfare needs and designing the projects to address them. And, as with other caring companies, while these initiatives were not driven by economic motives, the company discovered financial benefits – albeit obliquely.

Indeed, the quality of the ingredients is fundamental to the final quality of the product. In each type of tea sold by Traditional Medicinals, only one or two ingredients are active, while the rest of the plants in the teabag mitigate the undesirable side effects of the active ingredient. For instance, in the company's laxative product, only 35% of the formula consists of the active ingredient. While this ingredient alone can produce bowel movements, its potency can also cause cramps or bloating. To minimize these side effects, the remaining 65% of the teabag is filled with "inactive" plants.

Here is where supplier improvements had an unexpected impact: as producers enhanced their farming methods, they began growing increasingly potent active plants. This way, the company discovered it needed far less of these active – and costlier than inactive – ingredients per teabag. It led to a significant reduction in production costs and a corresponding increase in margins.

That said, at no point was the company's care for farming communities subordinated to economic interests. Furthermore, while Traditional Medicinals helped producers improve their methods, it refused to act as their sole client, avoiding the risk of creating their dependency. The producers would then be able to sell their products at a higher price to other clients. As Drake Sadler explains: "It's not charity at all. It's business."

And business it is. Today, Traditional Medicinals, with close to 300 employees, is the North American leader in medicinal herbal teas. As a private company, its revenues are not disclosed but are estimated to fall between $100 million and $500 million.

Interestingly, while it remains privately held and Drake Sadler has vowed that it will never be sold, the company has still managed to attract private equity investment. One notable investor is The Builders Fund, whose partner, Tripp Baird, explained their motivation: "We decided to invest … because [of] shared values and a shared vision for the purpose and potential of business as a force for good in the world."[29] He also made recommendations for purpose-driven companies and investors:

> Start from the long-term, aspirational goals and work back from there to strategy and an operating blueprint. Financial returns become a natural by-product of that alignment rather than the fundamental goal.[30]

His fund can achieve an eventual exit only by selling its equity to a buyer who shares similar values and vision. While the fund is committed to a long-term investment, it remains confident that a suitable buyer will be found when the time comes.

THE SECRET OF DOING GOOD AT LARGE SCALE

We began this chapter by asking whether caring companies can achieve massive positive impact and, in doing so, prove that businesses can play a pivotal role in revitalizing capitalism. The half-dozen caring companies we highlighted – ranging from multinational corporations to medium-sized businesses, spanning numerous countries and industries – demonstrate that such impact is indeed possible. "Caring" was the aspect that enabled their employees to take fruitful initiatives for the common good. But paradoxically, it is the fact that they were "companies" – thus capable of scaling – that made the impact of these initiatives, run through business processes, massive. Indeed, the scaling capacity is what distinguishes a company from a one-person enterprise.

In Chapter 3, we explained that caring companies deliberately choose to prioritize doing good locally and immediately for members of their business ecosystem – customers, suppliers, and the local communities – rather than focusing on philanthropy "targets" who are removed in space and time. While this narrow focus is far more effective, it may initially appear to be a limitation to doing good, given that the number of a company's clients, suppliers, or the size of its local community is inherently finite. However, this is precisely where scale, even in the case of small and medium-sized businesses, becomes a game changer.

As we will explore in the next chapter, caring companies reject the notion of maximizing economies of scale at all costs. Even so, like any company, they naturally interact with large numbers of customers, manage hundreds of suppliers, and operate in multiple locations. What sets them apart from traditional businesses are the spontaneous initiatives taken by their employees – those who go above and beyond to care for a specific customer, supplier, or host community. Often, these employees underestimate or ignore the potential impact of such efforts when scaled up.

> Yet companies, by their very nature, excel at scaling up what works, and this is where the true magnitude of their impact on society emerges. This scaling capacity is like the hidden power that can turn caring companies into a force for good at national or global level.

Even SMEs demonstrate this capacity to scale impact. For instance, Sterimed's initiative of sharing protective masks with a few neighboring businesses might seem like a small act, but scaling it up to 25 million imported masks in a single month alleviated an epidemic crisis across all of France. Similarly, Traditional Medicinals' initiative of helping a single supplier in a developing country improve their welfare or production methods might, by itself, yield limited results. Yet extending that same support to 160 suppliers – one supplier after another – across 35 countries has made this impact global.

Large corporations, of course, have an even greater scaling capacity. Integrating one young petty criminal into REMA 1000's workforce might have a limited social impact, but integrating hundreds can significantly reduce Norway's social costs and enhance its public safety. Similarly, reducing noise and nuisances by building one neighborhood-friendly gas station at Uno-X might seem minor, but constructing dozens of such stations in a caring way created a notable cumulative impact. And while Handelsbanken providing a credit line to one struggling small business during an economic crisis might offer limited benefits in isolation, offering this support to all the SMEs reduced Sweden's and UK's risk of plunging into recession.

In Chapter 4, we mentioned Adam Smith's belief that mutual sympathy was a far more natural basis for human interaction than self-interest. However, he doubted whether businesses, unlike private individuals, could maintain mutual sympathy with thousands of customers or suppliers. The caring companies have turned what Smith saw as a shortcoming into a strength.

By believing they can build meaningful, caring relationships with every member of their business ecosystem, these companies leveraged their scaling capacity and made a massive positive impact on thousands of such people.

These stories show that caring companies can scale their impact from local acts to national outcomes. But if the benefits are so clear – socially and economically – why haven't such companies become the norm rather than the exception? Why do so many organizations, even with the will to care, remain stuck in outdated ways? To answer these questions, we must examine not just business practices, but the deep-rooted beliefs that underpin them. This takes us to the heart of our next chapter: a whole new paradigm.

CHAPTER EIGHT

A WHOLE NEW PARADIGM

We resist the invasion of armies; we don't resist the invasion of ideas.
– Victor Hugo[1]

For caring companies to emerge in numbers, something deep must change: the very way we think about business. Despite compelling examples of impact, many leaders hesitate – not because they lack purpose, but because they are bound by inherited assumptions. They operate in belief systems where care is seen as optional or even as a sign of weakness, where self-interest is the driver, and where profits are treated as purpose. To move from scattered successes to systemic shift, we must confront the beliefs that quietly govern modern capitalism. And that begins with those willing to challenge the current belief system – not with theory, but with action.

"I never had any plans to set up a private clinic," remarked Timo Joensuu.[2] The founder of Docrates, a leading cancer clinic in Helsinki, Finland, was almost embarrassed when he recounted how he became an entrepreneur.

In the 2000s, this renowned oncologist felt a certain disillusionment with his profession that had been building for some time. As a young doctor involved in therapeutic trials, he was struck by the significantly greater attention given to volunteers in clinical trials compared to "ordinary" patients. To him, every patient deserved the same high level of care and respect.

Later, working as an oncologist in a large public hospital, he observed how treatment in public healthcare was highly standardized. Specifically, most therapies were administered without precisely targeting the cancer tumor. Often, radiation or chemotherapy was delivered across a broad area to maximize effectiveness – but at the cost of increased adverse effects in other parts of the body.

By leveraging advanced genetic characterization for more precise diagnosis and radiotherapy, Joensuu developed a treatment protocol that extended the average survival rate for advanced prostate cancer patients to 8.35 years – far exceeding the typical two to three years. He published and promoted his findings, yet this only deepened his frustration: his team was simply overwhelmed by the surge of patients seeking care. Neither the hospital's limited resources nor, more critically, its bureaucratic, silo-type structure could accommodate this demand. As Joensuu put it: "A patient has to call the urologist, then make an appointment for chemotherapy, then radiotherapy, and along the way, he has to see another specialist – to whom he has to tell his whole story again …"

This might seem like an unavoidable consequence of the highly specialized nature of advanced medical treatment. But this very challenge sparked Joensuu's radical vision:

> To create a multidisciplinary department [that takes] complete care of the patient, who [will] no longer run after the medical team, but where the medical team will run after the patient!

In 2003, Joensuu's colleagues at the university hospital were taken aback by his vision, while he himself struggled to see how he could bring it to life.

Feeling stuck, he accepted an invitation to attend an offsite seminar with Finnish philosopher Esa Saarinen on the island of Cyprus. It was during this philosophical retreat that Joensuu experienced his "Aha" moment. "I realized that I didn't have to do other people's work or compare myself to them," he recalls. "I understood what it meant to do a good job – and to do it as a team. So, I told myself: 'I can do my job and do it well. I'm capable of making a real impact in this world.'" That was the turning point. He decided to stop lamenting his circumstances, waiting for others to act, and instead to take matters into his own hands.

Together with a team of doctors, nurses, and specialists drawn to his project, Joensuu set out to reimagine how cancer patients should be treated.

"What would be your dream hospital?" he asked them.

"Windows in the radiation-protected rooms," suggested one doctor.

"An in-house cyclotron to manufacture radioactive drugs on the same floor as medical imaging," proposed another.

"An integrated control room to manage MRI, SPECT, and PET-CT scans," added a third.

"A soundproof room for servers," a technician chimed in.

And then came a truly unique idea: instead of the usual heavy bunker door leading to the radiotherapy machine, why not use a simple wooden door – with a labyrinthine entryway to ensure radiation protection?

Docrates' story highlights the challenges of building a genuinely caring company. Why did it take Joensuu so long to launch his uncompromisingly patient-centered private clinic? And why do so many other leaders – who harbor similar doubts about their own organizations – fail to take bold action to transform them into truly caring enterprises?

More broadly, this raises a fundamental question: If the social and – consequently – economic benefits of caring companies are so compelling and far-reaching, why isn't it already the dominant paradigm today?

A PARADIGM SHIFT

Since we began writing about caring companies in 2019, we have encountered many objections. Here are some of the most common:

- "This is great, but if I'm the only one acting this way, how can I avoid being taken advantage of by those who only worry about closing deals?"
- "When we started, my company was caring, but over time, it became more focused on profits than on our customers or host community."
- "We've grown so large that the kind of close relationships with customers and suppliers you describe are simply no longer feasible."

These – and many other concerns we've heard – raise valid challenges. But they also highlight something deeper: the difficulty of shifting from one paradigm to another.

Thomas Kuhn – first a physicist, later a historian and philosopher of science – introduced the concept of intellectual paradigms in his groundbreaking book, *The Structure of Scientific Revolutions*, one of the most widely cited academic works of all time.[3] Before Kuhn's book, the prevailing view of scientific progress was that of a steady accumulation of knowledge. Kuhn disputed this notion.

For him, a paradigm functions as a "thought matrix" shared by a given scientific community. It encompasses all the theories, landmark experiments, and established methods that scientists rely on daily – shaping the worldview of their discipline. A paradigm not only defines the direction of research but also dictates what kinds of questions you can ask and what types of answers are considered valid.

However, when persistent problems emerge – ones that resist resolution – or when experiments reveal anomalies that contradict existing theories, the discipline enters a crisis.

Such a crisis, Kuhn argued, can only be resolved by overturning the old "thought matrix" and replacing it with a new paradigm – a revolution in both thinking and practice within the scientific community.

Yet, this kind of intellectual upheaval is never easy. People struggle to abandon long-held beliefs and the familiar practices that structure their professional lives. As a result, Kuhn proposed that scientific progress occurs through disruptions rather than through a smooth, linear evolution.

Applied to business, this insight helps us understand why so many corporate leaders hesitate to embrace the caring company paradigm. To do so, we must first examine the dominant business paradigm of our time – along with its core assumptions and deeply ingrained beliefs.

THE DOMINANT PARADIGM AND ITS BELIEFS

The three common objections we received illustrate the three core beliefs that prevent leaders from adopting the caring company paradigm:

- The belief that the economy is solely about transactions
- The belief that profits must be maximized
- The belief that economies of scale are the surest path to prosperity

Belief 1: Business = Transactions

In Chapter 4, through the story of The FruitGuys, we explored the belief that transactions form the foundation of business – and how this company challenged it. In essence, this belief rests on the following assumptions:

- Human beings are motivated solely by self-interest.
- In every economic exchange, they will seek to maximize their self-interest.
- All transactions are voluntary and take the form of free contracts.
- The interplay of self-interests through transactions naturally creates the "common good" for society, without anyone intentionally pursuing it – an assumption known as the "invisible hand."

The FruitGuys and other caring companies challenge these assumptions:

- Self-interest alone cannot explain why LSDH goes out of its way to warmly welcome its suppliers' drivers.
- Profit maximization does not justify The FruitGuys purchasing nonstandard fruits from a supplier or driving three hours to deliver products to a remote, small customer.
- Transactions alone are insufficient to improve the welfare of Traditional Medicinals' plant producers and create shared benefits.

These facts do not fit the view of business as based on self-interested transactions. But they do fit seamlessly the view of business as based on authentic relationships and its underlying assumptions:

- Employees and members of the business ecosystem – clients, suppliers, and the host community – are primarily driven by a human need to establish authentic social relationships.
- Trust-based relationships are more beneficial for everyone than purely transactional exchanges.

- Taking a long-term perspective in economic interactions is more advantageous than focusing on short-term gains.
- Companies contribute to the common good more effectively by caring for the members of their business ecosystem and integrating this care into their core processes, rather than relying on distant, one-off initiatives or the hypothetical "invisible hand."

Moreover, authentic, trust-based relationships do not exclude contracts. Contracts serve a clear purpose: they make the counterpart predictable because she "plays by the rules." Legal contracts underlying transactions rely on one type of rules – those enforced by the courts. Yet, moral contracts underpinning trustful relationships also rest on a set of rules – a moral code upheld by the community that shares them. As the German economist Alfred Koch noted, individuals who respect contracts – legal or moral – form a society rather than a herd. The difference between these two types of contracts lies in the fact that it is often far more efficient to achieve the counterpart's predictability through a moral contract rather than a legal one. And it's not only a question of the cost of drafting legal contracts. It's also a matter of emotional and relational burden.

Indeed, research shows that even transaction-focused, traditional businesspeople rarely resort to enforcing contracts – a move that may offer compensation but almost certainly severs the relationship. Instead, they prefer to reach out-of-court arrangements, preserving the relationship they've built with the other party.[4] While caring companies do sign formal contracts when required, they bet on a moral contract through trustful relationships thereby simplifying their business life.

Finally, authentic, trust-based relationships built on unconditional care do not exclude profits. Caring companies act out of a genuine commitment to the members of their ecosystem – not in pursuit of financial rewards, which may or may not materialize. Nevertheless, these rewards often arise, driven by the universal norm of reciprocity and the ethical foundations inherent to all business relationships. For most business actors, receiving unconditional care does not imply that a caring company is giving away something for free – rather, they recognize its value and are willing to reward such a company.

Belief 2: We Must Maximize Profits

In Southern Florida's swamps, the alligators' most efficient diet would be to feed exclusively on large fish, which in turn prey on prawns. However, nature's solution is broader: in addition to large fish, alligators also consume turtles and snakes – both of which also feed on prawns.

This diverse diet is not about expanding the alligators' gastronomic choices; rather, it serves as a built-in safeguard against the disappearance or illness of any single food source. If large fish were to vanish, alligators could still survive by shifting to turtles or snakes. Yet, alligators do not hunt or consume everything in their ecosystem, as that would mean too much effort wasted on inefficient sources of calories.

This example, proposed by American and Belgian researchers Goerner, Lietaer, and Ulanowicz, challenges prevailing economic thought: rather than maximizing short-term efficiency, the most successful organisms seek to maximize their long-term survival. As these researchers have demonstrated, every living organism operates within an "optimal window of vitality" that best supports its survival over time.[5] This window corresponds to the peak of an inverted U-shaped curve, representing the optimal balance, the sweet spot between efficiency and resilience – the capacity to adapt to new disturbances. Figure 8.1 illustrates how species maximize their sustainability by striking this balance between efficiency and resilience. Furthermore, it demonstrates how an excessive focus on efficiency alone ultimately undermines sustainability.

This model helps explain many of the challenges facing modern capitalism. Specifically, a company puts its survival at risk when it seeks to maximize efficiency at the expense of resilience.

Figure 8.1 Sustainability as a function of efficiency and resilience.

Source: Adapted from [6].

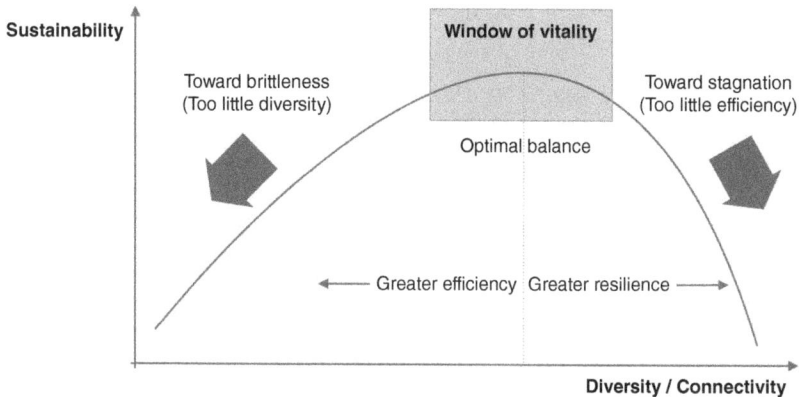

Sustainability

Window of vitality

Toward brittleness
(Too little diversity)

Toward stagnation
(Too little efficiency)

Optimal balance

←— Greater efficiency Greater resilience —→

Diversity / Connectivity

During the COVID-19 crisis, for example, global supply chains collapsed, exposing the vulnerabilities of businesses that had prioritized cost-cutting through offshoring, particularly to China. Those long supply chains, combined with just-in-time inventory systems, were extremely efficient, but extremely brittle. When the pandemic disrupted the system, hundreds of businesses collapsed almost overnight. Efficiency had made them profitable, but fragile. This is not a theoretical observation nor is it limited to the COVID-19 period. Several studies on corporate survival indicate that many approaches aiming to maximize efficiency – such as outsourcing or full automation – ultimately undermine sustainability.[7] The reason for this is that these approaches drive companies out of their "window of vitality."

Paradoxically, one of the very practices designed to enhance resilience – risk management – can instead make companies more vulnerable. Business plans, budgeting, and other forecasting tools, while intended to anticipate the future, can inadvertently rigidify organizations, leaving them brittle – either by resisting change or by outright disregarding any fact or event that challenge their established framework. Employees often hear or say, "It can't be done because it's not in the business plan or the budget." Unlike those businesses, caring companies do not seek to maximize economic efficiency at all costs. In fact, many explicitly state that their primary goal is longevity – to remain viable and thriving for as long as possible. We have seen how Handelsbanken valued long-term survival, Wallander building a bank that can last for a century – and how that commitment has helped it weather repeated financial crises that crippled other banks or forced them into government bailouts.

Another example is Reitan Retail. As Berit Hvalryg put it:

All the decisions that we have made are within our values. And this is also because in the Reitan group we have an *eternal* perspective. We don't know what the business is … in ten years and twenty years, but we know that we have an eternal perspective.[8]

Just like living organisms, caring companies value economic efficiency – but as a constraint, never as a goal. They embrace the philosophy that "you have to breathe in order to live, not live in order to breathe" – and certainly not to inhale as much air as possible.

In the second season of the *Fargo* TV series, police officer Lou Solverson engages in a conversation with philosopher-mafia-leader Mike Mulligan, following the typically polite Midwestern style:

"We're not meant to take on more than we can handle … So this need for conquest, trying to own things that aren't meant to be owned … that's a problem, right? Not a solution."

"You're saying capitalism is the problem?" asks the philosopher.

"No. Greed," replies the officer.

A compelling corporate example of self-imposed profit constraints is Clinitex, a 4,000-employee French leader in B2B cleaning services. Clinitex applies a concept it calls the "satiety threshold" – a self-imposed limit on economic results. Each year, the company determines the level of sales and profits needed to cover its survival needs: repaying bank debts, financing gain-sharing programs, maintaining sufficient working capital, building risk reserves, and ensuring adequate funds to pay shareholder dividends.

During the COVID-19 crisis, when its survival was at risk, Clinitex mobilized all its employees to boost economic performance. And by September 2020, the company had reached its satiety threshold. CEO Edouard Pick reassured his employees: "Relax! We crossed the finish line faster than expected!"[9] In other words, once the company's survival was secured, there was no need for an exceptional effort to further boost economic results.

Remarkably, most companies striving to maximize profits fail to do so in a sustainable manner. A study by American researchers Wiggins and Ruefli analyzing the financial performance of 6,772 companies over 25 years found that only 5% achieved a single 10-year period of superior return on assets, while merely 2% sustained above-average Tobin's Q for any 10-year stretch.[10] Over a 20-year horizon, only four firms met the above-average Tobin's Q criterion. Furthermore, this study focused exclusively on companies that survived the full 25-year period, excluding those that failed along the way – suggesting that the true financial success rate may be even lower. In other words, maximizing efficiency and financial performance makes companies fragile and leads to underperformance for most of them.

In addition to rejecting efficiency maximization, caring companies also avoid the other extreme – maximizing resilience – precisely because they are naturally resilient already. For instance, they do not minimize the number of suppliers to increase profits, but neither do they expand their supplier base excessively, as managing too many relationships would dilute their ability to genuinely care for each partner.

Finally, unlike employees in traditional companies, who focus on executing transactions to minimize risk, those in caring companies prioritize deepening relationships to remain open to the unexpected. Specifically, instead of telling a client, "That's not our problem – it's not in the contract," they say, "Please let us know as early as possible if anything changes in your situation so we can work together to find a solution and adapt." By operating at the optimal balance between economic efficiency and resilience, caring companies maximize their long-term sustainability. Yet, by nurturing strong relationships within their business ecosystem, they also – obliquely – achieve higher profits, as we have seen in previous chapters.

> In other words, in caring companies, profits remain where they belong: a constraint and a consequence, but never a goal in itself.

Many companies, driven by genuine concern for social and environmental issues, have embraced the various available approaches – from philanthropy to CSR, to B-Corp and Benefit Corporation. Yet, they have rarely questioned their belief in profit maximization as the key or at least a primary goal of their business activities. However, companies that prioritize the social and environmental good of their business ecosystem members over profit – treating profits as a constraint rather than the ultimate objective – realize that a radical transformation is necessary. This includes the gradual reintegration of philanthropic or CSR initiatives into the core business (as with Reitan Retail's Røbel project seen in Chapter 7).

Belief 3: Economies of Scale Are the Surest Path to Prosperity

Another deeply ingrained belief that caring companies challenge is the necessity of economies of scale. This idea dates back to the Industrial Revolution and was already evident in the nineteenth-century cotton mills described in Chapter 1. It gained even more traction in twentieth-century business practices. As Henry Ford famously put it:

> The experience of the Ford Motor Co. has been that mass production precedes mass consumption and makes it possible, by reducing costs and thus permitting both greater use-convenience and price-convenience … If production is increased 500%, costs may be cut 50%, and this decrease in cost, with its accompanying decrease in selling price, will probably multiply by 10 the number of people who can conveniently buy the product.[11]

The basic rationale behind economies of scale is quite simple: as production increases, fixed costs are spread over a larger number of units, thereby boosting margins. Countless examples reinforce this belief. For instance, the Boeing 737 is the cheapest aircraft to produce in its category, largely because Boeing has made nearly 12,000 of them to date – more than any other civil aircraft in history.

> However, an increasing body of evidence suggests that in many cases, mass production and massive corporations do not lead to economies of scale, but rather to *diseconomies* of scale.

The concept of diseconomies of scale was first introduced by British scholar Alfred Marshall in his 1890 book, *Principles of Economics.*[12] Marshall identified several diseconomies of scale, such as rising coordination costs, reduced flexibility, and declining employee motivation. Each of these is an obvious and very real cost of getting bigger – as anyone who has seen modern businesses operate knows. But we too often ignore or discount the costs of these diseconomies because they are incompatible with the dominant business paradigm.

Likewise, Nobel Prize-winning economist Ronald Coase, in his theory of the firm, argued that as a company grows, the cost of internal transactions increases. He proposed that there is an optimal firm size, beyond which the marginal cost of each additional transaction exceeds the cost of outsourcing it to external providers.

Despite these insights, the belief in economies of scale has remained deeply entrenched in most companies. Still, some visionary business leaders and thinkers have challenged this notion. In the 1950s and 1960s, Ernst Schumacher, then head of the British National Coal Board, which employed more than 800,000 people, reorganized the company into small, autonomous units he called quasi-firms. He later popularized his ideas in his 1973 book, *Small Is Beautiful*.[13] Schumacher explained that the purpose of such a decentralized structure is to balance the tension between order, which ensures the company's long-term stability, and human freedom and creativity, which enable adaptation to changing conditions. As Schumacher put it:

> In any organization, large or small, there must be a certain clarity and orderliness … Yet orderliness as such, is static and lifeless; so there must also be plenty of elbow-room … for breaking through the established order to do the thing never done before …
>
> Therefore any organization has to strive continuously for the orderliness of order and the disorderliness of creative freedom. And the specific danger inherent in large scale organization is that its natural bias … favors order, at the expense of creative freedom.[14]

As we saw in Chapter 3, recent evolutionary research by Robin Dunbar provides another explanation for the optimal organizational size: the cognitive limit to the number of people with whom one can maintain stable social relationships is 150. Some business leaders have recognized this human constraint and integrated it into their organizational models. We have already discussed how, in the early 1970s, Jan Wallander decentralized his bank, allowing each branch to operate as a small company with its own P&L responsibility.

A decade prior, in the beginning of the 1960s, Bill Gore established a guiding principle for W.L. Gore & Associates: never build a plant for more than 150 employees.[15] If additional production capacity was needed, Gore would simply construct another small-scale plant rather than expand an existing one.

Similarly, Japanese entrepreneurs Kuniyasu Sakai and Hiroshi Sekiyama adopted the same approach to manage the growth of their high-tech manufacturing corporations. They called it *bunsha*, meaning company spin-off, a strategy they used to create more than 40 successful, independent companies.[16] In a similar spirit, Kyocera Corporation's founder, Kazuo Inamori, developed "Amoeba management," an approach based on small and autonomous units.[17]

You may wonder why, despite the theories and practices that challenge economies of scale, many large corporations continue to pursue them.

One explanation might well be that, although often inefficient and rigid, large corporations strive to become even larger to attain "too big to fail" status. Their sheer size greatly increases the likelihood of being bailed out – either by their creditors, banks, or governments – in the event of bankruptcy. Through such bailouts, these corporations shift the cost of their inefficiencies onto taxpayers, effectively socializing their financial risks.

Yet, their contributions to society outside of crises are far less significant. Research shows that large corporations are not the job-creation engines they are often portrayed to be. Instead, they tend to erode surrounding economic networks – even as they contribute to GDP growth.[18] It is often called "the Walmart effect," but it is also exhibited by Amazon and numerous other large corporations.[19] Nor are large corporations "tax machines." For example, in 2018, profitable large corporations paid an average effective federal tax rate of 9% in the United States.[20] In fact, large corporations benefit disproportionately from tax provisions that allow them to pay effective tax rates well below the statutory rate.

In short, like any highly centralized company with several hundred employees or more, large corporations suffer from diseconomies of scale. The difference is that they offload these costs onto society – or onto large banks that continue lending to them, despite their inefficiencies.

Unlike these corporations, whose belief in economies of scale lead to such effects, caring companies do not risk them. Their size – or, in the case of large caring companies, the size of their autonomous business units – is optimized to strike a balance between economic efficiency and authentic relationships, both within the company and across their business ecosystem.

The previous discussion explains why leaders who adhere to the dominant business paradigm – rooted in transactions, profit maximization, and economies of scale – struggle to accept the caring company philosophy. Conversely, we have shown how abandoning this paradigm enabled the leaders described in this book to successfully build their caring companies. Yet, despite the notable impact of several dozen caring companies – some of which have achieved nationwide social and environmental impact – their success has not (yet) forced a paradigm shift. A handful of companies, no matter how influential, will not, by themselves, revitalize capitalism. The key question, then, is: How do we trigger a paradigm shift that engages thousands – rather than just dozens – of business leaders to transform their companies?

UNDERSTANDING TRANSITIONS

When Nobel Prize-winning Professor Muhammad Yunus started Grameen Bank in Bangladesh in 1976, it was a small experiment. The story began when he personally lent $27 total to a group of 42 women in Jobra village, near Chittagong University, where he was teaching. Soon, Yunus officially founded Grameen Bank, proving that microcredit could empower the poor and enable them to retain the profits of their labor. As of July 2024, the bank has served more than 10 million borrowers, disbursing more than $38 billion in loans.[21] Thus, this "small experiment" evolved into a global movement, reshaping both thinking and practice in economic development across poor regions – Laurent, while young, actively participated in it in Chile.

Yunus' success can be partly explained by his rejection of the dominant belief in banking that poor people are not creditworthy. However, this still leaves a key question: How did a handful of local micro-credit banks grow to become a global movement?

Margaret Wheatley and the Berkana Institute have devoted significant effort to both understanding and facilitating large-scale systemic transitions.[22] She and her colleagues draw a distinction between "dying systems," which operate under an old and increasingly contested paradigm, and "emerging systems," which pioneer a new paradigm. For Wheatley, pioneers face significant challenges when attempting to bring their ideas and practices into the mainstream. They must invent the future while still navigating the constraints of the past; reassure their supporters, who want them to look familiar; and overcome resistance from adversaries, who hope they will fail.[23]

Based on Berkana's experience in facilitating systemic transitions, Wheatley proposes a process centered around communities of practice. This approach unfolds in four key phases:

- **Naming:** Identifying the pioneers leading the shift
- **Connecting:** Bringing them together in communities of practice to foster shared learning
- **Nourishing:** Providing them with the resources needed to grow and evolve
- **Illuminating:** Telling their stories to raise public awareness of the new paradigm and inspire more leaders to embrace it

This cycle of naming, connecting, nourishing, and illuminating offers a roadmap for how caring companies can contribute to a society-wide paradigm shift.

Both authors have first-hand experience with such transformative movements. In 2009, when Isaac coauthored a book with Brian M. Carney on freedom-based or "liberated" companies, there were only a few dozen of such companies worldwide – each one isolated from the others.[24] However, around this time, a dozen leaders in France and Belgium began transforming their companies – shifting their managerial frameworks from control and subordination to trust and freedom of action. By 2010, this second generation of liberating leaders reached out to Isaac and Laurent, and in 2011, the two of us connected them, launching and coordinating a community of practice. This community was further nourished through articles, books, videos, social networks, learning expeditions, and direct coaching and mentoring. Finally, the community organized two one-day forums, each attracting more than 500 business participants from Europe and North America, eager to learn about liberated company practices – directly presented by the employees and leaders who had implemented them.

Additionally, community members actively engaged with the business media, securing coverage in prime-time TV programs akin to *CBS 60 Minutes*, as well as in the widely viewed documentary *Happiness at Work*. A highly successful comic strip further popularized the concept of liberated companies, making it accessible to a broader audience.[25] Simultaneously, Laurent led a series of learning expedition programs with an association of more than 8,000 French-speaking CEOs across 38 countries. These expeditions aimed to identify, connect, and nourish several dozen aspiring liberating leaders.

These Berkana-style initiatives – even though we only discovered their theoretical foundation in 2016 – have played a crucial role in helping hundreds of companies to become liberated. Among them are large multinationals such as Decathlon and Michelin, as well as divisions of several other publicly traded corporations. The impact has also extended beyond the private sector, influencing public service administrations such as the Belgian Ministries of Transportation and Social Security and the French Social Security.[26]

Liberated companies began to emerge in the 2010s and can be seen, in many ways, as a culmination of broader paradigmatic shifts in management – particularly in how organizations approach employee trust and autonomy (see Figure 8.2). Unlike in science, however, management paradigms tend to coexist, and a single company may transition from one to another with a change in CEO or ownership, for instance. Contrary to the views of Hegel and some management theorists, we do not subscribe to the

Figure 8.2   Timeline of the diffusion of key managerial frameworks in relation to employee trust and autonomy.

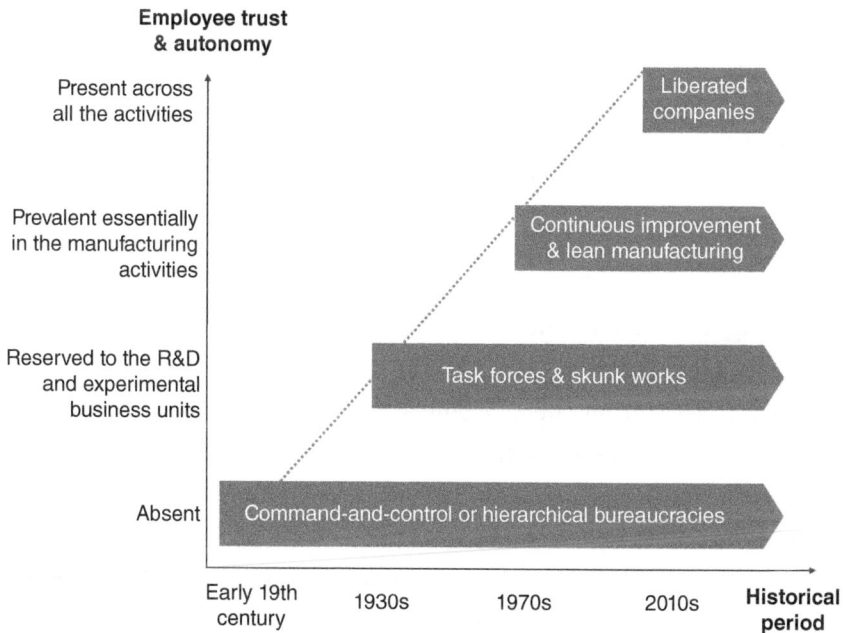

idea of a predetermined direction in history – nor have we observed such a pattern in practice.

A movement similar to the liberated companies' one – this time spanning different regions and countries – is entirely possible for caring companies. This book describes and explains the reality of caring companies. Some readers may even realize that their own companies already embody this philosophy. There is no reason why, once identified, these leaders would not be eager to connect in coordinated communities of practice, learn from one another, and inspire others by sharing their experiences.

True, we sometimes hear leaders asking whether there are examples of those who have failed in their attempts to transform their companies. It's an understandable concern, given the complexity and challenges inherent in any radical organizational transformation. It's also reasonable to assume that one can learn much from the mistakes of others – but not always.

In fact, when it comes to a challenge as profound as building a successful organization – both socially and economically – a leader will gain far more insight from those who have succeeded. As Odd Reitan, the founder and president of Reitan Retail, explains:

> I love positive, enthusiastic people and hate the opposite … If you face trouble in your world, seek support from those who are successful. It doesn't help much to cry with people who have the same problems as you.[27]

Joining a community of leaders driving successful transformations is a powerful learning tool.

Finally, research on "tipping points" shows that convincing an entire population is not necessary to trigger a fundamental shift in how things are done. Instead, a small but decisive group of people can play a crucial role in spreading an idea or behavior throughout society.[28] Environmental and situational factors also play a crucial role in major societal shifts. Under new conditions, a series of small, cumulative changes can eventually trigger large-scale transformations. This process can sometimes appear sudden and unexpected, as illustrated by Nassim Taleb's concept of the "black swan" phenomenon – an unpredictable event that reshapes the world in ways no one foresaw.[29]

Regardless of the "truth" of any particular view of human nature, narratives (whether about people or society) shape reality when they are widely accepted as true. The key insight is that a new paradigm does more than offer an alternative story about reality; it also creates its own language – its own vocabulary and grammar. This is what Thomas Kuhn refers to when he speaks of the incommensurability of paradigms. Specifically, this means that the "thought matrix" of one paradigm cannot simply be translated into the language of another. For instance, in the Copernican view of the universe, one can say that "planets orbit the sun," but this sentence is meaningless in Ptolemaic astronomy, where the sun itself is considered a planet.

Kuhn warns that concepts from one theory cannot be directly mapped onto another. To truly grasp a new theory, one must learn an entirely new language – one that frames reality differently:

> Anything that can be said in one language can, with sufficient imagination and effort, be understood by a speaker of another. What is prerequisite to such understanding, however, is not translation but language learning.[30]

For the caring company philosophy to evolve into a dominant paradigm in business, the key challenge lies in creating and spreading an entirely new language.

This is precisely the role of communities of practice – they serve as learning spaces where leaders and practitioners can develop, share, and internalize this new language, gradually making it the norm in business discourse and practice around them.

CARING COMPANIES, ECONOMICS, AND POLITICS

Though you may admire the caring company paradigm and see the transition needed to make it dominant, you may still doubt whether this shift can happen at the scale of the entire capitalist system. The following discussion may help overcome your skepticism.

Capitalism is not monolithic.

Fernand Braudel, the renowned French historian and founder of the world-famous *École des Annales* school of historical science, demonstrated in his work that preindustrial societies were structured around three distinct levels of economic activity.

The first level is what Braudel calls material civilization – a realm comprising local producers focused primarily on subsistence. Until the eighteenth century, the vast majority of humanity operated at this level, living within self-sufficient economies.

The second level is the market economy, which includes local markets, shops, and peddlers, as well as more sophisticated trading hubs such as fairs and town markets. Braudel highlights that the market economy is defined by regulated, law-abiding, and transparent trade – one that is conducted "eye-to-eye and hand-to-hand."[31] At this level of the free market economy, businesses are so deeply embedded in their local communities that they have no real choice but to care for others – since these "others" are often cousins, friends, or friends of friends.

The third level, however, consists of merchants – a category of economic actors *disconnected* from local ties and regulations. According to Braudel, only this third level is capitalism proper:

> [Another] type of exchange replaced the normal collective market and substituted for it individual transactions based on arbitrary financial

arrangements ... Here we are dealing with unequal exchanges in which competition – the basic law of the ... market economy – had little place and in which the dealer had two trump cards: he had broken off relations between the producer and the person who eventually received the merchandise (only the dealer knew the market conditions at both ends of the chain and hence the profit to be expected); and he had ready cash, which served as his chief ally.[32]

Progressively, this type of capital-centered actor appears in various parts of the world under the names of *mercader* in Spain, *katari* in India, *negoziante* in Italy, *négociant* in France, or *Kaufmann* in Germany. For Braudel, merchants are "chiefly concerned with exporting and long-distance trade." He notes: "Need I comment that these capitalists, both in Islam and in Christendom, were friends of the prince and helpers or exploiters of the state?"[33] Braudel provides further examples of merchants leveraging their proximity to power to restrict or eliminate competition.

This kind of influence of "capitalists" on governments has never ceased. In the late 1890s, for example, John Rockefeller strongly supported the career of President William McKinley with whom he shared views on protectionist policies, which would defend his companies against foreign competition. Today, the largest technology companies continue this tradition, using their influence to shape regulations in their favor.

All criticisms of capitalism implicitly target this third level of economic activity – and, as we will explore in Chapter 9, the fourth: the level of the financialized corporation. Critics do not take issue with the neighborhood plumber or the local fruit vendor at the weekly town market. These small entrepreneurs operate "eye-to-eye," making it easy for customers to compare options and hold them accountable. If they fail to care for their customers and communities, their reputation will eventually put them out of business.

The absence of caring, then, originates primarily – though not exclusively – from large, impersonal organizations. It is no coincidence that, in French, Italian, and Spanish legal terminology, corporations are referred to as "anonymous societies." And actually, it is impossible to really care anonymously because caring always involves two real, specific persons. We can see this in the difference between small towns and the city. In small towns inhabitants often don't lock their front door or their cars because they know one another. No one is anonymous.[34] But large corporations can be compared not only to big cities where inhabitants are anonymous and mistrusting, but also to particularly disturbing type of individuals. As Canadian scholar Joel Bakan observes, many of these corporations – which often control budgets rivaling those of nation-states – demonstrate no consciousness, no empathy, no regard for social norms, and no sense of guilt – traits commonly associated with psychopathy.[35]

Actually, already at the end of eighteenth century, Adam Smith warned in *The Wealth of Nations* of the dangers of merchants:

> People of the same trade seldom meet together, even for merriment and diversion, but the conversation ends in a conspiracy against the public, or in some contrivance to raise prices.[36]

Later in his book, Adam Smith strongly condemned the "merchant classes." In his view, they fabricated the concept of "balance of trade" as a way to deceive policymakers, persuading them to grant monopolies, advantages, and subsidies – particularly in North America. Smith observed that these privileges ultimately made merchants richer while impoverishing the rest of the nation.[37] He concludes that the key skill for statesmen is judgment – knowing how and when to balance the necessity of free trade with the need to limit what he calls the "merchants' conspiracy."[38]

The previous debate may seem theoretical, but it carries significant practical implications for the future of capitalism. Indeed, many critics of capitalism conflate free markets with capitalism as defined by Braudel. It was Lenin who initially merged these two concepts. Obsessed with preventing the restoration of capitalism in Russia, he wrote that "even within the socialist world, the village market, having once regained its freedom, might well reconstitute the whole tree of capitalism."[39] Unfortunately, that theoretical error led to the deportation and death of millions of so-called "kulaks" – independent peasant-producers – resulting in nationwide famines. And ironically, the Soviet economy was never able to function sustainably without town markets.

Braudel was also aware of the consequences of this mistake – confusing the two economic levels. Writing during the Cold War, he observed:

> What I personally regret ... is the refusal in both the capitalist world and the socialist world to draw a distinction between capitalism and the market economy. To those in the West who attack the misdeeds of capitalism, politicians and economists reply that these wrongdoings are a lesser evil, the indispensable reverse side of the free-enterprise-and-market-economy coin. I do not believe that.[40]

Figure 8.3 illustrates the extent to which various historical economic actors placed trust in their clients, suppliers, and local communities.

Figure 8.3 Timeline of key businesses' evolving reliance on trust-based relationships with their ecosystem.

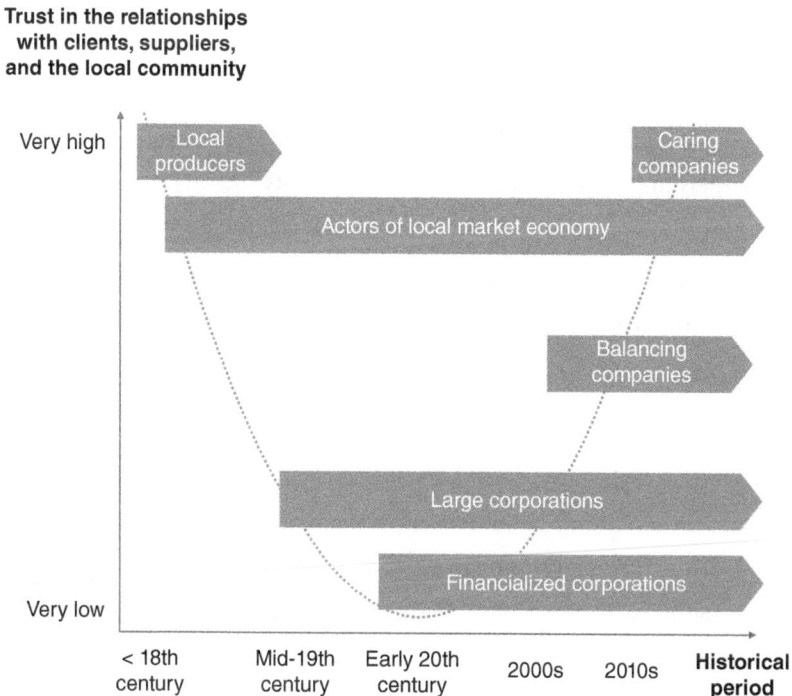

Trust in the relationships with clients, suppliers, and the local community

In contrast to the linear progression of paradigms depicted in Figure 8.2, this evolution follows a distinct U-shaped pattern. Trust was once a cornerstone of businesses in the preindustrial era, but over time, it virtually vanished from large-scale and financialized corporations. It is only in the early twenty-first century that trust has begun to re-emerge, embodied by what we identify as "caring companies": organizations that signal a return to earlier values, albeit at a greater scale and – naturally – within a fundamentally different context.

Revitalizing our economic system is a demanding task. Superficial measures will not suffice, nor can we rely on yet another swing between state-driven policies and the Chicago School approach of the 1990s.

Our societies deserve better. To revitalize capitalism, its key actors must break free from the old paradigm of self-interested transactions, profit maximization, and economies of scale.

Instead, they need to embrace a new paradigm:

- Building authentic relationships
- Operating within their "window of vitality"
- Harnessing the power of autonomous local business units

Moreover, caring companies thrive in free markets, ask for no special favors from the government, and contribute daily to the common

> Caring companies are leading the way, embodying this new paradigm. They cultivate caring relationships with all members of their business ecosystem, prioritizing social value for them, view profits as both a necessary constraint and a natural consequence, and favor smaller business units to deepen these caring relationships.

good – as Mrs. Sloan would say, "one village after the other." You never know how close the next tipping point is.

But to understand how we move forward, we must first understand how we got here. If today's caring companies represent a return to a more human, relationship-centered way of doing business, what caused us to stray so far from it in the first place? To answer that, we must revisit the pivotal moments and key figures that helped shape modern capitalism – moments when choices were made that still echo through today's business practices. The story begins over a century ago, in a spa town in the French Alps.

CHAPTER NINE

HEART-TO-HEART: THE FUTURE OF BUSINESS AND CAPITALISM

If ... we do it with love – for our customers, our employees, and our suppliers – the experience becomes meaningful on multiple levels. When we also integrate methods and products that align with our values, we begin to take better care of the planet and slowly start to change things for the better.

– Dominique Tremblay[1]

Today, Aix-les-Bains is a peaceful spa town nestled in the foothills of the French Alps. But at the dawn of the twentieth century, thanks in part to the advent of the telegraph, it bore witness to one of the most dramatic upheavals that financial markets had ever seen up to that point.

The stock-market panic of 1901 and its aftermath may seem as remote from our subject as Aix-les-Bains is from Wall Street. But the events of 1901, and one of its protagonists in particular, played a key role in giving birth to what might be thought of as capitalism in its modern, "financialized," form. Knowing how it began may help us better understand how to reform or replace it.

At the turn of the twentieth century, Aix-les-Bains was a favored destination of European royalty and aristocracy as well as the world's wealthiest capitalists. Officially, they all came for the hot springs and health treatments, but that didn't stop them from enjoying evenings filled with concerts, balls, and galas in the lavish salons of the casino Grand-Cercle – and more. Other halls offered ample gambling opportunities, far from the prying eyes of New York or Paris press.

However, one American financier – who owned a significant stake in the US steel and railroad industries – wasn't interested in such diversions. On April 4, 1901, he embarked from New York with a female companion on an ocean liner for one of his months-long European business and pleasure trips. Having left someone to oversee his vast business empire, he looked forward to thoroughly relaxing. He would not.

Barely settled in his Aix-les-Bains hotel one month later, he received a cable from his New York office regarding his holdings in the Northern Pacific Railroad. Several years earlier, he had amassed 25% of the railroad's stock at $16 per share, gaining effective control over the company. But beginning in March, a railroad tycoon, Edward Harriman, began quietly buying the railroad's stock, driving the share price to $96 – the day the financier boarded the sea liner. Perhaps due to his disdain for Harriman, he wasn't ready to change his plans.

He might have regretted it, while reading the cable which said that the share price had surged to $115, and Harriman was on track to surpass the financier's holdings.

"Buy 150,000 shares," ordered the financier.

The cable, sent from the spa resort, triggered seismic effects. Harriman met the challenge, and within days, the Northern Pacific share price sky-rocketed to $1,000. This frenzy created a global panic on the New York Stock Exchange, as investors sold every other stock – most of which lost half their value on average – to buy the star stock.

After a flurry of cables – by now, any notion of a "relaxing" stay at the spa long gone – a truce between the warring sides was negotiated, dividing control over a large portion of the US railroads. Yet, the 35% to 40% of US railroads the financier now controlled was far from his only asset. He also owned between 60% and 70% of the US steel industry, along with shipping lines, utilities, and more. In fact, just two months before his departure, he acquired the nation's largest steel company from Andrew Carnegie.

By now, you may have no difficulty identifying our protagonist: John Pierpont Morgan.[2] But here is a harder puzzle: just six years earlier, Morgan had been a discreet broker for English and other European investors in American securities. What enabled this financier to become the largest owner of America's most important industrial assets in less than a decade? And even more puzzling: How could Morgan believe he could run such a vast business empire remotely, through cables, for months?

Though worth $25 million (just under $1 billion in today's dollars) and ranked among the 100 wealthiest Americans, by January 1895, Morgan was still viewed as a mere "peddler of bonds" to Europeans. Yet, it was precisely his European relationships that opened the door to his rise. The Rothschild bank in London invited him to join them as an American partner – or rather, to be their American face – in lending $62 million in gold to the US government, saving it from default.

Relying on a decade of experience reorganizing smaller railroads – a process known as "Morganization" – Morgan now set his sights on redrawing the entire US railroad and steel industries. His motive was neither ego nor power but rather a continuation of his lifelong role: serving as an agent for transatlantic capital.

It is often said that the secret of finance is using other people's money. But that's only half the truth. The other half is that managing others' money requires fiduciary responsibility: preserving the principal investment and delivering the expected return – if the financier expects those clients to come back. This responsibility demanded investment in low-risk assets.

Morgan's financial genius lay in his ability to see beyond the traditional conduit role of channeling transatlantic capital into existing low-risk securities. Instead, he devised a bold strategy: acquiring high-risk assets – such as railroads – wresting them from entrepreneurs and speculative financiers and transforming them into safe, stable holdings for his European clients. It was this strategy that elevated Morgan into the largest owner of American industrial assets – and, more importantly, a trusted steward of his European clients' capital.

Until May 4, 1901.

That day, by triggering the stock market panic that ended with a truce with Harriman, Morgan shattered this trust. Alarmed by the instability of the American market, English, French, and other European investors – the primary buyers of US securities – withdrew $200 million (equivalent to nearly $7.5 billion today) in the following year.

At the same time, Morgan's steel empire – the first $1 billion company in history – mostly acquired from Carnegie only three months earlier, failed to achieve performance gains through economies of scale. Worse still, in 1904, his railroad trust was dismantled by President Theodore Roosevelt's antitrust actions. And by 1912, his broader "money trust" became the subject of an extensive congressional investigation.

In short, the key to understanding the puzzles of both Morgan's swift accumulation of vast industrial assets and of his belief in managing them from afar lies in his transformation from a prudent and responsible steward of others' finances into a bold and aggressive investor. This shift both foreshadowed and paved the way for the financialization of the economy as a whole, which – we argue – constitutes a "fourth level" of capitalism, one that the historian Fernand Braudel, discussed in Chapter 8, did not describe. But J.P. Morgan's story holds an even deeper significance.

Until – and including – the 1895 Gold Reserve Crisis, Morgan maintained authentic relationships with his transatlantic clients, often meeting them personally. At that time, he functioned within the sweet spot between ensuring the safety of his clients' investments and generating sufficient returns for them. Finally, as an industrialist he operated rather decentralized small railroads, utilities, and shipping lanes, trying to benefit from the boom in these industries.

Paradoxically, Morgan was both a financier and a mid-sized industrialist, whose approach bore some resemblance to the new capitalist enterprise paradigm outlined in Chapter 8. Yet, through his high-risk and aggressive strategies, he ultimately abandoned all three core principles of this paradigm. First, he compromised the trust-based relationships, that his father – and later he himself – had carefully maintained with clients, by offering them speculative and risky railroad securities. Next, he shifted away from the "window of vitality" in favor of maximizing financial returns at any cost. Finally, he forsook decentralized industrial structures in pursuit of economies of scale and monopolistic returns. In other words, Morgan pioneered a capitalist enterprise model defined by escalating risks in the relentless pursuit of ever-higher profits – a model that would soon become the primary target of today's critics of capitalism. Such critiques abound.

CAPITALISM ON TRIAL

We opened Chapter 2 with a text by Dee Hock, criticizing financialized – or, as he called them, monetized – corporations.

We now invite you to guess the authors of the following passage:

> As citizens, as consumers, as employees … we affirm our determination to change an economic system in which we no longer believe … It's high time we take the necessary measures and stop living beyond our means, to the credit of the planet, other peoples and future generations.

You may think that the authors are militant ecologists. They aren't. In fact, the authors and signatories of this 2018 *Student Manifesto for an Ecological Awakening* are 34,000 students at elite French universities and *Grandes Ecoles*, the equivalent of the US Ivy League and top institutes of technology.[3] They added their voices to the long list of grievances against capitalism as we know it.

This third level capitalism, as Braudel described it (see Chapter 8) started with cash-ready merchants. And as we showed in J. P. Morgan's story, it evolved into the fourth level in the final quarter of the nineteenth century, with bold, capital-rich financiers acquiring entire industries in order to transform those assets into financialized corporations.

These capitalists earned the name of robber barons and even at the time were criticized by trade unions, newspapers, and politicians. Thus, during his 1901–1909 tenure, President Theodore Roosevelt curtailed the economic power of some of them, including Morgan and Harriman, and earned the nickname of "trust buster." But capitalism was on trial for decades before that and continues to be today.

Here are some key grievances against capitalism.

The first one is that capitalism doesn't care for people. Since Karl Marx, this is the most common accusation made against it. Working conditions in nineteenth century factories in the West were despicable, as we described in Chapter 1. Yet, such – or even worse in some cases – working conditions still exist in many places of the world: today more than 160 million children are working to earn a living and an estimated 50 million people are kept in so-called "modern" slavery, like the Uyghurs in China and other oppressed populations.[4] These violations of human rights are happening within a global capitalist economy relying on its international supply chains. Despite the regular denunciation of these practices, businesses ignore them or pay lip-service to them in their pursuit of ever-higher profits.

In the wealthy countries that are members of the Organization for Economic Cooperation and Development, employees have their rights and working conditions protected. But they still suffer psychologically. Indeed, only 31% of US employees are "engaged" in their work – that is, they find it meaningful and fulfilling. The majority – 52% – are disengaged, working simply to earn a paycheck, while 17% are "actively disengaged," so angry that they show up in order to sabotage their engaged colleagues' work.[5] Despite all their sermons and pledges, businesses still view people as "human resources," that is, something to be exploited to make profit – just as Marx said.

The second main grievance against capitalism is that it creates unbearable inequality. Like the insufficient care for people, this grievance is not new. Marx pointed to capital accumulation in the hands of a few as a key characteristic of capitalism. The case has been re-opened recently with French economist Thomas Piketty's book *Capital in the Twenty-first Century*, whose success – whatever its shortcomings – tells a lot about the relevance of the topic today. According to the Federal Reserve, the gap between the super-rich and the rest of the population has never been so big. In the United States, the top 0.1% alone possess more than five times the wealth of the bottom 50% of population – and this gap has only grown over the past 35 years (see Table 9.1).

Table 9.1 Wealth in the United States by Wealth Percentile Group

	Q3 1989	Q3 2024	Change 1989–2024 in USD
Top 0.1%	$1.76 trillion (8.6% of total)	$22.13 trillion (13.8%)	× 12.57
Bottom 50%	$0.71 trillion (3.5%)	$3.89 trillion (2.4%)	× 5.47

Source: Adapted from [6][6].

The problem is not inequality itself but the fact that the weakest of the bottom part of society lacks means for a shelter, for food, and for education.

The third grievance against capitalism is that it is destroying the environment. This one is more recent. In Chapter 2 we described the nine earth boundaries that our current economic model is threatening. Yet, most businesses are run in an unsustainable manner, ignoring them. Some argue that capitalism has enough internal dynamism to find solutions to the problems it has created in the first place. Such optimism disregards the degree to which we are now navigating uncharted waters, ecologically speaking.

Take one boundary – of novel entities, such as plastics, pesticides, industrial chemicals, and antibiotics. We human beings are in danger from the way these entities enter into our bodies. In 2024, a team of Swiss experts found that, out of more than 14,000 known food contact chemicals, 25% enter our blood, urine, hair, umbilical cords, placentas, and breast milk, and 80 of those chemicals cause cancer, decrease fertility, cause birth defects, or are toxic to humans.[7] Pesticides are also threatening human life, particularly through the decline of wild bees, which – as the main pollinators of wild plants and many crops – are crucial to the stability of ecosystems and agriculture.[8] Yet, large chemical corporations seem to ignore these issues. Worse, they have often lobbied against any limitation on their activity, as in the case of the regulation on toxic substances proposed by the European Union.[9]

Or take a more recent threat to the environment – the race to generative AI by Big Tech. According to the report *Electricity 2024: Analysis and forecast to 2026*, "electricity consumption from data centers, AI, and the cryptocurrency sector could double by 2026," thus dramatically increasing CO_2 emissions.[10] This race also accelerates the use of rare earth elements, not to mention how the development of electric vehicles is driving their demand to unprecedented levels.[11]

The fourth grievance against capitalism is that unelected capitalists wield power over elected officials. Lobbying is highly regulated in many European countries, while in others, and in the governing bodies of the EU, it is freely allowed, as in the United States. In the former, businesses often circumvent regulations through corporate "public relations." Whether it's called PR or lobbying, however, the result is the same: influence over governments and legislators.

Moreover, companies find direct and indirect ways to finance political campaigns. Thus, according to the US Federal Election Commission, as of September 30, 2024, corporate political action committees (PACs) had disbursed $353.6 million to presidential and congressional candidates during the 2024 campaign.[12] Furthermore, in 2024, crypto corporations contributed $119 million to a nonpartisan super PAC dedicated to electing pro-crypto candidates, accounting for 44% of all corporate contributions.[13] It is not a coincidence that a number of measures favoring the crypto industry were announced as early as January 2025.

What's more, in many countries, large chunks of mass media are owned by corporations or billionaires, whose main activities have little relation to media. Jeff Bezos' ownership of *Washington Post* or the Gates Foundation's support of many media in the world are not exceptional.[14] Owning media is another way to wield influence over public opinion, and thus over governments and politicians.

The fifth and final grievance: capitalism is accused of undermining societies, destroying the cultural soil on which it grows. Indeed, well-functioning free markets require free individuals, able to make reasonable choices, with sufficient critical thinking. This isn't the case in a consumerist society. Pervasive advertising results in visual and mental stimulation of consumer desires. But since most of these desires remain unfulfilled, people end up with high levels of frustration. Pleasure is fleeting and needs constant resupply. Joy is sacrificed on the altar of pleasure.

All these critiques of third- and fourth-level capitalism are well grounded. Yet, most businesses seem to ignore them or to believe that they can be addressed by the "invisible hand" or the power of innovation.

Unsurprisingly, numerous solutions have emerged and are presented as alternatives to capitalist enterprise.

ALTERNATIVES TO CAPITALIST ENTERPRISE

The following discussion focuses on these alternatives. However, a short comment is due on the alternatives to the capitalist system itself.

Such alternatives have been attempted since the 1917 Communist takeover in Russia, extending after World War II to Central and Eastern European countries under Soviet dominance, as well as, later, to China, Vietnam, Laos, Cambodia, North Korea, and Cuba. They all established economic systems based on central planning, centralized decision-making, state ownership of companies, and collective farming. Their economic – but also social and human – failures have been most clearly proven by what economists call "natural experiments."

Two notable natural experiments occurred in Germany after World War II and in Korea after the Korean War. In the case of East and West

Germany, the key difference lay in their political and economic systems, while in the case of North and South Korea, the primary distinction was economic – South Korea remaining authoritarian until 1987.

The superiority of the capitalist countries – whether in economic, social, or human terms – was undeniable. The two communist regimes became so oppressive that East Germany and North Korea were forced to seal their borders with their capitalist counterparts so extremely that any attempt to cross them meant almost-certain death. Despite this, over the decades, hundreds risked their lives to breach these deadly barriers, desperate to escape a system that promised paradise in rhetoric but delivered a nightmare in reality.

Now, let's shift our focus to alternatives to capitalist enterprise that operate within free-market economies.

Social Enterprises

Social enterprises are an often-mentioned alternative. Researchers define it as "organizations or ventures that combine a social purpose with pursuit of financial success in the private marketplace."[15] However, there is no clear consensus on the definition of social enterprises, as the term encompasses traditional nonprofits alongside "new legal forms of social businesses, social cooperatives, inter-sector partnerships, corporate social responsibility programs of for-profit corporations, and myriad combinations of these models."[16]

The Global State of Social Enterprise (GSSE) 2024 report defines social enterprise as "a business that puts people and the planet first."[17] This should exclude the previously mentioned CSR programs, as well as Benefit Corporations and B Corps discussed in Chapter 2, since the former prioritize profits above all else, while the latter aim to balance profit with social and environmental goals. According to the GSSE report, there are 1.3 million social enterprises in the United States and more than 8 million worldwide. Furthermore, social enterprises account for 2% of global GDP – a significant figure. Given their ability to achieve social and environmental goals when successful, they present a credible alternative to for-profit businesses, which often pursue these goals only marginally.

However, there is one critical issue preventing social enterprises from being a true alternative: most are not self-sustaining. According to the GSSE report, "typically, social enterprises seek, on average, financing that amounts to about 75 percent of their yearly revenue."[18] These funds come from public and private grants, as well as equity and debt financing. In other words, three-quarters of social enterprises' revenues do not stem from business activities but from fundraising efforts. These funds originate either from for-profit corporations – often through their foundations – or from tax revenues channeled by public agencies.

Put simply, the majority of social enterprises would not survive without being embedded in capitalist economies that generate profits and taxes, a portion of which is redirected to them. Since social enterprises rely on capitalist businesses for financing – directly or indirectly – they can hardly be considered an alternative to them.

Cooperatives

Another frequently cited alternative to capitalist enterprise is worker cooperatives. Unlike corporations, cooperatives are owned by their members and operate for mutual benefit. Cooperatives' shared ownership, democratic decision-making, and their focus on members' economic and social well-being are key features that have traditionally attracted people critical of capitalist enterprise. Worker cooperatives must be clearly distinguished from producer cooperatives – businesses in which producers pool their output for mutual benefit. Worker cooperatives must also be differentiated from client- or consumer-owned cooperatives. Among cooperatives generating annual revenues exceeding $10 billion only the Basque group Mondragon qualifies as a worker cooperative.[19] Our focus is exclusively on worker cooperatives, as only these entities are historically regarded as viable alternatives to traditional capitalist enterprises.

Worker cooperatives emerged as a response to the harsh realities of wage laborers. Just a few generations ago, their predecessors were land-owning peasants who enjoyed a degree of autonomy and self-realization through their labor. The notion of co-owning one's workplace was thus envisioned as a means of reclaiming similar work and life conditions as well as economic agency.[20]

Thus, in the early nineteenth century, the French philosopher Charles Fourier (1772–1837) proposed economic organizations based on cooperation and communal living. His ideas inspired Robert Owen, whom we discussed in Chapter 1, and who sought to create "villages of cooperation" in Britain – eventually establishing one, albeit short-lived, in the United States. In 1844, Fourier's influence extended to the Rochdale Pioneers in England, who founded what is considered the first modern worker cooperative.

According to *Cooperatives and Employment: Second Global Report*, around 27 million people are employed in worker cooperatives or similar cooperative models, including 16 million salaried employees and 11 million worker-members – a figure that represents nearly 1% of the global workforce.[21] An additional 252 million individuals – primarily self-employed producer-members – work directly within the economic scope of cooperatives. Combined with those employed within cooperatives themselves, the worker cooperative economy accounts for an over 279 million people, representing nearly 10% of the global workforce – a testament to their economic significance.[22] However, as a result of their growth, worker cooperatives and similar models began to employ nonmember workers who today, often outnumber worker-members.[23] Therefore, cooperatives face labor issues similar to that of capitalist businesses.

The first is one of the employees' rights. This typical to the capitalist business issue is amplified by the fact that in worker cooperatives the worker-members are also employees. Indeed, International Organisation of Industrial and Service Cooperatives (CICOPA) – the main organization of worker-cooperatives – still discusses whether worker-members "should give up their freedom and rights as owners of cooperatives to gain rights and protection as employees?" or how can cooperatives manage a situation in which worker-members "claim their rights as employees by referring to labor laws without assuming their responsibility as owners?"[24]

The second challenge concerns wages. In traditional capitalist businesses, the interests of owners and employees are inherently misaligned: owners seek to contain labor costs, while employees aim to maximize their earnings. Salary levels are typically determined through individual or collective bargaining. Such an adversarial framework is ill-suited for worker cooperatives, where many employees are also the owners. Instead, worker-members strive to optimize the total value they derive from both wages and equity – a balancing act akin to chasing two rabbits at once. As discussed in Chapter 2, capitalist businesses faced with this duality tend to prioritize profit maximization, with social concerns treated as constraints rather than core goals. In contrast, the relatively low individual equity value in worker cooperatives makes social considerations – such as higher employment stability versus lower wages – more prominent.[25] As one study of worker cooperatives explains, "it is more difficult for a conventional firm [than for a worker cooperative] to elicit agreement for pay cuts in exchange for job preservation, since the firm has an incentive not to increase pay when business recover."[26] Similarly, driven by the egalitarian principle, the ratio between the lowest and highest salaries in worker cooperatives typically ranges from 1:1 to 1:6 – significantly narrower than in comparable capitalist businesses.[27]

Finally, beyond a certain size – which, as discussed in Chapter 3, is around 150 employees – like in every organization, worker cooperatives face the challenge of coordinating activities among individuals who lack direct relationships. By default, they will adopt a command-and-control structure, which fails to address employees' fundamental psychological needs (see Chapter 5). Consequently, just as in traditional businesses, this often results in employee disengagement – but in cooperatives, where many employees are also co-owners, such a reality can generate even more frustration, as it seems so at odds with the very principles of the cooperative movement.

To illustrate, several years ago, one of us, delivered a keynote address to a worker cooperative employing more than 3,000 people, including 650 worker-members. After the speech, he was approached by two audience members who asked for a private conversation. We moved to a quiet corner of the large hall, where they introduced themselves as local union representatives and worker-members. Speaking discreetly – away from the prying eyes of executives – they shared their concerns about the toxic workplace culture within the cooperative. While they may have been venting frustrations, such hostility, while not uncommon in traditional corporations, is not supposed to happen in a worker cooperative – and yet, it did. Moreover, based on our observations and research, we have found that large cooperatives tend to interact with customers and suppliers much like traditional capitalist enterprises do – primarily through transactions rather than genuine relationships.

All the noted unresolved challenges undermine the worker cooperatives movement, and they exist – we submit – because of the false belief it has gradually adopted. Recall that worker cooperatives emerged as a *mean* to the early Industrial Revolution labor's autonomy and self-realization. With time however, worker cooperative legal form became an end, ignoring that its nonmembers employees don't enjoy these very autonomy and self-realization.

In short, worker cooperatives seem to many as a "silver bullet" social measure. Yet, as discussed in Chapter 1, only a bundle of coherent and mutually supporting social measure can achieve such goals as employee autonomy and self-realization.[28] Many such social measures, we suggest, could emerge from engaging the employees – both members and non-members – in the co-construction of the workplace allowing autonomy and self-realization. The corporate liberation movement, discussed in Chapter 8, involving businesses, public administration, and some worker cooperatives shows that it is possible. Such engagement of employees in the co-construction of their work environment has been already promoted within the syndicalism. For example, in the 1930s and 1940s, a former syndicalist and management thinker Hyacinthe Dubreuil studied and described the experiences and principles of such work environments. Likewise, reflecting on syndicalism, the American philosopher Christopher Lasch concluded:

> It was not ownership so much as the opportunity for invention and self-reliance that made work interesting, and the same advantages could be recreated in factories … once the workers themselves began to exercise responsibility for the design of production.[29]

In contrast to worker cooperatives, caring companies – similarly to liberated companies – foster authentic relationships with their employees who serve as the bridge to these companies' business ecosystem members. As a result, caring companies tend to be more prosperous – often outperforming their profit-focused competitors. As such, they represent a fundamentally different approach to running a capitalist enterprise.

A compelling example of this can be found in a recent case of a North American mid-sized manufacturer that successfully transformed itself from a traditional and rather stagnant business into a caring company that prospers.

FROM HEART TO HEART

In November 2024, one of us received a LinkedIn message from Dominique Tremblay, who held an intriguing title: CEO and Organizational Coach. This Canadian leader had come across our TED Talk on the concept of a caring company, then sought out our writings to share and discuss them with his colleagues. "Without realizing it," he wrote, "our management principles closely align with what you describe so well, and that inspires me tremendously."[30]

Tremblay's company, PMB, is situated across the river from Quebec City. This 120-employee manufacturer of metallic structures is anything but conventional:

- It operates without a strategic plan.
- It declines requests for proposals.
- It has intentionally stopped working with certain clients.
- It has significantly increased salaries – particularly for frontline workers – along with vacation time.
- Its owner and CEO at the time chose to take a sabbatical year – a decision he upheld despite the onset of COVID-19.
- Although manufacturing conditions are challenging, employees genuinely enjoy coming to work.

PMB is also unconventional for the unexpected outcomes of its unusual approach:

- Once PMB partners with a client, it becomes that client's preferred supplier within six months – despite charging higher prices than its competitors.
- Though PMB has increased its payroll expenses, the ratio of payroll to the revenues has decreased year after year.

- During the CEO's absence, the company tripled its profits compared to the already strong results of the previous year – and did so despite COVID-19.
- In 2022, PMB was named *Company of the Year* by the regional Chamber of Commerce and, in addition, won both the *High Performer (Medium and Large Company)* and the *Exceptional Manufacturer* awards – the first time a single company had ever won so many honors in this competition.[31]

While accepting the awards on stage, standing before an audience of 700 business leaders, Dominique Tremblay declared:

> We acted out of love – love for our colleagues, our clients, our suppliers … We can work with our hearts, and there is no contradiction between performance and love.[32]

"There was a long silence in the room – about 20 seconds," Tremblay recalled. "Then, the audience erupted in applause."

Tremblay grew up in an entrepreneurial environment: his parents ran a car-repair business, which he believes was also a caring company. He vividly remembers his father inviting clients who had been shaken by a car accident earlier in the day home for a dinner. While the mechanics repaired the vehicle, his father cared for the clients' well-being.

From an early age, Tremblay was driven to create positive change – to make things more humane. At just 18, he had an unusual moment of clarity:

> I was struck by how few years I had left – 50 years … to make a difference, to care, and to contribute to a better world. Would I be a good steward of those years? Fifty years in the vast history of humanity was merely a drop in the ocean. I might as well live fully – not just survive or endure. I might as well pursue what enriches life, what is nourishing and fulfilling, rather than retreat into myself and give up.

He studied theology and became the pastor of a 200-member community at the age of 25, but left the role, unsatisfied with the tangible impact of his ministry. Tremblay then pursued a graduate degree in ethics, launching and running a co-working café all the while. As his family grew, he trained in architectural and technical drafting, driven by a long-standing interest in structures where "people can gather."

When in 2012, Tremblay interviewed with PMB for a technical draftsman position, he warned the owners Bussières family, that managing him wouldn't be easy. He explained that he needed leaders who practiced what they preached – or as they say in Québécois French, "*Il faut que les bottines suivent les babines*" (the boots must follow the lips).

It didn't take long for Tremblay to confront the owners, pointing out that while the company claimed to uphold certain values, its actual practices exposed a different story. "Put your house in order," he said. That evening, he told his wife, "I need to update my résumé. I think I'll be fired tomorrow." He wasn't. But this pattern repeated itself time and again – until, in 2017, Steve Bussières, who had since become the sole owner of PMB, offered Tremblay the opportunity to lead the company's transformation into a liberated company.

In Chapter 8, we discussed how hundreds of companies across French-speaking countries, including Canada, embraced this philosophy to transform themselves. But at the time, Tremblay had never heard of it. Bussières simply sent him a YouTube link. "That was the extent of my instructions," Tremblay recalled with a smile. "But I accepted."

His first step? Spending six months on the frontline. "I needed to understand their reality – their needs, their hopes, their joys, and their frustrations."

At the time, PMB had an aspirational vision: "To take care of our clients, employees, and the company." But as Tremblay often reminded the owner and his colleagues, the real challenge is to put these aspirations into practice. To turn it into reality – and to implement the liberated company philosophy, which is fundamentally about unconditional care for employees – he drew on an approach he had developed in graduate school: "love in action."

This may sound unusual, even out of place in a corporate setting. But in practice, it meant equipping employees with tools to engage in meaningful dialogue, to use what he called "conscious communication." Unlike many executives, who dictate what needs to change, Tremblay firmly believed that PMB's employees were the ones who knew best what should be transformed. He began asking his colleagues, "What would help you do your work better?" or even, "If you dared to really listen to your heart, what part of your work would you want to change?" His role was to facilitate the implementation of his colleagues' ideas. Over time, this approach became embedded in the company's culture, with every team conducting a 15-minute daily meeting to discuss the needs of each team member, of the team, of the company, and of the clients.

An operator, Jocelyn Fortier, immediately embraced the emerging workplace culture. In his previous jobs, he had experienced both extremes: a rigid environment – what he described as a "prison," where even the shopfloor bathrooms were locked outside of break times and Halloween candies were banned because unwrapping them "wasted work time" – transformed into a care- and trust-based culture.[33] A new plant general manager (GM) would walk the shopfloor every morning, greeting employees with a genuine "How are you?" and often recalling a family concern or a movie discussed days before.

As Fortier's trust in the GM grew, he approached him with a serious issue. The GM's response surprised him:

> You're asking me to make a decision. The only decision I'll make is to trust you. You're the one who knows this best. When you find the solution, come back – we'll celebrate it together.

"It took four or five months," Fortier recounted, "but it completely transformed the company."

He saw the same kind of leadership in Tremblay and told him early on: "Caring for people, showing them love – that speaks to me." Fortier concluded in our interview:

> I love taking care of people – and I love when people take care of me too ... I've never met anyone who didn't appreciate that. Sure, some people didn't connect with the company and chose to leave – but even then, they felt well-treated, and that mattered to them ... Just because we're a business doesn't mean we can't be human.

Fast forward to 2019, together with PMB's finance director, Tremblay led the development of a comprehensive financial dashboard, which they saw as "a tool to empower [all employees] and to set meaningful goals – if we truly wanted to take care." Addressing his team, he emphasized: "We need to be both functional and efficient. If we go bankrupt, we won't be able to work together or take care of our clients." However, his focus was never on financial goals but rather on working together to enhance efficiency and allowing PMB, as a result, to share its success with employees, clients, and partners.

This approach also led to challenging conversations with some clients and suppliers. While it's easy to see what PMB might discuss with its suppliers, it may be less obvious how it could push back on clients. Tremblay explained:

> The clients we retained had to bring us joy. We needed to genuinely appreciate their purpose and the products they created. That's why we only work on projects we truly believe in and collaborate with partners who share our commitment to people and the environment – ideally, both.

As an oblique result, existing clients increased their orders, while new clients, drawn by word-of-mouth, began approaching PMB on their own. And these were just some of the indirect benefits.

In 2020, despite the challenges of COVID-19, PMB had its best year yet and, for the first time, shared its profits. At the end of December, through an equivalent of an American 401(k) plan, employees – regardless of salary level – each received a little over $4,000.

By 2024, with a 120-person workforce, PMB had distributed nearly $700,000 to its employees.

Considering this journey, Tremblay said:

> People now have the opportunity to better prepare for retirement or pursue projects they never thought they could afford. That brings me immense joy … And we haven't forgotten our sole shareholder in all this – he's never made as much money in his life.

But all these oblique financial rewards – and taking care of the owner as discussed in Chapter 6 – came from PMB making a difference for its clients, suppliers, and the local community though its unconditional care for them, and for PMB's employees. As Tremblay expressed it:

> Local businesses and organizations can make a huge, tangible difference and witness the results of their contributions. [For] a renovation company … it's incredibly rewarding to see before-and-after images of completed projects. It improves the daily lives of different families. It creates beauty. A cleaning service … relieves busy people and enhances the comfort of their homes. A bakery? It ultimately creates happiness! The scent of fresh bread in the morning, the line of customers selecting pastries, the smiles …

As he reflected on his life choices and PMB's broader aspirations, Tremblay concluded:

> My choice remains to get involved and take action locally – by building or shaping organizations that are visible and deeply rooted. To see and know the people I work with. To learn to love them, and to allow myself to be transformed by that relation. To be a direct witness to the fruits of our collective effort …

I want us to reinvent work and life within organizations as something fundamentally human … I hope the path we're exploring here at PMB, in such a tangible and local way, inspires others. I hope we're proving that doing things differently – and with love – actually works.[34]

YOU CAN CARE TODAY

PMB's story shows that becoming a genuinely caring company is both possible and challenging. This PMB owner's WHY of social innovation was highly important but simple declarations and even sincere intentions are not enough. A leader willing and able to transform a transaction-based, profit-driven business into a caring company must step up. PMB's owner was willing to transform his company but – to his credit – acknowledged that he was unable to do so himself. Instead, he entrusted a subordinate – Tremblay – who showed the potential for necessary leadership and became the WHO of social innovation. Moreover, once he installed Tremblay as a leader, Bussières was wise enough to step aside. In doing so, he also transformed himself – not into a transformational leader, but into someone who enabled another to fulfill that role.

This transformation was not easy – for the owner, for Tremblay, or for his colleagues. It was difficult because any transformation inevitably encounters myriad challenges – especially when the WHAT of social innovation involves a bundle of mutually supportive measures rather than a one-off silver bullet. Yet together, they proved that it was possible.

It is possible for your company too.

The real question is: Does your company have a choice? More broadly, can we – as participants in today's capitalist system – afford to continue with business as usual? Specifically, can we sustain businesses that are purely transactional and profit-driven?

Sustainability is a popular corporate buzzword, but true sustainability, and true prosperity, seem to demand that we rebuild our businesses on the basis of caring relationships that are oriented toward the benefit – rather than the exploitation – of clients, suppliers, and local communities.

We have shown in this book how caring companies offer a viable alternative to conventional business practices.

By transforming their core processes to prioritize unconditional care for their clients, suppliers, and host communities, these companies reaped the loyalty of the first, the dedication of the second, and the goodwill of the third. The result of this approach was financial prosperity – not as a primary goal, but as a natural consequence.

The diverse range of caring companies we've explored – small, medium-sized, and large; industrial, retail, and service-based; private and public; operating across North America, Europe, and Asia – demonstrate that this alternative, successful way of doing business is possible. They define success as committing to the good of those they interact with daily, betting that such unconditional care will ultimately be rewarded with prosperity. They operate within what we saw as being the "window of vitality" – a synthesis between the relational depth of early eye-to-eye capitalism and the operational efficiency of modern business practices.

As human beings, we are built to care. As we saw in Chapter 3, early anthropological evidence shows that caring for others has both psychological and survival benefits for those who care. But we've created an economic system that far too often seems to punish rather than reward this fundamental drive. The companies and leaders in this book have shown that there is a different way and that a business does not need to forsake the focus on financial results to take this better, more natural path.

To the contrary, the caring companies in this book are outcompeting their peers already. But status quo bias is strong, and the establishment always resists new approaches until they can no longer be ignored. The capitalist "system" won't fix itself.

Whoever you are – a business owner or a simple employee, a student or an academic, a public servant or an investor – you can join this movement toward a caring, heart-to-heart economy. You can take action now, exactly wherever you are. By bringing true care into your business dealings, your relations with colleagues, customers, suppliers, and members of host communities you may well trigger the tipping point – the moment where, together, we will transform our economic paradigm for the benefit of all.

Don't wait. The evidence is unmistakable, the need is urgent, and the time is now. We can build an economy based on true caring. It starts with each of us. It starts with you.

WHAT'S NEXT?

If you would like to join the caring company's global community of practice and are interested in receiving regular updates, please visit the book's website:

www.thecaringcompanybook.com

There, you will find guidance on how to deepen your understanding of what it takes to become a caring company – and how to connect with purpose-driven leaders like yourself.

NOTES

INTRODUCTION

1. See Maddison, A. (1991). *Dynamic Forces in Capitalist Development*. Oxford: Oxford University Press; and Maddison, A. (2004, August). Contours of the world economy and the art of macro-measurement 1500–2001. *Ruggles Lecture, IARIW 28th General Conference, Cork, Ireland.*
2. See the French economic historian Anne Fontaine's major analysis: Fontaine, A. (2014). *Le Marché: Histoire et Usages d'une Conquête Sociale* [The Market: History and Uses of a Social Conquest]. Paris: Gallimard.
3. The 2016 Deloitte Millennial Survey. Deloitte. https://www2.deloitte.com/content/dam/Deloitte/global/Documents/About-Deloitte/gx-millenial-survey-2016-exec-summary.pdf (accessed 10 July 2025).
4. Gen Zs and millennials at work. Deloitte. https://www.deloitte.com/us/en/insights/topics/talent/2025-gen-z-millennial-survey.html (accessed 10 July 2025).
5. The business of building a better world: Global CEOs' priorities for a more sustainable future. Wall Street Journal Intelligence Survey for NTT. https://partners.wsj.com/ntt/vision-for-a-sustainable-future/the-business-of-building-a-better-world/ (accessed 18 November 2024).
6. 2023 Gen Z and Millennial Survey. Deloitte. https://www2.deloitte.com/content/dam/Deloitte/global/Documents/deloitte-2023-genz-millennial-survey.pdf (accessed 10 July 2025).

CHAPTER 1

1. Crainer, S. Peter Drucker: From Vienna to Qingdao, Thinkers50, https://thinkers50.com/blog/peter-drucker-from-vienna-to-qingdao/ (accessed 4 June 2025).
2. The description of Owen's life and activities is partially based on Owen, R. (1857). *The Life of Robert Owen, Written by Himself.* http://www.robert-owen-museum.org.uk/manchester (accessed 18 December 2017); New Lanark Trust (2012). *The Story of Robert Owen*; Harrison, J. F. C. (1972). Robert Owen's quest for the new moral world in America. In D. Pitzer (ed.), *Robert Owen's American Legacy: Proceedings of the Robert Owen Bicentennial Conference.* Indianapolis: Indiana Historical Society; Simon, O. (2017). *Robert Owen's Experiment at New Lanark.* London: Palgrave MacMillan. Finally, the description includes the observations from our visit at New Lanark in January 2018.
3. To determine Owen's historical incomes – or the incomes of his businesses – for the present moment, we apply an income/wealth deflator, encompassing wages, profits, and asset values. Specifically, we select the real wage/real wealth value of that historical income; selecting the relative to GDP income value would require to multiply the real wage/real wealth value by 15. See www.measuringworth.com/ukcompare.
4. For example, the maximum average workweek is 48 hours in the UK and Germany and is 52 hours in South Korea.
5. Owen, R. (1813–1814). *A New View of Society: Or, Essays on the Principle of the Formation of the Human Character, and the Application of the Principle to Practice.* London: Cadell and Davies.
6. Sinek, S. (2009). *Start with Why.* New York: Penguin Business.
7. Carney, B. M. and Getz, I. (2009/2016). *Freedom, Inc.* New York: Crown Business (revised edition 2016).
8. Understanding the limitations of such forecasting doesn't mean that budgeting – the process of envisioning financial resources required for the year ahead – is useless. However, it is often done on a fixed date of the year and based on various assumptions – bets – about the next year's economic and geopolitical realities. Moreover, traditional budgeting serves as a top-down control tool, which can lead to a lack of accountability and demotivation among the controlled managers. Alternatives such as the Beyond Budgeting Round Table approach offer the benefits of budgeting while avoiding its pitfalls.
9. Kay, J. (2010). *Obliquity: Why Our Goals Are Best Achieved Indirectly.* London: Profile Books; Kay, J. (2012). Obliquity. *Capitalism and Society* 7(1).

10. Wooden, J. and Jamison, S. (2007). *The Essential Wooden: A Lifetime of Lessons on Leaders and Leadership*. New York: McGraw-Hill, p. 33.
11. Ibid., p. 140.
12. Xu, H. and Ruef, M. (2005). The myth of the risk-tolerant entrepreneur. *Strategic Organization* 2(4): 331–355. https://doi.org/10.1177/1476127004047617.
13. Kawasaki, G. (2004). *The Art of the Start: The Time-Tested, Battle-Hardened Guide for Anyone Starting Anything*. New York: Portfolio, p. 40.
14. Sarasvathy, S. D. (2001). Causation and effectuation: Toward a theoretical shift from economic inevitability to entrepreneurial contingency. *Academy of Management Review* 26(2): 243–263.
15. Lohr, S. (2011, January 18). Can Apple find more hits without its tastemaker? *New York Times*. https://www.cnbc.com/2011/01/18/can-apple-find-more-hits-without-its-tastemaker.html (accessed 13 January 2025).
16. Zachary, G. P. and Yamada, K. (1993, May 25). What's next? Steve Jobs's vision, so on target at Apple, now is falling short. *Wall Street Journal*.
17. Speech to Decathlon employees in Villeneuve-d'Ascq, France on 28 November 2017. We used ChatGPT-4o to translate all the French texts in this book, except where an official translation already existed. We then further reviewed the translations in collaboration with several of the book's editors.
18. Combs, J., Liu, Y., Hall, A. et al. (2006). How much do high-performance work practices matter? A meta-analysis of their effects on organizational performance. *Personnel Psychology* 59(3): 501–528; Huselid, M. A. (1995). The impact of human resource management practices on turnover, productivity, and corporate financial performance. *Academy of Management Journal* 38: 635–672; Ichniowski, C., Kochan, T. A., Levine, D. et al. (1996). What works at work: Overview and assessment. *Industrial Relations* 35(3): 299–333; MacDuffie, J. P. (1995). Human resource bundles and manufacturing performance: Organizational logic and flexible production systems in the world auto industry. *Industrial and Labor Relations Review* 48: 197–221.
19. Ichniowski et al., ibid., p. 319; emphasis of the authors.
20. Hastings, R. and Meyer, E. (2020). *No Rules Rules: Netflix and the Culture of Reinvention*. New York: Penguin Press.
21. Caredda, S. (2020, September 13). Netflix culture deck. https://sergiocaredda.eu/inspiration/netflix-culture-deck (accessed October 31, 2024).
22. Kahneman, D. and Deaton, A. (2010). High income improves evaluation of life but not emotional well-being. *Proceedings of the National Academy of Sciences* 107(38): 16489–16493. https://doi.org/10.1073/pnas.1011492107.

23. Rosenblatt, L. (2022, December 25). Seattle celebrity CEO Dan Price's rise and fall at Gravity Payments. *Seattle Times.* https://www.seattletimes.com/business/seattle-celebrity-ceo-dan-prices-rise-and-fall-at-gravity-payments/ (accessed 1 November 2024). Further post-2022 Gravity issues we evoke also come from this investigative report with 40 people close to Gravity or Price.

24. Wooden and Jamison, pp. 125–126.

25. O'Toole, J. (2019). *The Enlightened Capitalists: Cautionary Tales of Business Pioneers Who Tried to Do Well by Doing Good.* Harper Business, p. 427. Most of these cases have not endured beyond the tenure of the original leader at the helm of the company. However, effectiveness, as we define it, is not synonymous with the sustainability of specific organizational practices. Corporate observers recognize that a large portion of incoming CEOs initiate "reorganizations," and if they do not, their boards often demand them. Companies with innovative social practices are no exception to this rule. Yet, when social measures fail to persist after a leadership change, it does not imply they were ineffective. Consider UCLA's basketball legacy: after John Wooden's departure, the team won only one additional championship, and that was 20 years later. This, however, does not negate the impact of the innovations Wooden introduced during his tenure. His innovations were undeniably effective, as evidenced by UCLA's unprecedented 10 championships in 12 years – a record that continues to inspire generations of coaches.

CHAPTER 2

1. Hock, D. (2005). *One from Many.* San Francisco: Berrett-Koehler, pp. 140–141.

2. Ibid., pp. 141–142.

3. Much of this section owes to Latapí Agudelo, M. A., Jóhannsdóttir, L., and Davídsdóttir, B. (2019). A literature review of the history and evolution of corporate social responsibility. *International Journal of Corporate Social Responsibility* 4(1): 1–23. https://doi.org/10.1186/s40991-018-0039-y.

4. Caiazza, S., Galloppo, G., and Lattanzio, G. (2023). Industrial accidents: the mediating effect of corporate social responsibility and environmental policy measures. *Corporate Social Responsibility and Environmental Management* 30(3): 1191–1203.

5. The limits to growth. Wikipedia. https://en.wikipedia.org/wiki/The_Limits_to_Growth (accessed 11 November 2024).

6. Utz, S. (2019). Corporate scandals and the reliability of ESG assessments: evidence from an international sample. *Review of Managerial Science* 13(2): 483–511.

7. Richardson, K., Steffen, W., Lucht, W. et al. (2023). Earth beyond six of nine planetary boundaries. *Science Advances* 9(37): eadh2458. https://doi.org/10.1126/sciadv.adh2458.

8. According to a 2024 Gallup survey, among 17 US institutions, only 6% of Americans express a "great deal of confidence" in big business – ranking it above only television news and Congress. Interestingly, small businesses receive the highest level of public confidence among all institutions, ranking just ahead of the military and police. https://news.gallup.com/poll/647303/confidence-institutions-mostly-flat-police.aspx (accessed 19 November 2024). See also our discussion in Chapter 3 "The Virtues of Local Government" section.

9. Wilson, J. and Melero, D. (2024). Spain flood survivors hurl mud at the royals and top government officials. AP. https://apnews.com/article/spain-floods-king-protest-mud-a8525bd82cf4cc3fc6273d535cbb9d66 (accessed 19 November 2024).

10. Latapí Agudelo, M.A., Jóhannsdóttir, L., and Davídsdóttir, B. (2019).

11. Paris Agreement. Wikipedia. https://en.wikipedia.org/wiki/Paris_Agreement (accessed 25 October 2024).

12. Bowen, H. (1953). *Social Responsibilities of the Businessman*. New York: Harper & Brothers, p. 6.

13. Friedman, M. (1962). *Capitalism and Freedom*. Chicago: University of Chicago Press.

14. Friedman, M. (1970). A Friedman doctrine – The social responsibility of business is to increase its profits. *New York Times*. https://www.nytimes.com/1970/09/13/archives/a-friedman-doctrine-the-social-responsibility-of-business-is-to.html (accessed 10 October 2024).

15. Schiller, B. (2024, March 19). The most innovative corporate social responsibility companies in 2024. *Fast Company*. https://www.fastcompany.com/91038535/corporate-social-responsibility-most-innovative-companies-2024 (accessed 11 November 2024).

16. Elkington, J. (1997). *Partnerships from Cannibals with Forks: The Triple Bottom Line of 21st-century Business*. Oxford: Capstone Publishing Limited.

17. Chandler, D. and Werther Jr., W. B., (2005). Strategic Corporate Social Responsibility as global brand insurance. *Business Horizons* 48(3): 267–276.

18. Porter, M. E. and Kramer, M. R. (2011). Creating shared value. *Harvard Business Review* 89(1–2): 62–77.

19. Schwab, K. and Kroos, H. (1971). *Moderne Unternehmensführung im Maschinenbau.* Frankfurt am Main: Maschinenbau-Verlag.
20. This notion would be developed later by Freeman, R. E., Martin, K., and Parmar, B. (2007). Stakeholder capitalism. *Journal of Business Ethics* 74(4): 303–314.
21. Schwab, K. and Vanham, P. (2021). *Stakeholder Capitalism: A Global Economy that Works for Progress, People, and Planet.* New York: Wiley.
22. Freeman, R. E. (1984). *Strategic Management: A Stakeholder Approach.* Boston: Pitman.
23. The state of stakeholder capitalism with Edward Freeman, the "father" of the movement. YouTube. https://youtu.be/n2VgTTGMFMo?feature= shared&t=429 (accessed 8 November 2024).
24. There is more to say about stakeholder capitalism (SC) than this book space allows. We have described Schwab's view of SC, as the most dominating one. However, there are other SC conceptions. For example, Freeman views SC as a management approach, while Bebchuk and Tallarita view it as a governance imperative. It is also interesting to note that while Schwab calls corporations simply to engage stakeholders, Freeman calls them to create as much value as possible for stakeholders. Our interpretation of SC is close to Freeman's, that is we consider that SC calls to maximize each stakeholder's value through the change of the ways the company is managed. This SC view is similar to the balancing approaches of TBL and of B-Corps (see following text). We thank Peter Vanham for his ideas on the different conceptions of SC.
25. Weinrebgroup (2021, May 18). Hiring of chief sustainability officers surged in 2020; rise in women, little diversity. https://weinrebgroup.com/hiring-of-chief-sustainability-officers-surged-in-2020-rise-in-women-little-diversity/ (accessed 21 October 2024).
26. Grewal, J., and Serafeim, G. (2020). Research on corporate sustainability: Review and directions for future research. *Foundations and Trends in Accounting* 14(2): 73–127. http://dx.doi.org/10.2139/ssrn.3687330
27. Building the Movement. B Corporation. https://www.bcorporation.net/en-us/movement/ (accessed 7 October 2024).
28. Danone North America. B Corporation. https://www.bcorporation.net/en-us/find-a-b-corp/company/danone-north-america/ (accessed October 8, 2024).
29. Measuring a company's entire social and environmental impact. B Corporation. https://www.bcorporation.net/en-us/certification/ (accessed 7 October 2024).

30. Ibid.
31. In particular, the 1919 *Dodge v. Ford Motor Co.* decision often cited as establishing the principle of shareholder primacy, is frequently portrayed as restricting executives from making decisions that do not directly maximize shareholder interests. However, in subsequent legal actions against corporate management, this seminal case has rarely served as a binding legal precedent. US courts have largely upheld executives' discretion to consider broader stakeholder interests, provided such decisions are made in good faith and align with the corporation's overall best interests. For further discussion, see Blount, J. and Offei-Danso, K. (2012). The Benefit Corporation: A questionable solution to a non-existent problem. *St. Mary's Law Journal* 44: 617–670; Reiser, D. B. and Dean, S. A. (2017). *Social Enterprise Law: Trust, Public Benefit, and Capital Markets*. Oxford: Oxford University Press.
32. World Economic Forum, Stakeholder Metrics Initiative. https://www.weforum.org/stakeholdercapitalism/our-community/ (accessed 30 October 2024).
33. US SIF Foundation, Report on US Sustainable and Impact Investing Trends, 2020 quoted by Larcker, D. F., Tayan, B., and Watts, E. M. (2022). Seven myths of ESG. *European Financial Management* 28(4): 869–882.
34. KPMG, The numbers that are changing the world. https://assets.kpmg.com/content/dam/kpmg/ie/pdf/2019/10/ie-numbers-that-are-changing-the-world.pdf (accessed 7 October 2024).
35. Nelson, M. (2024, February 23) Responsible investment funds tripled in size in the decade to 2022. *PA Future.* https://future.portfolio-adviser.com/responsible-investment-funds-tripled-in-size-in-the-decade-to-2022/ (accessed 7 October 2024).
36. Prahalad, C. K. and Hammond, A. (2002). Serving the world's poor, profitably. *Harvard Business Review* 80(9): 48–57.
37. Mackey, J. (2011). What conscious capitalism really is. *California Management Review* 53 (3): 83–90; Mackey, J. and Sisodia, R. (2013). *Conscious Capitalism: Liberating the Heroic Spirit of Business*. Boston: Harvard Business Review Press.
38. Capitalism can be a powerful force for good. Conscious Capitalism. https://www.consciouscapitalism.org/mission-and-vision (accessed 9 October 2024).
39. Bird, A. (2009, October 1). McKinsey conversations with global leaders: Paul Polman of Unilever. *McKinsey Quarterly*, p. 9.
40. Purpose of a Corporation. Business Roundtable https://opportunity.businessroundtable.org/ourcommitment (accessed 8 October 2024).

41. Fink, L. (2022). The Power of Capitalism. BlackRock. https://www.blackrock. com/corporate/investor-relations/larry-fink-ceo-letter (accessed 8 October 2024).

42. Ibid.

43. Elkington, J. (2018, June 25). 25 years ago I coined the phrase "Triple Bottom Line." Here's why it's time to rethink it. *Harvard Business Review*. https://hbr. org/2018/06/25-years-ago-i-coined-the-phrase-triple-bottom-line-heres-why-im-giving-up-on-it (accessed 8 October 2024).

44. Ibid.

45. ORPEA: Further very strong growth in activity in Q3 2021. Businesswire. https://www.businesswire.com/news/home/20211103005912/en/ORPEA-Further-Very-Strong-Growth-in-Activity-in-Q3-2021 (accessed 11 November 2024).

46. Castanet, V. (2022). *Les Fossoyeurs : Révélations sur le Système qui Maltraite nos Aînés*. Paris: Fayard.

47. Larcker, D. F., Tayan, B., and Watts, E. (2021, November 4). Seven myths of ESG. Rock Center for Corporate Governance at Stanford University.

48. Atz, U., Van Holt, T., Liu, Z. Z. et al. (2022). Does sustainability generate better financial performance? Review, meta-analysis, and propositions. *Journal of Sustainable Finance & Investment* 13(1): 802–825. https://doi.org/10.1080/20430795.2022.2106934.

49. Zobrist, J. F. (2020). L'essentiel du management par la confiance d'un petit patron naïf et paresseux. https://liberteetcie.com/2025/03/zobrist-2 (accessed 17 March 2025).

50. Bebchuk, L. A. and Tallarita, R. (2020). The illusory promise of stakeholder governance. *Cornell Law Review* 106: 91; Bebchuk, L. A. and Tallarita, R. (2022). Will corporations deliver value to all stakeholders? *Vanderbilt Law Review* 75: 1031.

51. Dorff, M. B. (2023). *Becoming a Public Benefit Corporation: Express Your Values, Energize Stakeholders, Make the World a Better Place*. Berrett-Koehler Publishers. https://www.sup.org/books/business/becoming-public-benefit-corporation (accessed 15 January 2025).

52. In 2025, the contribution is over $1000.

53. Martin, R. L. (2010). The age of customer capitalism. *Harvard Business Review* 88(1): 58–65; Martin, R. L. (2011). *Fixing the Game: Bubbles, Crashes, and What Capitalism Can Learn from the NFL*. Boston: Harvard Business Review Press.

54. Beasley, N. (1948). *Main Street Merchant: The Story of the J.C. Penney Company.* New York: McGraw-Hill Book Company, p. 94.
55. Hock, D. (2005). *One from Many.* San Francisco: Berrett-Koehler, p. 142.

CHAPTER 3

1. Char, R. (1979). *Fenêtres dormantes et porte sur le toit.* Paris: Gallimard, p. 578. A leading French poet René Char (1907–1988) stopped writing poetry during World War II to fight in a partisan resistance against the Nazis.
2. Tolstoy, L. (1888). Lucerne. In *A Russian Proprietor, and Other Stories* (trans. Nathan Haskell Dole). New York: Thomas Y. Crowell & Co., p. 117. Apparently, this event did indeed occur, as the narrator encourages the reader to verify the list of those present at the Schweitzerhof on that date by consulting the local newspapers. The Schweitzerhof Hotel still exists. Little has changed in it since the time of the novel, as we observed during our visit there in January 2025.
3. Ibid., pp. 118–119.
4. Dale, B. (2023). *SBF: How the FTX Bankruptcy Unwound Crypto's Very Bad Good Guy.* Wiley.
5. Jaeger, B. and Van Vugt, M. (2022). Psychological barriers to effective altruism: An evolutionary perspective. *Current Opinion in Psychology* 44: 130–134, p. 130. https://doi.org/10.1016/j.copsyc.2021.09.008.
6. Small, D. A. and Loewenstein, G. (2003). Helping a victim or helping the victim: Altruism and identifiability. *Journal of Risk and Uncertainty* 26: 5–16.
7. Burum, B., Nowak, M. A., and Hoffman, M. (2020). An evolutionary explanation for ineffective altruism. *Nature Human Behaviour* 4: 1245–1257.
8. Hardy, C. L. and Van Vugt, M. (2006). Nice guys finish first: The competitive altruism hypothesis. *Personality and Social Psychology Bulletin* 32: 1402–1413.
9. Leading American moral psychologist Jonathan Haidt has explored the intriguing link between autism and utilitarianism in his 2012 book *The Righteous Mind: Why Good People Are Divided by Politics and Religion.* New York, NY: Pantheon Books. He concluded that both autistic individuals and utilitarians tend to be strong systemizers and low empathizers. For example, Jeremy Bentham, the founder of utilitarianism, reportedly exhibited behaviors that would today be considered characteristic of Asperger's syndrome. Furthermore, anecdotal evidence surrounding Sam Bankman-Fried – including his apparent emotional detachment and

obsession with optimization – has led many commentators to speculate about his possible autism, although no public diagnosis has ever been confirmed. Similar traits are often observed in other Silicon Valley archetypes, where a preference for logic, systems-thinking, and radical efficiency sometimes overshadows traditional social cues.

10. Spikins, P. (2017). Prehistoric origins: The compassion of far distant strangers. In P. Gilbert (ed.), *Compassion: Concepts, Research and Applications* (pp. 16–30). London: Routledge, p. 16. The word "weakness" is emphasized by Spikins.

11. Dunbar, R. I. (2014). The social brain: Psychological underpinnings and implications for the structure of organizations. *Current Directions in Psychological Science* 23(2): 109–114.

12. Ibid., p. 110.

13. The exact lines found in Plautus' play *Asinaria* are: "Lupus est homo homini, non homo, quom qualis sit non novit" which means "A man is a wolf rather than a man to another man, when he hasn't yet found out what he's like." The quote suggests that this attitude stems from a fear of the unknown rather than from any alleged innate propensity for violence.

14. This episode is based on the personal interview with Haim Sheffi on 8 February 2015; on his interview in Klare, J. (2014, November 22). Man muss leben weiter, kannst nichts machen. *Frankfurter Allgemeine Sonntagszeitung*. https://www.faz.net/aktuell/gesellschaft/menschen/altenheim-in-haifa-man-muss-leben-weiter-kannst-nichts-machen-13268276.html (accessed 10 April 2025); and on his video interview on 8 January 1998, Survivors of the Shoah Visual History Foundation, Code: 39832-13.

15. Despite Hungary being a Nazi Germany ally and enacting anti-Jewish laws and, since 1941, sending thousands of Jewish men to forced labor camps, its authorities had steadily refused German demands to deport its Jewish population.

16. Deci, E. L. and Ryan, R. M. (1985). *Intrinsic Motivation and Self-Determination in Human Behavior*. New York: Springer US.

17. Marcus, G. (2004). *The Birth of the Mind*. New York: Basic Books.

18. van der Kolk, B. (2014). *The Body Keeps the Score: Brain, Mind, and Body in the Healing of Trauma*. Viking; see also the work of Gabor Maté.

19. Levinas, E. (1995). *Difficile Liberté*. Paris: Albin Michel, pp. 21–22.

20. Stanley Milgram's famous psychological experiment, conducted in the 1960s, provides further evidence to support this concept. In the study, participants were instructed by the lead researcher to administer electric shocks of increasing intensity to a person in another room. Unbeknownst to the participants,

the individual was an actor who did not actually receive shocks. Despite hearing realistic-sounding cries of pain, many participants continued to deliver shocks as instructed, even up to potentially fatal intensities. Interestingly, when the "victim" was in the same room, participants showed greater hesitation in causing harm. This reluctance increased further when they were required to physically interact with the "victim," such as tightening the cables on the individual's wrist at the researcher's direction. These findings highlight the profound impact of physical proximity and human connection on ethical decision-making.

21. Dominique Birman's article, *Le Monde*, 14 December 1957. Following this article, Sartre, who was an unconditional supporter of Algerian independentists, broke up with Camus.

22. Murdoch, I. (1970). *The Sovereignty of Good*. London: Routledge & Kegan Paul.

23. Brooks, D. (2023). *How to Know a Person: The Art of Seeing Others Deeply and Being Deeply Seen*. Random House, p. 38.

24. du Bouchet, A. (1969, winter). Tournant au plus vite le dos au fatras de l'art. *L'Éphémère* 12: 538–550, p. 539.

25. Dostoevsky, F. (1866/1914). *Crime and Punishment* (transl. by Constance Garnett). William Heinemann (published by Planet PDF, http://www.planet-pdf.com), pp. 126–127.

26. Ibid., p. 466.

27. Dostoevsky, F. (1873/1916). *The Possessed* (transl. by Constance Garnett). New York: The Macmillan Company, pp. 421–422.

28. Jones, J. M. (2023, October 13). Americans trust local government most, congress least. Gallup. https://news.gallup.com/poll/512651/americans-trust-local-government-congress-least.aspx (accessed 24 November 2024).

29. Brenan, M. (2024, July 15). U.S. confidence in institutions mostly flat, but police up. Gallup. https://news.gallup.com/poll/647303/confidence-institutions-mostly-flat-police.aspx (accessed 24 November 2024).

30. OECD, Governance. https://www.oecd-ilibrary.org/governance/trust-in-the-local-government-is-usually-higher-than-trust-in-the-regional-and-national-governments_54ca6845-en (accessed 24 November 2024).

31. Brenan, M. (2024, July 15).

32. Lasch, C. (1990, April). Conservatism against itself. *First Things* 2: 17–23.

33. Aristotle. (1998). *Politics* (C. D. C. Reeve, Trans.). Indianapolis: Hackett Publishing, 1261b30–1262a1. (Original work published ca. 350 BCE).

34. Ostrom, E. (1990). *Governing the Commons: The Evolution of Institutions for Collective Action*. Cambridge, UK: Cambridge University Press.

CHAPTER 4

1. Weil, S. and Bousquet, J. (2014). *Correspondance 1942, Quel Est Donc ton Tourment?* Paris: Editions Claire Paulhan.
2. Smith, A. (1776/1976). *An Inquiry into the Nature and Causes of the Wealth of Nations.* London: W. Strahan and T. Cadell, Vol. 1, Book III, Chapter 4. (Oxford University Press, 1976 edition)
3. de Tocqueville, A. (2010). *De la Démocratie en Amérique.* Flammarion, p. 186.
4. Châteauform' is written with an apostrophe at the end of the word, but for simplicity's sake, we have written it Châteauform without the apostrophe in the rest of the book.
5. Ibid., Vol. 1, Book I, Chapter 2.
6. Self-Interest Rightly Understood. https://www.adamsmithworks.org/documents/self-interest-rightly-understood? (accessed on 24 February 2025).
7. Smith, A. *The Theory of Moral Sentiments.* Book 1, Chapter 5.
8. Smith, A. *An Inquiry into the Nature and Causes of the Wealth of Nations.* Vol. 1, Book III, Chapter 4.
9. See for example: Sterelny, K., Joyce, R., Calcott, B. et al. (eds.) (2024). *Cooperation and Its Evolution.* New York: Penguin Random House; Raihanni, N. (2023). *The Social Instinct.* New York: St. Martin's Griffin; and the classic Axelrod, R. (2006). *The Evolution of Cooperation* (revised edition). New York: Basic Books.
10. Servigne, P. and Chapelle, G. (2019). *L'Entraide: L'Autre Loi de la Jungle.* Paris: Les liens qui libèrent.
11. Lecture given at ESCP Business School as part of Isaac Getz's seminar, May 2002, Paris.
12. Kula ring: https://en.wikipedia.org/wiki/Kula_ring (accessed 17 December 2024).
13. Grout, P. (2023). *E-Squared: Nine Do-It-Yourself Energy Experiments That Prove Your Thoughts Create Your Reality* (10th anniversary edition). Carlsbad, CA: Hay House LLC.
14. Bruni, L. (2012). *The Wound and the Blessing: Economics, Relationships, and Happiness.* Hyde Park, NY: New City Press.
15. Brooks, D. (2024). *How to Know a Person: The Art of Seeing Others Deeply and Being Deeply Seen.* New York: Random House, p. 98.
16. Ibid., p. 99.
17. Murdoch, I. (1970). *The Sovereignty of Good.* London: Routledge, p. 36. All subsequent quotes from Murdoch are drawn from this page.

18. In the early 1980s, a philosophical current known as the "ethics of care" emerged with the publication of Carol Gilligan's *In a Different Voice* (1982). It was further developed through the work of Joan Tronto, who, in *Moral Boundaries* (1993), explicitly identified "attentiveness" as the first moral element of care.

19. Grant, A. (2013). *Give and Take: Why Helping Others Drives Our Success*. New York: Viking Penguin; Grant, A. (2013). In the company of givers and takers. *Harvard Business Review* 91(4): 90–97; Grant, A. (2013, April). Givers take all: The hidden dimension of corporate culture. *The McKinsey Quarterly*.

20. Video interview with Chris Mittelstaedt, 23 April 2025.

CHAPTER 5

1. A line from an essay *Genshi Shiroku* by this late Edo-period Confucianist is quoted by Haruo Naito, Eisai President in Eisai (2010). *hhc Book: Blue Book*, internal Eisai document, Eisai Knowledge Creation Department, p. 8.

2. Eisai. (2010). *hhc Book: Blue Book*, p. 55. The rest of Naito's quotes from this speech are on the same page 55.

3. "Human health care" is a pioneering approach to nursing practices conceived in the mid-nineteenth century by a British nurse Florence Nightingale. Nightingale advocated for compassionate and personalized care that respected the dignity of patients, addressing not just disease but the overall well-being of individuals. Eisai not only took Nightingale term for their own corporate vision, but also her handwritten in small letters *hhc* as its logo.

4. By the term "vision" we intendedly express here only one aspect of what authors like Collins and Porras identify as such: an inspiring purpose, a dream destination, ideal final state the leader and the company seek to reach (Collins, J. C. and Porras, J. I. (1994). *Built to Last: Successful Habits of Visionary Companies*. Harper Business). This type of corporate visions is usually expressed in one inspiring sentence such as "Relieving the suffering of patients and their families" for Naito and Eisai, "Making a small dent in the universe" for Steve Jobs and Apple, or "To organize the world's information and make it universally accessible and useful" for Google. A company having a vision is not necessarily a caring company, but all caring companies have an inspiring vision.

5. Personal interview, 22 April 2016.

6. The emphasis on the shame can be traced back to medieval Japan, but also reflects the heritage of Chinese religious traditions. As Hesna Cailliau explains: "In all societies influenced by Chinese culture, as opposed to the

Judeo-Christian tradition, the principal source of unhappiness is not guilt but shame, the fear of social judgment, of dishonoring one's family." (Cailliau, H. (2015). *Le Paradoxe du Poisson Rouge: Une Voie Chinoise pour Réussir*. Paris: Éditions Saint-Simon, pp. 97–98).

7. Eisai. (2010). *hhc Book: Blue Book*, p. 199.

8. This story is borrowed from Carney, B. M. and Getz, I. *Freedom, Inc.*

9. Le Cunff, A.-L. (2025). *Tiny Experiments*. Avery, p. 17.

10. Godart, F., Henry, B., and Berrada, M. (2017). Biscuits Poult SAS: Can alternative organizational designs be successful? *INSEAD Case Study* 12/2017-6332. https://publishing.insead.edu/case/biscuits-poult (accessed 1 December 2024).

11. In psychological research, a potential hypothesis could be that such leaders possess a lower threshold for questioning the alignment between their beliefs and actions.

12. Ellis, R. D. (1996). *Eros in a Narcissistic Culture: An Analysis Anchored in the Life World*. Dordrecht: Kluwer Academic, pp. 131–132.

13. Of course, this suggestion does not apply to emergencies. One such emergency is a breach of a company's behavioral norms, such as publicly disrespecting someone or lying. In such cases, everyone expects a caring leader to take swift action. Paradoxically, traditional leaders who act swiftly to address business problems often procrastinate when it comes to people problems – allowing bad apples to poison the barrel.

14. This idea as applied to business has been first formulated by a French business philosopher Jean-Christian Fauvet. His ideas will be further explored later in this chapter.

15. It is often said that leaders need to spend a major effort to share and get the buy-in for their vision. From our observation to over a hundred corporate transformations, it may be true for visions-strategies involving rational objectives and timelines. However, from our experience, when leaders share inspiring visions aligned with their own values, such visions resonate well with the majority of their associates.

16. Fauvet, J.-C. (2004). *L'Elan Sociodynamique*. Paris: Éditions d'Organisation, p. 107.

17. Tremblay, D. (2024). *Pour Arrêter de se Tuer à l'Ouvrage* [To Stop Working Yourself to Death], unpublished book, p. 173.

18. "To get it done" may be one name for this habit. An alternative name is what the leading coaching thinker Marshall Goldsmith calls "Telling the world how smart you are," that is overly showcasing your intelligence or expertise. It is usually related to the inflated ego issues. If you have such an urge to climb to the stage, it may be a good topic to work on yourself or with a coach.

19. Levinas, *Difficile Liberté*, op. cit., pp. 204–205.
20. Zobrist, J.-F. (2022). *Ce que l'entreprise libérée doit à Jean-Christian Fauvet* (unpublished), p. 79.
21. Wooden, J. and Jamison, S., p. 88.
22. This case is taken from Getz, I. and Robinson, A. G. (2003). *Vos Idées Changent Tout!* Paris: Eyrolles. See also, Getz, I. and Robinson, A. G. (2003). Innovate or die: Is that a fact? *Creativity and Innovation Management* 12: 130–136.
23. To identify every other work practice that prevented people from doing their best, Townsend and AVIS managers were asking questions such as: "What made you mad today?", "What took too long?", "What was misunderstood today?", "What costs too much?", "What was wasted", "What was too complicated?", "What's just plain silly?", "What job took too many people, and what job involved too many actions?" Townsend explained that you don't ask all people all those questions. You try one on one person, then move to another area and try another question on another person. Acting on these questions allowed to realize the "We try harder" vision (see Carney and Getz, *Freedom, Inc.*, pp. 153–154).
24. Goldsmith, M. (2007). *What Got You Here Won't Get You There*. Grand Central Publishing.
25. Wooden and Jamison, p. 168.
26. Wooden and Jamison, p. 43.
27. Goldsmith, M. Recognizing your needs. https://marshallgoldsmith.com/articles/recognizing-your-needs/ (accessed 1 December 2024).
28. Kegan, R. and Lahey, L. L. (2009). *Immunity to Change: How to Overcome It and Unlock the Potential in Yourself and Your Organization*. Boston, MA: Harvard Business Review Press.
29. Xavier Huillard presentation at Peter Drucker Global Forum, 29 November 2018, Vienna, Austria.
30. Kegan and Lahey, *Immunity to Change*.
31. Kegan, R. and Lahey, L. L. (2001). The real reason people won't change. *Harvard Business Review* 79(10): 85–92.
32. Hardy, C. L. and Van Vugt, M. (2006). Nice guys finish first: The competitive altruism hypothesis. *Personality and Social Psychology Bulletin* 32: 1402–1413.
33. Ibid., 1412.
34. Deci, E. L. and Ryan, R. M. (1985). *Intrinsic Motivation and Self-determination in Human Behavior*. New York: Plenum Press.
35. Wooden and Jamison, p. 88.
36. Eisai. (2010). *hhc Book: Blue Book*, p. 16. The following quotes from Matsuno are taken from the pp. 16–19.

37. Taylor, M. J., Hoerauf, A., and Bockarie, M. (2010). Lymphatic filariasis and onchocerciasis. *The Lancet* 376 (9747): 1175–1185.
38. Each person requires between 6 and 12 tablets for a complete treatment course. For 2.5 billon tablets, the range of individuals is thus between 170.8 million and 341.7 million.
39. Largest Companies by Marketcap: Eisai. https://companiesmarketcap.com/eisai/revenue/ (accessed 12 December 2024).
40. Brooks, D. (2023). *How to Know a Person.*

CHAPTER 6

1. Lavelle, L. (2004). *Règles de la Vie Quotidienne.* Paris: Arfuyen, pp. 78 and 119.
2. Stubbart, C. I. and Knight, M. B. (2006). The case of the disappearing firms: Empirical evidence and implications. *Journal of Organizational Behavior* 27: 79–100.
3. *Handelsbanken Annual and Sustainability Report 2023*, p. 5.
4. Wallander, J. (2003). *Decentralisation: Why and How to Make it Work.* Stockholm: SNS Förlag, p. 111.
5. Ibid., p. 102. More on the "Beyond budgeting" approach can be found at www. bbrt.org.
6. Wallander, J. *Decentralisation*, pp. 38–39.
7. *Handelsbanken Annual and Sustainability Report 2023*, p. 5.
8. Ibid., p. 1.
9. *Financial Times* magazine *The Banker.* https://www.handelsbanken.co.uk/en/about-us/press-and-media/news/handelsbanken-wins-bank-of-the-year (accessed 30 December 2024).
10. Ranked top for customer satisfaction. Handelsbanken. https://www.handelsbanken.co.uk/en/satisfaction-survey (accessed 14 August 2025).
11. Global finance names the world's 50 safest commercial banks 2024. Global Finance. https://s44650.pcdn.co/wp-content/uploads/2024/10/Safest-Banks-2024-50-Safest-Commercial-Banks-GFMAG.pdf (accessed 30 December 2024).
12. Quick facts about Handelsbanken. Handelsbanken. https://www.handelsbanken.com/en/press-and-media/quick-facts (accessed 30 December 2024).
13. Nylander, J. (2009, September 7). World's best stock share is Swedish. *Swedish Wire.* https://www.swedishwire.com/business/902-worlds-best-stock-share-is-swedish (accessed 30 December 2024).

14. Wallander, J. *Decentralisation*, p. 24.
15. Ibid., p. 133.
16. Ibid., p. 23.
17. Ibid., p. 26.
18. In the 1960s, when Wallander became familiar with the literature of motivational psychology, the current leading theory of motivation by Deci and Ryan, mentioned in Chapter 5, had not been yet developed. Although Deci and Ryan's three empirically established universal needs – relatedness, competence, and autonomy – are slightly different from Maslow's postulated higher needs – belonging, self-esteem, and self-fulfillment – the key logic is the same. Without satisfaction of these universal needs, humans will not be motivated to act to advance a company's vision. Like McGregor before them, Deci and Ryan have also established empirically the link between the type of managerial organization and employees' satisfaction of their universal needs: "field studies in ... organizations ... show[ed] in real-world settings that providing autonomy support, relative to control, was associated with more positive outcomes, including greater intrinsic motivation, increased satisfaction, and enhanced well-being" (Deci, E. L. and Ryan, R. M. (2000). The "what" and "why" of goal pursuits: Human needs and the self-determination of behavior. *Psychological Inquiry* 11(4): 227–268, p. 234).
19. Wallander, J. *Decentralisation*, p. 37.
20. Ibid., p. 38.
21. Weil, S. (1949/2014). *L'Enracinement : Prélude à une Déclaration des Devoirs Envers l'Etre Humain*. Paris: Flammarion, pp. 86–87 (our translation).
22. Ibid., p. 89.
23. Handelsbanken removes CEO due to culture clash. EuropeanCEO. https://www.europeanceo.com/business-and-management/handelsbanken-removes-ceo-due-to-culture-clash/ (accessed 12 July 2025).
24. Personal interview, 5 May 2017.
25. Personal communication, 15 August 2025.
26. Wallander, J. *Decentralisation*, p. 133.
27. Our history. Handelsbanken. https://www.handelsbanken.com/en/about-the-group/our-story (accessed 3 January 2025).
28. Our history. Reitan Retail. https://www.reitanretail.no/en/about/our-history (accessed 4 January 2025).
29. See on this topic Segall, K. (2012). *Insanely Simple: The Obsession That Drives Apple's Success*. New York: Portfolio.
30. Personal interview, 4 May 2017.
31. Wallander, J. *Decentralisation*, p. 137.

32. Personal interview, 2 May 2017.

33. Talk at Réseau Oudinot on 21 October 2021, https://youtu.be/I60Viw8tiZ8 (accessed 20 January 2025). In our observation, the CEO of a company facing acquisition often holds a particularly strong position, as a significant share of the company's value lies in the strength of its executive team – beginning with the CEO.

CHAPTER 7

1. Personal interview, 5 May 2017.

2. Sheff, D. (1985, February). Interview: Steven Jobs – candid conversation. *Playboy* 32(2): 49–184, p. 184.

3. Ibid.

4. Ibid.

5. Personal disclosure: While one of us is an enthusiastic supporter of Apple, the other refrains from using Apple devices. Nonetheless, we both acknowledge the significant contributions Apple computers have made to the industry. At the same time, we are fully aware of the limitations of Apple in terms of proactively addressing social and environmental issues (such as the responsibility of the company for the bad labor conditions of its supplier Foxconn). And we are aware of the ongoing public debate regarding the negative impact of smartphones on society, and particularly teenagers, a trend that gained momentum with the widespread adoption of Apple's iPhones.

6. Ibid., p. 58.

7. Personal interview, 27 February 2019.

8. Personal interview, 3 May 2017. All the following quotes from Reitan Retail employees are from the personal interviews on 3 and 4 May 2017.

9. Cohn, A., Maréchal, M. A., Tannenbaum, D. et al. (2019). Civic honesty around the globe. *Science*, 365(6448): 70–73. https://doi.org/10.1126/science.aau8712.

10. Pøbelprosjektet AS. Ashoka. https://www.ashoka.org/en-us/fellow/eddi-eids-v%C3%A5g (accessed 25 January 2025).

11. De Soto, H. (2016). How to win the war on terror. *Project Syndicate*. https://www.project-syndicate.org/onpoint/how-to-win-the-war-on-terror-by-hernando-de-soto-2016-01 (accessed 16 January 2025).

12. Rekawek, K. (2018). Who are the European Jihadis. *Globsec.* https://www. globsec.org/what-we-do/publications/who-are-european-jihadis-crimi- nals-terrorists-and-back-midterm-report (accessed 16 January 2025).

13. Waronker, S. et al. (2009). *A New Model for Education.* The New American Academy. Internal document, p. 2.

14. Ibid., p. 41.

15. Evaluative comments for The New American Academy Charter School: Renewal site visit report 2022-2023. The New American Academy. https:// www.nysed.gov/sites/default/files/programs/charter-schools/evaluative- comments-for-the-new-american-academy-charter-school-2022-2023- renewal-sv.pdf (accessed 1 February 2025).

16. Parquette Silva, L. (2017, Nov. 10). PoliticsNY. https://politicsny.com/2017/ 11/10/serving-brooklyn-community-one-child-time/ (accessed 1 February 2025).

17. Personal interview, 18 August 2025.

18. Personal interview, 27 February 2019.

19. Personal interview, 18 August 2025.

20. Kantar et BearingPoint classement service clients 2024 [customer service ranking in France in 2024 by Kantar and BearingPoint], https://www.podi- umdelarelationclient.fr/podium-2024/laureats-2024/ (accessed 13 February 2025).

21. Personal interview, 5 May 2017.

22. La Banque WIR consolide sa position de force grâce à un résultat record. Banque WIR. https://www.wir.ch/fr/news-detail/la-banque-wir-consolide- sa-position-de-force-grace-a-un-resultat-record (accessed 27 January 2025).

23. Bénéfice de 13,5 millions de francs pour la banque WIR. https://www.wir. ch/fr/news-detail/wir-bank-mit-135-millionen-franken-gewinn (accessed 18 January 2019).

24. The WIR, the complementary Swiss currency since 1934, Institute of Social Currency. https://www.theeconomyjournal.eu/texto-diario/mostrar/758830/ wir-moneda-complementaria-suiza-activo-desde-1934 (accessed 27 January 2025).

25. Sterimed's story is partially based on our article Getz, I. and Marbacher L. (Autumn 2020). A lesson in creating successful companies that care. *Strategy + Business* 100: 28–31. https://www.strategy-business.com/article/ A-lesson-in-creating-successful-companies-that-care (accessed 18 January 2025).

26. Video interview, 1 May 2020. The following Hyvernat's quotes come from this interview.

27. Podcast de ETIRadio.Tv with Thibaut Hyvernat, 11 January 2021, https://podcast.ausha.co/eti-radio-tv/thibaut-hyvernat-groupe-sterimed (accessed 4 April 2024).

28. All the quotes in this section are from the personal interview with Drake Sadler, 19 January 2016.

29. https://bthechange.com/success-through-community-traditional-medicinals-found-investor-through-seeking-shared-values-45c3cdc41d71 (accessed 20 January 2025).

30. Ibid.

CHAPTER 8

1. Hugo V. (1877). *Histoire d'un Crime – La Chute* (original edition), p. 341, https://victorhugoressources.paris.fr/mini-sites/Histoire_crime/Appels_Texte_nu.htm (accessed January 27, 2025).

2. This and the following quotes of Joensuu come from the personal interview, 2 May 2016.

3. Kuhn, T. S. (2012). *The Structure of Scientific Revolutions* (4th ed.) Chicago: The University of Chicago Press.

4. In the early 1960s, Stewart Macaulay, a law professor at the University of Wisconsin, conducted interviews with executives from 43 companies and lawyers from six law firms to examine how contracts are used in business practice. He found that deals are often sealed with a simple verbal agreement, and even when written contracts are exchanged, the parties seldom review all the terms – particularly the fine print. More strikingly, even when a formal contract is in place and disputes arise – whether over a canceled order, an unpaid invoice, or a noncompliant service – parties rarely resort to litigation. Macaulay's findings have since been corroborated by numerous studies. In 2004, he noted that the likelihood of a dispute over a legal commercial contract ending up in court is about as low as that of a drug trafficking deal being litigated. Rather than invoking the legal system, contracting parties typically prefer to "settle in the shadow of the law." Businesspeople offered two main reasons for this approach. First, economic relationships are built on good faith and shaped by the unwritten social norms of commerce – such as the principle that "invoices must be paid." Second, the ongoing

relationship between parties is often valued more highly than any single dispute. See Macaulay, S. (1963). Non-contractual relations in business: A preliminary study. *American Sociological Review* 28(1): 55–67; Macaulay, S. (2004). Freedom from contract: Solutions in search of a problem ? *Wisconsin Law Review* 2004(2): 777–820.

5. Goerner, S. J., Lietaer, B., and Ulanowicz, R. E. (2009). Quantifying economic sustainability: Implications for free-enterprise theory, policy and practice. *Ecological Economics* 69(1): 76–81. https://doi.org/10.1016/j.ecolecon.2009.07.018.

6. Ibid., p. 77.

7. Govindarajan, V. and Srivastava, A. (2016). The scary truth about corporate survival. *Harvard Business Review* 12: 24–25. https://hbr.org/2016/12/the-scary-truth-about-corporate-survival (accessed 26 February 2025); Garelli, S. (2016, December). Why you will probably live longer than most big companies. IMD. https://www.imd.org/research-knowledge/disruption/articles/why-you-will-probably-live-longer-than-most-big-companies/ (accessed February 26, 2025).

8. Personal interview, 3 May 2017.

9. Pick, T. (2021). *Bienvenue Chez les Fous*. Paris: Diateino, p. 173.

10. Wiggins, R. R. and Ruefli, T. W. (2002). Sustained competitive advantage: Temporal dynamics and the incidence and persistence of superior economic performance. *Organization Science* 13(1): 81–105. Tobin's Q is the ratio of a company's market value to the replacement cost of its assets.

11. Henry Ford on mass production. Britannica Money. https://www.britannica.com/money/Henry-Ford-on-mass-production (accessed 8 January 2025).

12. Marshall, A. (1890). *Principles of Economics*. London: Macmillan and Co.

13. Schumacher, E. F. (1978). *Small Is Beautiful: A Study of Economics as If People Mattered*. London: Blond & Briggs.

14. Ibid., p. 178.

15. Over time, the size limit of 150 has been adjusted and currently the plants have around 250 employees.

16. Sakai, K. and Sekiyama, H. (1992). *Bunsha: Improving Your Business Through Company Division*. New York: Weatherhill.

17. Inamori, K. (2012). *Amoeba Management: The Dynamic Management System for Rapid Market Response*. Boca Raton: CRC Press.

18. Goerner, S. J., Lietaer, B., and Ulanowicz, R. E. (2009).

19. Milliot, J. (2022, Nov. 4). ABA report charts damage done to retailers by Amazon's expansion. *Publishers Weekly*. https://www.publishersweekly.com/

pw/by-topic/industry-news/bookselling/article/90870-aba-report-charts-damage-done-to-retailers-by-amazon-s-expansion.html (accessed 14 January 2025).

20. Six charts that show how low corporate tax revenues are in the US right now. Peter G. Peterson Foundation. https://www.pgpf.org/article/six-charts-that-show-how-low-corporate-tax-revenues-are-in-the-united-states-right-now (accessed 26 January 2025).

21. Biography of Nobel Laureate Dr. Muhammad Yunus. Grameen Bank. https://www.grameenbank.org.bd/about/founder (accessed on 16 January 2025).

22. Wheatley, M. J. and Frieze, D. (2011). *Walk Out Walk On: A Learning Journey into Communities Daring to Live the Future Now.* Berrett-Koehler Publishers. https://walkoutwalkon.net/walking-out-on/are-you-a-walk-out/ (accessed 15 January 2025).

23. Wheatley, M. J. (2002). Using emergence to take social innovation to scale. https://berkana.org/resources/pioneering-a-new-paradigm/ (accessed 16 January 2025).

24. Carney, B. M. and Getz, I. *Freedom, Inc.*

25. Simmat, B. and Bercovici, P. (2016). *Les Entreprises Libérées.* Paris: Les Arènes.

26. Getz, I. and Arnaud, G. (2024). The liberated company theoretical concept: Current issues and the intimidating complexity of organizational design. *Journal of Organization Design* 13(4): 125–145. https://doi.org/10.1007/s41469-024-00170-4.

27. *Blue Book*, internal Reitan Retail document, quoted by Kristin Genton. Personal interview with Odd Reitan, Kristin Genton, and Berit Hvalryg, 27 February 2019.

28. There are diverging points of view regarding the proportion of people required to initiate a large-scale change. Recent research suggests that 25% is the critical threshold for a marginal belief to transition into mainstream acceptance (Centola, D., Becker, J., Brackbill, D. et al. (2018). Experimental evidence for tipping points in social convention. *Science* 360(6393): 1116–1119). Meanwhile, other studies propose the "3% rule": within an organization, just 3% of employees – key influencers – can effectively reach and influence approximately 85% of their colleagues (Innovisor, How to Rethink Change with the Three Percent Rule. https://www.innovisor.com/2017/05/30/how-to-rethink-change-with-the-three-percent-rule/, accessed 21 January 2025).

29. Taleb, N. N. (2007). *The Black Swan: The Impact of the Highly Improbable.* New York: Random House.

30. Kuhn, T. S. (2000). *The Road Since Structure, Philosophical Essays* (J. Conant and J. Haugeland, eds.). Chicago: The University of Chicago Press, p. 60.
31. Braudel, F. (1977). *Afterthoughts on Material Civilization and Capitalism.* Baltimore, MA: The Johns Hopkins University Press, p. 51. https://archive. org/download/BraudelFernandCivilizationAndCapitalism/BraudelFernand-AfterthoughtsOnMaterialCivilizationAn.pdf (accessed 17 January 2025).
32. Ibid., p. 53.
33. Ibid., p. 57.
34. We thank Brian Carney for this observation and confirm that one of us lived in such a small town in Massachusetts for several years.
35. Bakan, J. (2005). *The Corporation: The Pathological Pursuit of Profit and Power.* New York: Free Press.
36. Smith, A. *Wealth of Nations,* Book I.x.c.27.
37. Ibid., Book IV.i.1–45.
38. A very interesting and more detailed analysis on Adam Smith's view about the influence of merchants on politics can be found in Sagar, P. (2018). Adam Smith and the conspiracy of the merchants. *Global Intellectual History.* https:// doi.org/10.1080/23801883.2018.1530066 (accessed on 23 January 2025).
39. Braudel, F., p. 62.
40. Braudel, F., pp. 114–115.

CHAPTER 9

1. Tremblay, D. *Pour Arrêter de se Tuer à l'Ouvrage.*
2. The story of J. P. Morgan draws heavily on Wheeler, G. (1973). *Pierpont Morgan and Friends: The Anatomy of a Myth.* Englewood Cliffs, NJ: Prentice-Hall.
3. Studies and first job: getting actively involved in a wake-up call on the environment. Ecological Awakening. https://pour-un-reveil-ecologique.org/en/ (accessed 18 February 2025).
4. Child Labour: Global estimates 2020, trends and the road forward. UNICEF/ILO. https://data.unicef.org/resources/child-labour-2020-global-estimates-trends-and-the-road-forward/; 50 million people worldwide in modern slavery, ILO. https://www.ilo.org/resource/news/50-million-people-worldwide-modern-slavery-0 (both reports accessed 13 February 2025).
5. Harter, J. (2025, Jan. 14). U.S. Employee Engagement Sinks to 10-Year Low. Gallup. https://www.gallup.com/workplace/654911/employee-engagement-sinks-year-low.aspx (accessed 13 February 2025). The Gallup figures are worse for most other countries.

6. Board of Governors of the Federal Reserve System. Distribution of Household Wealth in the U.S. since 1989, https://www.federalreserve.gov/releases/z1/dataviz/dfa/distribute/table/#quarter:129;series:Net%20worth;demographic:-networth;population:all;units:shares (accessed on 10 February 2025).

7. Aksenfeld, R. (2024, Nov. 25). Thousands of chemicals from food packaging found in humans, a major study reveals. Mongabay. https://news.mongabay.com/2024/11/thousands-of-chemicals-from-food-packaging-found-in-humans-a-major-study-reveals/ (accessed 13 February 2025). See also: Persson, L., Carney Almroth, B. M., Collins, C. D. et al. (2022). Outside the safe operating space of the planetary boundary for novel entities. *Environmental Science & Technology* 56(3): 1510–1521. https://doi.org/10.1021/acs.est.1c04158.

8. Bernardes, R. C., Botina, L. L., Araújo, R. D. S. et al. (2022). Artificial intelligence-aided meta-analysis of toxicological assessment of agrochemicals in bees. *Frontiers in Ecology and Evolution*, 10: 845608. https://doi.org/10.3389/fevo.2022.845608.

9. See for example: Foucart, S., Horel, S., and Mandard, S. (2022, Oct. 19). Les lobbys de l'industrie chimique ont gagné: la Commission européenne enterre le plan d'interdiction des substances toxiques pour la santé et l'environnement. *Le Monde*. https://www.lemonde.fr/planete/article/2022/10/19/les-lobbies-de-l-industrie-chimique-ont-gagne-la-commission-europeenne-enterre-le-plan-d-interdiction-des-substances-toxiques-pour-la-sante-et-l-environnement_6146397_3244.html (accessed 13 February 2025); Wenger, C., Secher, T., Mohammed, H. et al. Disarming REACH-An insight to lobbying in the European Union. https://www.academia.edu/8515935/Disarming_REACH_An_Insight_to_Lobbying_in_the_European_Union (accessed 13 February 2025).

10. *Electricity 2024: Analysis and forecast to 2026*. International Energy Agency, p. 8; see also De Vries, A. (2023). The growing energy footprint of artificial intelligence. *Joule* 7(10): 2191–2194.

11. Pitron, G. (2023). *The Rare Metals War: The Dark Side of Clean Energy and Digital Technologies*. Scribe Publications.

12. Statistical summary of 21-month campaign activity of the 2023-2024 election cycle. Federal Election Commission. https://www.fec.gov/updates/statistical-summary-of-21-month-campaign-activity-of-the-2023-2024-election-cycle (accessed 17 February 2025).

13. https://www.citizen.org/article/big-crypto-big-spending-2024/ (accessed 17 February 2025).

14. https://medium.com/mediapowermonitor/gates-foundation-the-rich-disruptor-be774b83493e (accessed 17 February 2025).
15. Young, D. R. and Lecy, J. D. (2014). Defining the universe of social enterprise: Competing metaphors. *VOLUNTAS: International Journal of Voluntary and Nonprofit Organizations* 25(5): 1307–1332, p. 1308. https://papers.ssrn.com/sol3/Delivery.cfm (accessed 18 February 2025).
16. Ibid.
17. The State of Social Enterprise: A Review of Global Data 2013–2023, Schwab Foundation for Social Entrepreneurship and the World Economic Forum, 2024, p. 5. https://www3.weforum.org/docs/WEF_The_State_of_Social_Enterprise_2024.pdf (accessed 18 February 2025).
18. Ibid., p. 11.
19. Crédit Agricole (France), Rabobank (Netherlands), Desjardins Group (Canada), Raiffeisen (Austria), Zen-Noh (Japan), Fonterra (New Zealand), CHS Inc. (United States), REWE (Germany), Migros (Switzerland), S Group (Finland), and Mondragon (Spain).
20. Of course, this vision romanticized the experience of peasant life. In reality, many left their farms – often involuntarily, as noted in Chapter 1 – because subsistence agriculture could no longer support them. Nevertheless, the idea of collective ownership gained traction.
21. Hyungsik, E. (2017). *Cooperatives and Employment: Second Global Report – Contribution of Cooperatives to Decent Work in the Changing World of Work.* Brussels: CICOPA, p. 12. https://www.cicopa.coop/wp-content/uploads/2018/01/Cooperatives-and-Employment-Second-Global-Report-2017.pdf (accessed 31 March 2025). Note: Along worker cooperatives, the report aggregates the data from "user cooperatives," "producer cooperatives," "multi-stakeholder cooperatives," "secondary cooperatives," and "enterprise cooperatives."
22. Ibid.
23. Hyungsik, E. (2017), p. 21.
24. Hyungsik, E. (2017), p. 36.
25. For instance, in times of economic crisis, worker-members often prioritize employment stability over short-term income, even agreeing to temporary pay cuts. One study of Italian worker cooperatives, for example, found that their average wages were 14% lower than those in comparable capitalist firms – a trade-off that reflects the longer-term orientation and collective resilience of the cooperative model. See Pencavel, J., Pistaferri, L., and Schivardi, F. (2006). Wages, employment, and capital in capitalist and worker-owned

firms. *Industrial and Labor Relations Review* 60(1): 23–44. https://doi. org/10.1177/001979390606000102. Cooperatives in the Italian region of Emilia-Romagna account for 35% of the GDP; see Billiet A., Dufays F., Friedel, S. et al. (2021). The resilience of the cooperative model: How do cooperatives deal with the COVID-19 crisis? *Strategic Change* 30(2): 99–108. https://doi. org/10.1002/jsc.2393. A comparable willingness to accept salary reductions during the 2009 financial crisis was also evident at Mondragon, underscoring the cooperative model's capacity for collective sacrifice in pursuit of long-term stability; see *The Economist* (2009). All in this together. https://www.econo-mist.com/business/2009/03/26/all-in-this-together (accessed 31 March 2025).

26. Pérotin, V. (2016). What do we really know about workers' co-operatives? In A. Webster, L. Shaw, and R. Vorberg-Rugh (eds.), *Mainstreaming Co-operation: An Alternative for the Twenty-first Century?* Manchester: Manchester University Press, pp. 239–260. https://doi.org/10.7765/9781526100993.00019 (accessed 2 April 2025)

27. Pérotin, V. (2016).

28. In a similar vein, employee ownership – through ESOP or 401(k) plans – is also presented as such a "silver bullet" social measure. Yet, according to a large study of employee-owned firms, they do less long-term investment, take fewer risks, show slower growth, and create fewer jobs than comparable capitalistic firms; see Faleye, O., Mehrotra, V., and Morck, R. (2006). When labor has a voice in corporate governance. *Journal of Financial and Quantitative Analysis* 41(3): 489–510.

29. Lasch, C. (1990). Conservatism against itself. *Human Life Review* 16: 47–61. https://firstthings.com/conservatism-against-itself/ (accessed 31 March 2025).

30. Personal interview with Dominque Tremblay, 17 April 2025; Personal com-munication with Dominque Tremblay, 17 November 2024.

31. Les Pléiades. CCI Grand Lévis. https://cciglevis.ca/les-pleiades/ (accessed 11 February 2025).

32. Tremblay, D. (2024). *Pour Arrêter de se Tuer à l'Ouvrage* [To Stop Working Yourself to Death], unpublished book, Chapter 8. All Dominque Tremblay's quotes come from his book, our video interview on 27 November 2024, and from his personal written communication with us.

33. Fortier's quotes in the following paragraphs are based on the personal inter-view with him on 17 April 2025.

34. Tremblay, D. (2024), op. cit., pp. 167, 180.

GLOSSARY

Balancing approaches   Strategies in which companies seek to generate profit while simultaneously advancing social and environmental goals. Examples include Corporate Social Responsibility (CSR), the Triple Bottom Line (or 3P – Profit, People, Planet), B-Corp, Benefit Corporation, and Stakeholder Capitalism. While rooted in good intentions, these approaches often prove inadequate because social and environmental goals remain marginal rather than being embedded within the core business processes. Balancing approaches also rely on the unrealistic assumption that multiple objectives can be simultaneously optimized. When tensions inevitably arise, profit imperatives tend to override other considerations, revealing the inherent fragility of such balancing actions or initiatives.

Business ecosystem   A company's clients, suppliers, and members of the local communities where it operates (including local governments, other local businesses, schools and universities, local NGOs, etc.). Traditional companies interact with members of their business ecosystems through transactions; caring companies do that through caring relationships.

Caring company A company that serves members of its business ecosystem – clients, suppliers, and the local community – unconditionally and through its core business processes. By doing so, it enjoys unrivalled long-term prosperity.

Caring relationship A caring relationship is grounded in the unconditional commitment to serving members of the company's business ecosystem. These relationships are built on trust and attention to these people as human beings with fundamental needs rather than as business partners driven solely by economic interests. Caring relationships go beyond transactional relationships necessary to operate a business (see Transactional relationship). Ultimately – and often within a short period – caring relationships generate greater economic value for the company than purely transactional ones.

Diseconomies of scale Occur when a company becomes so large that growing further actually makes it less efficient. Instead of enjoying lower costs per unit – as with economies of scale – costs begin to rise, productivity slows, and the company becomes less responsive to employees, customers, or market shifts. This happens because employee engagement drops as personal relationships are replaced by processes, metrics, and controls; decision-making gets bogged down in bureaucracy; and communication breaks down across siloed departments. According to research, diseconomies of scale typically begin to emerge once a company surpasses 150 employees.

Effective social innovation Effective social innovation consists in designing and implementing new business practices that generate social value. What makes it effective is that it rests on three pillars: WHY – innovations being ends in themselves, not simply the means to increase profits; WHAT – they must consist of a bundle of mutually supportive measures, systematically transforming both the way the business operates and the social conditions of employees, their families, and the local communities; WHO – these transformations should be led by business-persons at the helm of their companies or business units and with the cooperation of employees.

Heartset shift (leader's)   A leader's heartset shift is a profound process of self-transformation. It begins when a leader no longer asks, "How can we maximize profit?" but instead, "Where do I go to truly serve our eco-system members?" It is not simply a shift in management mindset – it is a fundamental reorientation of the leader's habits, beliefs, and inner compass (hence the concept of "heartset").

Managerial framework   A company's managerial framework encompasses the set of management systems and practices, organizational structure, and cultural habits that determine how it is run. In traditional companies, these frameworks are typically rooted in subordination and control. In contrast, caring companies operate within managerial frameworks grounded in trust, subsidiarity, autonomy, and responsibility.

Obliquity   The indirect path to achieving goals. Literally, obliquity describes the relationship between two lines that are neither perpendicular nor parallel – a connection that exists but is not immediately visible to the naked eye. In the case of caring companies, profits are not pursued directly but rather emerge obliquely – through the unconditional service of the members of their business ecosystems.

Profit as objective vs. profit as constraint and consequence   "Profit as objective" reflects the prevailing logic of modern capitalism: a company exists primarily to maximize shareholder returns. In contrast, "Profit as constraint and consequence" underpins the philosophy of caring companies. Here, profit is viewed as a discipline – a necessary financial constraint to ensure long-term vitality – but not as the business's fundamental purpose. That purpose is to deliver unconditional service to clients, suppliers, and the local communities. When a company excels in doing that, profit follows as a natural outcome.

Revamping (organizational)   A fundamental transformation of how a company functions – not merely tweaking policies or reorganizing reporting lines but transforming its managerial framework. For caring companies, this often means moving away from control-centric structures and management systems in favor of managerial frameworks that empower frontline teams – those closest to customers and operations – to make autonomous decisions. Such a shift enables a culture of unconditional service to the members of company's business ecosystem.

Steering through conversations   A leadership approach in which ongoing dialogue supplants control mechanisms as the primary means of guiding an organization with regard to its employees, members of its business ecosystem, and its shareholders. With respect to employees, rather than relying on budgets and top-down targets, leaders share vision and foster alignment through frequent, trust-based conversations with them. With respect to members of the business ecosystem, leaders cultivate trust-based relationships and dialogue with them in order to understand their needs and aspirations. As for shareholders, leaders make it clear through a dialogue with them that the company is not merely an investment vehicle, but an enterprise driven by a vision – to care for the members of its business ecosystem. They emphasize that the organization operates on the conviction that fulfilling this vision will – as a natural outcome – deliver superior financial performance.

Transactional relationship   A transactional relationship is grounded in mutual exchange and individual self-interest, forming a cornerstone of the dominant theories in economic science. Each party is primarily concerned with obtaining their desired outcome – be it a product, service, or payment – with limited regard for, or even at the detriment of, the other party's good. These relationships are typically short-lived and governed by contracts. While effective for straightforward or one-off interactions, they often fall short in fostering trust or sustaining long-term commitment.

Transformational leadership   Transformational leadership is a leadership style aimed not merely at enhancing performance, but at reshaping an organization's very purpose, values, and culture. Unlike transactional leaders – who prioritize financial goals, rules, and incentives – transformational leaders lead from a place of personal conviction. Authentic transformational leadership begins with a fundamental heartset shift in the leader, followed by a redefinition of the organization's purpose, a revamp of its managerial framework, and a redesign of business processes to more effectively serve that purpose. It is sustained by the leader's role as a steward of both the renewed purpose and processes.

Window of vitality   In nature, the most successful organisms strive to maximize their long-term survival, not just their short-term efficiency. To adapt to disturbances, they operate within a sweet spot – a state where efficiency is deliberately not maximized in order to foster resilience. Biologists call this optimal state the "window of vitality." Traditional companies, however, often fixate on efficiency alone, which in the long run undermines their sustainability. By contrast, caring companies intuitively remain in their sweet spot, and it is this positioning that secures their lasting prosperity despite inevitable crises.

ACKNOWLEDGMENTS

This book has two authors, but it was written and published thanks to the contributions of a diverse group of people from around the world.

Most importantly, we are indebted to the leaders of caring companies whose insights and proven practices inspired us. We owe our gratitude to Chris Mittelstaedt of The FruitGuys, Drake Sadler of Traditional Medicinals, Haruo Naito of Eisai, Emmanuel Vasseneix of LSDH, Daniel Abittan of Châteauform, Anders Bouvin of Handelsbanken, Kristin Genton, Berit Hvalryg, and Odd Reitan of Reitan Retail, Timo Joensuu of Docrates, and Dominique Tremblay of PBM. We are also thankful to the employees we met in these companies, who generously shared their experiences of what it means to work in companies that care.

Special thanks go to the Club of Caring CEOs, with whom we exchanged ideas in the early 2020s about the transformation toward caring companies – leaders who also field-tested these concepts.

Reflecting on how this book came to life, two Japanese sayings come to mind. The first is: "There are no coincidences." Indeed, our initial idea was to write a book about corporate transformation toward caring companies targeted at CEOs. While the idea was met with enthusiasm, it wasn't quite enough to bring it to fruition. Then, one day, Isaac gave a speech in London, where he was introduced to Clare Grist Taylor, a literary agent. It was through working with Clare that the idea for a broader focus – the future of capitalist enterprises and capitalism itself – was born. Thank you, Clare, for your insights, even if our paths have since diverged.

The second Japanese saying is: "Fate works in mysterious ways." Such a mysterious way took place when Isaac met Peter Vanham at his business school. Peter, an accomplished author, was the one who connected us with Wiley's Acquisitions Editor, Bill Falloon.

Bill not only believed in this book but also reviewed its final version and shared invaluable insights. Before his retirement, Bill thoughtfully entrusted our book to Gemma Valler, who masterfully oversaw its final stages of publication. We are also grateful to the Wiley team, particularly Katherine Cording, editorial assistant, who graciously guided us through the various stages of this book's development, and Susan Cerra, managing editor, for overseeing all aspects of production together with the exceptional content refinement specialist Jajneswar Chhotaray. Special thanks go to Gus A. Miklos, development editor, whose deep understanding of English, keen attention to detail, and kindness accompanied us like a guiding light throughout our writing.

Finally, Isaac would like to thank his institution, ESCP Business School, for its support. On a personal level, he is profoundly grateful for his family's unwavering support. Laurent, for his part, feels indebted to four people who have deeply inspired him and whose work is woven into these pages: Prof. Muhammad Yunus, Peter Senge, Johannes Partanen, and Esa Saarinen. He thanks his clients and partners, who have supported this project with understanding, and hopes that they have not felt overlooked during the writing of this book. He is also full of gratitude for the constant support of his wife Emmanuelle and each of their children.

Last but not least, both authors are deeply appreciative of Brian Carney, who edited our manuscript to refine its tone and generously shared his thoughtful feedback and ideas, which enriched this book.

We owe to all of you what is best in this book – and to ourselves, its shortcomings. Thank you.

ABOUT THE AUTHORS

Isaac Getz

Isaac is a professor at ESCP Business School – one of the world's top-ranked institutions with campuses in Paris, London, Berlin, Madrid, and Torino. Previously, he was a visiting professor at Cornell and Stanford.

He is best known as the co-author, with Brian Carney, of *Freedom, Inc.*, a book translated into 15 languages and recognized as a #1 bestseller and award-winning business book in France. He has also published half a dozen other books in English and French, including *Leadership Without Ego*, co-written with Bob Davids and Brian Carney. His work has been featured in *The Wall Street Journal, Forbes, Harvard Business Review, Financial Times, Strategy+Business, CNBC, Fox, Nikkei*, and other leading media worldwide. He was also named one of LinkedIn's Top 25 Voices in France.

Alongside Laurent Marbacher, Isaac has played a pivotal role in the rise of the corporate liberation movement across Europe and North America, helping hundreds of companies and institutions transition from traditional command-and-control structures to freedom- and responsibility-based organizations.

Isaac was a finalist for the *Thinkers50* Breakthrough Idea Award and he is once again nominated for this recognition with Laurent for this book, received the Marconi Creativity Award, and has been invited to speak at prestigious global events, including the Peter Drucker Global Forum in Vienna and the World Knowledge Forum in Seoul.

Isaac has been a senior advisor for several major corporations including Decathlon, Michelin, and Suez. He is a sought-after public speaker, delivering at executive conferences and keynotes around the world over the past 25 years. He's been also invited to give four TEDx talks, the most recent on the caring company.

Isaac's personal page: `isaacgetz.com`

Laurent Marbacher

Laurent is a trusted senior advisor, working closely with global leaders, particularly from family businesses and start-ups. He engages in deep dialogues with CEOs both on their personal journey and on the transformation of their companies.

Laurent has a background in social entrepreneurship. After studying at HEC Paris, he worked in Chile for four years where he launched with some friends the first micro-credit bank in the country with the support of Muhammad Yunus, Nobel Peace Prize Laureate, founder of the Grameen Bank. This pivotal experience shaped his later work in advancing leadership principles and organizational paradigms of the liberated company and the caring company. Laurent has been deeply influenced by Peter Senge and SOL (Society for Organizational Learning), as well as by Ignatian spirituality. He also trained as a team coach with the pioneering Team Academy in Finland.

A sought-after speaker, Laurent regularly addresses business audiences, particularly C-suite teams and boards of directors. He has also spoken at high-profile events (TEDx, World Economic Forum, Family Business Network ...).

Laurent's personal page and blog: `laurentmarbacher.com`

INDEX